The United States and Latin America after the Cold War

In assessing the relations between the United States and Latin America since the Berlin Wall fell in 1989, Russell Crandall argues that any lasting analysis must be viewed through a fresh framework, one that allows for the often unexpected episodes and outcomes in U.S.–Latin American relations. An academic and recent high-level U.S. policymaker, Crandall examines the policies of three post–Cold War presidential administrations (George H. W. Bush, Bill Clinton, and George W. Bush) through the prism of three critical areas: democracy, economics, and security. The author then introduces relevant case studies of U.S. policy in several Latin American countries, including Cuba, Brazil, Haiti, Colombia, Venezuela, Mexico, and Argentina.

Russell Crandall is currently Associate Professor of Politics at Davidson College. He has also served as the director for the Western Hemisphere at the National Security Council, special assistant for counterterrorism to the Joint Chiefs of Staff, and adviser for Latin American security to the assistant secretary of defense for international security affairs. He is the author of *Gunboat Democracy: U.S. Interventions in the Dominican Republic, Grenada, and Panama* (2006) and *Driven by Drugs: U.S. Policy toward Colombia* (2002).

Latin America

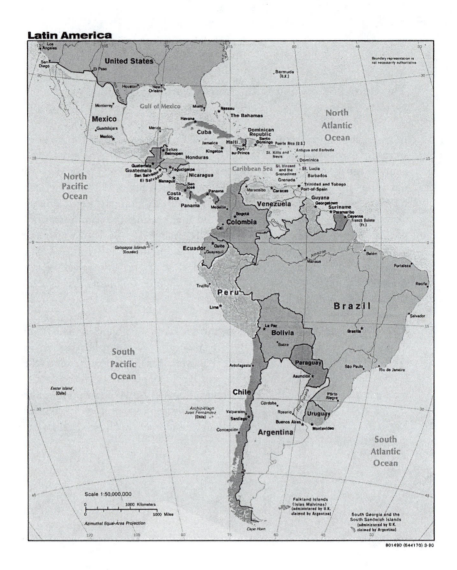

The United States and Latin America after the Cold War

RUSSELL CRANDALL
Davidson College

September
2008

With affection
for my alma mater,
Russell Crandall
'94

CAMBRIDGE
UNIVERSITY PRESS

CAMBRIDGE UNIVERSITY PRESS
Cambridge, New York, Melbourne, Madrid, Cape Town, Singapore, São Paulo, Delhi

Cambridge University Press
32 Avenue of the Americas, New York, NY 10013-2473, USA

www.cambridge.org
Information on this title: www.cambridge.org/9780521717953

First published 2008

Printed in the United States of America

A catalog record for this publication is available from the British Library.

Library of Congress Cataloging in Publication Data
Crandall, Russell, 1971–
    The United States and Latin America after the cold war / Russell C. Crandall.
      p.   cm.
    Includes bibliographical references and index.
    ISBN 978-0-521-88946-9 (hardback) – ISBN 978-0-521-71795-3 (pbk.)
      1. United States – Foreign relations – Latin America.   2. Latin America – Foreign
    relations – United States.   I. Title.
    F1418.C893 2008
    327.730809′049–dc22   2008000264

ISBN 978-0-521-88946-9 hardback
ISBN 978-0-521-71795-3 paperback

One distinct characteristic of teaching is that the energy spent in the endeavor is largely intended to influence the thinking and behavior of others. That is, teaching is not really about the teacher. Oftentimes, any teacher's impact on a student occurs long after the actual coursework has ended. In many of these cases, the teacher never becomes aware of what was in fact a tremendous influence on a student. In this sense, teaching is holding the faith that what is taught will actually matter – someday, somewhere.

I dedicate this book to one of my teachers, Don Dooley, whose profound influence on me continues to this day. A legendary cross-country coach at San Mateo High School in northern California, Don passed away far too young. I was thus especially blessed to have received his guidance and wisdom. Through tremendous examples of personal behavior but few spoken words, "Dooley" subtly but powerfully taught me to take responsibility for my own efforts, in this case long-distance running. Through him, I now understand that any true greatness requires passion, dedication, and humility.

Contents

Acknowledgments

I am grateful to all of the friends and colleagues without whom this book would not have been possible. All errors of fact or judgment, though, are entirely mine.

As scholars, we far too often underestimate the research and writing abilities of undergraduates. In many of my experiences, however, undergraduates are often asking the "big questions" that the rest of us have ignored or overlooked. During the life of this book project, I was blessed to have been able to rely on the enthusiasm and hard work of three fantastic Davidson College undergraduate research assistants: Katie Hunter, Marshall Worsham, and Peter Roady.

Former Davidson student Rebecca Stewart did an absolutely masterful job editing the manuscript and gave new meaning to the old saying "putting lipstick on a pig." Former students Josh Craft, Andrew Rhodes, John Foster, Eduardo Estrada, Adam Chalker, and Dane Erickson provided helpful comments on the manuscript.

I must also thank my Davidson colleague Ralph Levering, who was a constant source of encouragement during this entire project. Joe Gutenkast in the college's interlibrary loan office provided timely and cheerful support for my countless requests. My department chair Mary Thornberry and her assistant Kerrie Moore provided critical assistance, especially when I was teaching in Peru during the fall of 2007.

The Center for American Progress (CAP) in Washington, DC, was my "home away from home" during the life of this project. I have found CAP to be a wonderfully freewheeling, serious, and supportive intellectual environment. I am especially indebted to Denis McDonough, Dan Restrepo, Melody Barnes, and John Podesta for their wonderful hospitality.

The following colleagues, friends, and family provided important ideas or inspiration for this book: Bill Crandall Sr., Bill Crandall Jr., Chris Chivvis, Richard Feinberg, Riordan Roett, Jerry Haar, Brian Latell, Michael Shifter, Tom Shannon, Lawrence Petroni, Ramiro Orias, Augusto Chian, Jeff Dawson, Guadalupe Paz, Greg Weeks, and Kim Breier. My wife and colleague, Britta Crandall, contributed to the Brazil chapter using research from her current doctoral dissertation on U.S.-Brazilian relations. She also patiently edited the manuscript several times.

The research for this book was supported by generous grants from the Duke Endowment (via the Davidson Student Research Initiative), which funded my summer research assistants, and the Earhart Foundation, which supported my research travel. I owe a special thanks to Verna Case and Clark Ross at Davidson and Monty Brown at Earhart for their generous support for this project.

At Cambridge University Press, I was especially lucky to work with Lew Bateman. Lew's commitment to publishing controversial or contrarian perspectives is to be admired and hopefully replicated far more often than is the case. Cambridge's Emily Spangler patiently assisted me through all stages of the publishing process. Lastly, my agent and friend, Gillian MacKenzie, is remarkably talented and wise and a constant source of encouragement.

Arequipa, Peru
November 2007

The following colleagues, friends, and family provided important ideas or inspiration for this book: Bill Crandall Sr., Bill Crandall Jr., Chris Chivvis, Richard Feinberg, Riordan Roett, Jerry Haar, Brian Latell, Michael Shifter, Tom Shannon, Lawrence Petroni, Ramiro Orias, Augusto Chian, Jeff Dawson, Guadalupe Paz, Greg Weeks, and Kim Breier. My wife and colleague, Britta Crandall, contributed to the Brazil chapter using research from her current doctoral dissertation on U.S.-Brazilian relations. She also patiently edited the manuscript several times.

The research for this book was supported by generous grants from the Duke Endowment (via the Davidson Student Research Initiative), which funded my summer research assistants, and the Earhart Foundation, which supported my research travel. I owe a special thanks to Verna Case and Clark Ross at Davidson and Monty Brown at Earhart for their generous support for this project.

At Cambridge University Press, I was especially lucky to work with Lew Bateman. Lew's commitment to publishing controversial or contrarian perspectives is to be admired and hopefully replicated far more often than is the case. Cambridge's Emily Spangler patiently assisted me through all stages of the publishing process. Lastly, my agent and friend, Gillian MacKenzie, is remarkably talented and wise and a constant source of encouragement.

Arequipa, Peru
November 2007

Acknowledgments

I am grateful to all of the friends and colleagues without whom this book would not have been possible. All errors of fact or judgment, though, are entirely mine.

As scholars, we far too often underestimate the research and writing abilities of undergraduates. In many of my experiences, however, undergraduates are often asking the "big questions" that the rest of us have ignored or overlooked. During the life of this book project, I was blessed to have been able to rely on the enthusiasm and hard work of three fantastic Davidson College undergraduate research assistants: Katie Hunter, Marshall Worsham, and Peter Roady.

Former Davidson student Rebecca Stewart did an absolutely masterful job editing the manuscript and gave new meaning to the old saying "putting lipstick on a pig." Former students Josh Craft, Andrew Rhodes, John Foster, Eduardo Estrada, Adam Chalker, and Dane Erickson provided helpful comments on the manuscript.

I must also thank my Davidson colleague Ralph Levering, who was a constant source of encouragement during this entire project. Joe Gutenkast in the college's interlibrary loan office provided timely and cheerful support for my countless requests. My department chair Mary Thornberry and her assistant Kerrie Moore provided critical assistance, especially when I was teaching in Peru during the fall of 2007.

The Center for American Progress (CAP) in Washington, DC, was my "home away from home" during the life of this project. I have found CAP to be a wonderfully freewheeling, serious, and supportive intellectual environment. I am especially indebted to Denis McDonough, Dan Restrepo, Melody Barnes, and John Podesta for their wonderful hospitality.

Preface

In March 2007 President George W. Bush embarked on a week-long trip to Latin America. While in Uruguay, Bush met with his presidential counterpart, Tabaré Vásquez, who represents one of several left-leaning governments recently elected to power in the region. Polls in Uruguay before the visit suggested that only 12 percent of Uruguayans supported Bush's trip, yet more than 50 percent of the population endorsed entering into a free trade agreement with the United States.

As the two leaders signed U.S.-Uruguayan investment accords and relaxed at the Uruguayan presidential retreat, just across the Rio de la Plata in Argentina a different scene unfolded: the fiery Venezuelan president Hugo Chávez staged an "alternative" rally, denouncing Bush to chants of "Gringo, go home!" Attended by thousands of ardent supporters of Chávez's vehemently anti-American manifesto, the rally stole the headlines from Bush's unexpectedly warm reception from Uruguay's Vásquez.

Had casual observers of United States–Latin American relations not seen the footage or read media reports from these events, many might have already concluded that Bush and Vásquez would be too-strange bedfellows to meet amicably, much less to consider joint strategic objectives. In fact, many might have expected instead to see the leftist Vásquez join Chávez at his anti-Bush rally. Moreover, we might have assumed that, given their reported widespread dislike of President Bush, Uruguayans would have resoundingly rejected a free trade pact with the United States.

In U.S.–Latin American relations today, unexpected alliances, episodes, and outcomes abound. These new realities are in play largely because the end of the Cold War has diminished the ideological and strategic constraints that for decades dictated U.S. policy in Latin America. In this new era, what is often at the core of U.S. policies in Latin America is an interplay between international and domestic, or "intermestic," politics.

Consider the case of U.S. policy toward Colombia. During a 2000 congressional debate on the amount and type of assistance for the war-ravaged country, longtime Latin America policy "dove" Senator Christopher Dodd (D-CT) adopted one of the most "hawkish" positions in the Senate, reflected in his ardent support for sending Black Hawk helicopters to the Colombian military. Amid the acerbic debates in the 1980s over the nature of U.S. policy in Nicaragua, when a Marxist government was in power, Dodd repeatedly denounced what he contended to be President Ronald Reagan's overly militaristic policies toward the Central American country. In 2000, though, Dodd appeared to be supporting a "military solution" to Colombia's conflict through his support for the Black Hawks. Also, and in a clear indication of the increased role of domestic politics in the post–Cold War era, it is worth noting that the proposed helicopters were to be manufactured in Dodd's home state of Connecticut.

Before the fall of the Berlin Wall in 1989, U.S. policy in Latin America was concerned overwhelmingly with stopping communist expansion. Accordingly, the prevailing frameworks for studying U.S. policy in Latin America were equally grounded in anticommunism. Without this threat in the region, most U.S. policies are no longer driven by a "one-size-fits-all" approach. Because U.S. policy has moved beyond the Cold War, those studying the motivations and application of U.S. policy toward Latin America must equally adopt a fresh approach.

The United States' legacy in Latin America is the "Big Stick." President Theodore Roosevelt's pithy maxim, derived from an African proverb, "Speak softly and carry a big stick, and you will go far," epitomized the country's emergence as a self-appointed police force in Central America and the Caribbean at the beginning of the twentieth century. For our purposes, the Big Stick may be described as the assertion that, historically and at times presently, the United States has tended to act in an imperious, unilateral, and paternalistic manner in Latin America. This was certainly the case during the Cold War, when Washington used the Big Stick habitually in order to combat communism.

Although the United States might still act with a Big Stick, that is no longer the entire story of U.S. policy in Latin America. Rather, a variety of hemispheric developments – including not only the end of communism but also globalization and immigration from Latin America – has required and permitted the United States to adopt policies that do not fit this traditional approach. As a result, the years after the Cold War witnessed several key episodes in which the United States had every opportunity to yield the Big Stick but did not.

Acknowledging the need for this paradigm shift does not mean that observers must endorse the United States' paternalistic historic legacy in Latin America. Nor does it mean that we must necessarily agree with current and future U.S. policies in the region or that there are not elements of the past that still have a great influence on the United States' conduct in the region. It does mean, though, that we must be prepared to look at U.S. motivations and actions in Latin America through a new framework – one that takes into account current realities while not assuming that contemporary policies bear the same intent as in the recent past.

The United States and Latin America after the Cold War aims to shed light on what is new and what is old in Washington's Latin America policy playbook and focuses on four major developments influencing U.S. policies. First, the end of the Cold War dramatically increased the level of flexibility and choices for Washington in its dealings in the Western Hemisphere. Second, unlike during the Cold War, Latin American countries are increasingly democratic and sovereign; few would consider them to be the Cold War "pawns" of the United States or the Soviet Union as was the case in the prior era. This development provides Latin American countries with greater flexibility, similar to that which the United States has always had in the region. This new freedom has at times meant choosing to turn away from Washington to embrace other global powers such as China or Europe or, conversely, to adopt some of Washington's long-promoted policy priorities, such as trade expansion and liberalization.

Simply having to ask whether, for example, China will rival the United States for influence in Latin America reinforces the notion that it is no longer "business as usual" for Washington. Because Latin American countries have far more options than they did in previous eras, a cold shoulder from Washington might not mean as much as it once did; increasingly, to replace U.S. investment or development dollars, countries have the ability to turn to Asia, Europe, or even other energy-rich countries in the region.

Globalization, a third critical development influencing U.S. policy after the Cold War, catalyzes communication and interaction at an unprecedented rate between peoples and cultures in all corners of the world. Yet its dynamism and rapidity carry particular weight in the relationship between the United States and Latin America. For example, nongovernmental activists attempting to free American Lori Berenson, incarcerated in Peru for her alleged collaboration with a Peruvian terrorist organization, used the Internet to deliver their political message to a global audience. By increasing public pressure on Peruvian and U.S. officials, these new "actors" have forced both governments to respond to challenges that they could have ignored much more easily in previous eras.

Lastly, U.S. domestic politics today "spill over" increasingly into the formulation and implementation of U.S. policies in Latin America. Domestic politics have played an integral role in Latin American policy since the early decades of the U.S. republic. During the Cold War, however, the overarching, bipartisan U.S. effort to combat communism often superseded domestic interests. In the post–Cold War era, domestic politics again play an outsized role in policy toward Latin America. Today, almost all of the hot-button issues related to Latin America policy, such as drugs, immigration, and trade, have their roots in domestic policies.

In addition to considering a new approach for exploring how the U.S. government conducts its policy toward Latin America, this book explores the major events related to U.S.–Latin American relations during the past two decades. The post–Cold War era has thus far spanned three U.S. presidential administrations – those of George H. W. Bush, Bill Clinton, and George W. Bush – and the age of America's struggle against Islamic terrorism. We analyze the key episodes in U.S.–Latin American relations in the context of these three presidential administrations, as well as through the overriding themes of democracy, security, and economics. The events studied in this book should provide the evidence with which to recognize and analyze the emerging trends in the United States' actions toward Latin America.

The United States and Latin America after the Cold War seeks to inform and challenge observers of U.S.–Latin American relations who are coming of age well after the Cold War. It also seeks to help shape future policy decisions by deepening our understanding of what has transpired during the past quarter century. In a study of U.S.–Latin American relations since the Cold War, one should "expect the unexpected." Yet we will uncover these critical but often latent developments only if we push ourselves beyond the increasingly anachronistic frameworks of prior eras.

The United States and Latin America after the Cold War

I

Understanding U.S. Policy

Given that communism is no longer the existential threat it once was, Cold War–era approaches to U.S.–Latin American relations are no longer sufficient. The traditional Big Stick metaphor, though, remains a useful lens through which to examine the motivations and applications of U.S. policy in Latin America that were common before the end of the Cold War. The Big Stick refers to the way the United States wielded its overwhelming power, often through unilateral and domineering policies, to promote outcomes in line with its national security interests. Historically, the United States has dealt with Latin America (Central America and the Caribbean in particular) from a position of superiority, one from which it "told" Latin Americans more than it "asked" them.

Acknowledging the Big Stick's legacy is not intended to place a value judgment on U.S. actions in Latin America. Nor does this book seek to resolve the debate over the morality or efficacy of U.S. policies during the Cold War or earlier eras. Rather, our point is to characterize the United States' historical motivations in Latin America, so that, as the post–Cold War era nears the end of its second decade, we may better see why the Big Stick is not the entire story in today's context. Does the United States continue to determine outcomes in the region more by power and force than by cooperation and respect? How extensive is its power and influence? Is this influence beneficial or detrimental to Latin American interests? If U.S. policy is harmful or counterproductive, what should it look like instead? Before exploring these questions, we first must look back to the nature of U.S. policy during the Cold War, an era that still influences U.S. policies.

COLD WAR HANGOVER

If one word can describe the underlying issue that drove U.S. policy in Latin America during the Cold War, it is *security*. Successive Cold War–era American administrations – Republican and Democratic alike – developed and implemented their Latin American policies usually in direct reaction to the perceived security threat of communist revolution in the United States' very own "backyard." Democratic president John F. Kennedy, for instance, authorized the Bay of Pigs operation in 1961, in a failed attempt to spark a popular insurrection to overthrow Cuba's new Marxist revolutionary leader Fidel Castro. Kennedy's fateful decision was a response to Castro's stunning revolution in 1959 and Washington's fear that the Cuban leader would now attempt to "export" communist revolution to other Latin American countries.

A few years later, fearing that the Dominican Republic was vulnerable to exploitation by radical communist elements, Kennedy's successor, Lyndon Johnson, ordered upward of 20,000 American troops into the Dominican Republic to quell an incipient civil war. In the early 1970s, concerned that Chile was headed toward communism under newly elected President Salvador Allende, Republican president Richard Nixon oversaw covert efforts to undermine the leftist leader's democratic government. After declaring that the Soviet Union and Castro's Cuba were attempting to fan communist revolution across the Central American isthmus, Republican president Ronald Reagan spent hundreds of millions of dollars to shore up El Salvador's government and military. And in Nicaragua, the Reagan administration trained and funded a counterrevolutionary force committed to overthrowing the revolutionary government in Managua.

These episodes of U.S. policies in Latin America illustrate the intensity of the United States' preoccupation with Latin America during the Cold War. In the early 1960s President John F. Kennedy called Latin America "the most dangerous area in the world."[1] Two decades later, during the height of controversy over U.S. policies in Central America, U.S. ambassador to the United Nations Jeane Kirkpatrick claimed that Central America and the Caribbean had become "the most important place in the world for us."[2] To be sure,

---

[1] See Stephen G. Rabe, *The Most Dangerous Area in the World: John F. Kennedy Confronts Communist Revolution in Latin America* (Chapel Hill: University of North Carolina Press, 1999), 7.

[2] Quoted in Mark T. Gilderhus, *The Second Century: U.S.–Latin American Relations since 1889* (Wilmington: Scholarly Resources, 2000), 223.

rhetoric and style varied across administrations, but the overriding goal was the same: stop communism at all costs.

Washington's Cold War policy responses promoted U.S. national security interests over other potential priorities, such as democracy or the United States' image in the region. Defenders of this "security first" emphasis argue that, while it was not always pretty, Washington had to employ a variety of diplomatic and military means in order to defeat communism.

On the other hand, critics of U.S. policy claim that the United States relinquished its moral authority by engaging in activities that were antithetical to the country's democratic foundations and practices. They also argue that these policies were counterproductive, often producing as many enemies as friends in the region.[3] Such critics maintain that the Eisenhower administration's covert overthrow of leftist but democratic Guatemalan president Jacobo Arbenz in 1954 revealed Washington's willingness to abandon its democratic principles, further exposing the cynical and hypocritical nature of American policy in the region. Moreover, many governments and observers throughout Latin America concluded from Arbenz's overthrow that the United States was concerned not about democracy and sovereignty but about its narrow economic and strategic interests in the region.

Despite the disagreements between these two camps, there is no question that Washington used its enormous military and economic might as a Big Stick to ensure that events in the region concluded favorably for the United States. However, Washington did not rely solely on threats or force to promote its policies in the region; it also encouraged economic development and democracy programs as a means to promote "communist-free" outcomes. The first such policy was President Kennedy's Alliance for Progress and Peace Corps programs that began in the early 1960s. The United States also funded civil society groups to help foster peaceful democratic change in countries such as Chile in the late 1980s and Haiti in the early 1990s. In the case of Chile, the avidly anticommunist Reagan administration – in what became a policy that surprised many critics who assumed that Reagan would ignore the Chilean dictator's brutal excesses – funded the democratic opposition's effort to defeat right-wing dictator Augusto Pinochet in a 1988 national referendum.

Many observers greeted the end of the Cold War as an opportunity for the United States to adapt its policies in ways that would bolster U.S.–Latin American relations: no longer beholden to the overriding concern of communist expansion, Washington could shift its narrow focus on security

---

[3] See Julia Sweig, *Friendly Fire: Losing Friends and Making Enemies in the American Century* (New York: Public Affairs, 2006).

toward a more expansive and mutually beneficial set of policies.[4] This approach would see the United States finally focusing on issues often neglected during the Cold War, such as human rights, democracy, and economic reform.[5] For these observers, the post–Cold War era rekindled a latent "Wilsonian urge" to promote distinctively American notions of democracy and capitalism in the region.[6]

Other observers, however, forecasted a different outcome for the post–Cold War era. Rather than expecting enlightened policies and hemispheric engagement, these observers assumed that the United States would quickly forget Latin America. No longer a global hotspot, they surmised, the region now had to fear becoming an "Atlantis" from the U.S. perspective.[7] One scholar even argued that Latin America might end up "missing the Cold War" because it at least had kept Washington's rapt attention during this period.[8]

ESTABLISHMENT AND ANTI-IMPERIALIST SCHOOLS

A useful way to organize the conventional approach to studying U.S.–Latin America relations is to divide the varying perspectives into the Establishment and Anti-imperialist schools. While not entirely comprehensive, these two broad conceptual schools encompass the major ideologies in what is an often polarized and ideological realm of U.S.–Latin America relations.

The Establishment School

The Establishment school, whose adherents are often members of the U.S. foreign policy "establishment," believes that the United States usually acts

---

[4] For more of the optimistic scenario, see Jorge I. Domínguez, ed., *The Future of Inter-American Relations* (New York: Routledge, 2000), 5; Jorge G. Castañeda, "The Forgotten Relationship," *Foreign Affairs* 82, no. 3 (May–June 2003): 67–81; Kenneth Maxwell, "Avoiding the Imperial Temptation," *World Policy Journal* 16, no. 3 (Fall 1999): 57–68; Howard J. Wiarda, "After Miami: The Summit, the Peso Crisis, and the Future of U.S.–Latin American Relations," *Journal of Interamerican Studies and World Affairs* 37, no. 1 (Spring 1995): 43–69.

[5] Wiarda, "After Miami," 43–69.

[6] Joseph Tulchin and Ralph Espach, "A Call for Strategic Thinking," in *Latin America in the New International System*, ed. Joseph S. Tulchin and and Ralph H. Espach (Boulder, CO: Lynne Rienner Publishers, 2001), 11.

[7] Castañeda, "The Forgotten Relationship," 70.

[8] Michael Desch, "Why Latin America May Miss the Cold War: The United States and the Future of Inter-American Security Relations," in *International Security and Democracy: Latin America and the Caribbean in the Post–Cold War Era*, ed. Jorge I. Domínguez (Pittsburgh: University of Pittsburgh Press, 1998), 245–65.

in good faith in its dealings with Latin America and that Washington's espoused goals of democracy, human rights, and economic liberalization are benign and necessary for the region's stability and growth. The school also believes in the legitimacy and morality of the U.S. government, even if fierce (and often partisan) debates exist within the school as to what should constitute the specific nature of U.S. policies in Latin America.

The Establishment school viewed the end of the Cold War as an opportunity for improved U.S.–Latin American relations. No longer forced to fight communism, these analysts and scholars contended, U.S. policy-makers would take up issues of democracy and economic reform and trade liberalization. Thus, according to one Establishment adherent, "free from the strategic and ideological rigidities of the Cold War, Latin America in the mid-1990s looked forward to a more realistic and constructive relationship with the United States."[9] For the Establishment school, the potential exists for a "win-win" scenario in U.S.–Latin American relations.

Perhaps the greatest distinction among the various elements of the Establishment school is how they perceive threats in the region. More conservative Establishment policymakers and analysts are predisposed to see threats to American interests in matters such as drug trafficking, anti-American nationalism, and populist economic policies. For example, conservatives tend to be more alarmist about President Hugo Chávez's attempts at spreading a "Bolivarian Revolution" throughout Latin America and supporting Marxist guerrilla groups in Colombia than, say, about the excesses of a right-wing political leader or government. Conservatives tend to work in or with Republican administrations.[10]

The liberal side of the Establishment school is more willing to look at the "root causes" of drug cultivation or of Hugo Chávez's populism; its policy prescriptions tend more toward rewards, or "carrots," than punitive "sticks." For example, in describing his view of the motivations behind post–Cold War U.S. policies in the region, Tim Reiser, a senior Democratic staff member for Senator Patrick Leahy (D-VT), underlined the central tenets of the liberal wing of Establishment school:

Since the Cold War our interests have broadened. Today we are dealing with many challenges including terrorism, drug trafficking and organized crime, illegal immigrants, supporting elections and democratic institutions, military, police and

---

[9] Castañeda, "The Forgotten Relationship," 67.

[10] Robert Pastor provides a definition of liberals and conservatives in *Exiting the Whirlpool: U.S. Foreign Policy toward Latin America and the Caribbean* (Boulder, CO: Westview Press, 2001), 30–3.

judicial reform, and issues involving human rights, poverty, health and environmental protection. But these broader interests do not diminish the reality that an
overriding interest of the U.S. government in Latin America has been to promote an
investment climate where U.S. companies can increase their earnings.[11]

Although they might have more of a "social orientation" than their
conservative counterparts, Establishment liberals do not reject the legitimacy of U.S. leadership and power in the hemisphere. Nor do they consider
a secure hemispheric business environment and U.S. investment to be
contrary to the interests of Latin American countries. All of the post–Cold
War presidential administrations can be placed in the Establishment cate-
gory; in this sense, U.S. policies most often reflect Establishment principles.
The *analysis* of U.S. policy, though, is not limited to the Establishment
school.

The Anti-imperialist School

The "Anti-imperialist" school, a set of scholars and policy analysts who
adopt a more strident and critical tone toward the United States' objectives
in Latin America after the Cold War, views the United States' imperialist
legacy as the best predictor of how government officials in Washington will
act today and in the future. For the Anti-imperialists, the collapse of the
Soviet Union meant even fewer restraints on America's power; thus, the
United States could now reign "uncontested and complete."[12] Therefore,
instead of a new era of engagement and "goodwill," the Anti-imperialists
suggested that we should expect Washington to *increase* its control over
Latin America.[13]

According to this school, the United States would justify its more controlling policies in Latin America by intentionally replacing communism
with a variety of other "threats" to national security, such as drug trafficking, illegal immigration, and terrorism. During the first years of the
post–Cold War thaw, for example, some Anti-imperialists criticized U.S.
policies as too militaristic. More specifically, they felt that the U.S. military
had monopolized bureaucratic control of U.S.–Latin American relations,
resulting in policies that were overly "militarized" at the expense of

---

[11] Tim Reiser (Senior Democratic Staff Member, Senate Appropriations Committee), in an
interview with the author, Washington, DC, May 3, 2007.
[12] Peter H. Smith, *Talons of the Eagle: Dynamics of U.S.–Latin American Relations*, 2nd ed.
(New York: Oxford University Press, 2000), 6.
[13] Lars Schoultz, *Beneath the United States: A History of US Policy toward Latin America*
(Cambridge, MA: Harvard University Press, 1998), xiv.

diplomatic, political, or social alternatives.[14] In one particularly salient case, they claimed that, instead of helping the Colombian people find alternatives to illicit drug production, Washington instead had sent military hardware and advisers in order to increase its control over the country.

Unlike the Establishment school's view, the Anti-imperialist school sees a "win–lose" situation, in which the United States reaps military and financial benefits while Latin America pays the costs of reduced sovereignty and greater poverty. To get a sense of how the Anti-imperialist school might analyze a particular U.S. policy, consider policy activist Coletta Youngers's view regarding the U.S. military's motives for embracing the drug war in the late 1980s: "The escalation of the U.S. war on drugs coincided with the end of the Cold War and the struggle by U.S. policymakers and Pentagon strategists to develop a rationale for maintaining U.S. military might in the region, and protect the status of the United States as sole superpower."[15] Or take another Anti-imperialist explanation of the Clinton administration's motives for supporting the controversial Plan Colombia initiative in 2000. In this characterization, Washington is once again acting in its predictable and nefarious ways, all at the expense of Colombia's welfare:

Plan Colombia is heavily influenced by Washington's successful reassertion of hegemony in Central America following the so-called "peace accords." Washington's success [in Central America] was based on the use of state terror, mass displacement of population, large-scale and long-term military spending, military advisors, and the offer of a political settlement involving the reincorporation of the guerrilla commanders into politics ... Washington believes it can repeat the "terror for peace" formula of Central America via Plan Colombia in the Andean country.[16]

In light of these two differing schools, what then is the true nature of U.S. policy since the Cold War? Now that communism is no longer a threat, has Washington adopted a broader set of policies? Or is the United States using its unprecedented military, political, and economic might to increase its control over a region of the world that has historically been its subordinate?

There are no easy answers to these questions, and, while both the Establishment and the Anti-imperialist schools can at times provide accurate and useful interpretations and predictions, each one is incomplete as an overriding framework for interpreting the motivations and applications of

---

[14] See, for example, Adam Isacson, "Militarizing Latin America Policy," *Foreign Policy in Focus* 6, no. 21 (May 2001): 1–4.

[15] Coletta Youngers, "Cocaine Madness: Counternarcotics and Militarization in the Andes," *NACLA Report on the Americas* 34, no. 3 (2000): 17.

[16] James Petras, "The Geopolitics of Plan Colombia," *Monthly Review* 53, no. 1 (May 2001): 30–48.

U.S. policy in Latin America since the Cold War. Instead, we should continue to consider the premises of these two schools but not let their assumptions overwhelm a broader, more encompassing approach.

A NEW PERSPECTIVE

Developing a lasting, comprehensive, yet simple approach for understanding post–Cold War U.S. policy in the Western Hemisphere is not an easy task. In addition to recognizing the "structural" features, such as "power asymmetries," that shape the United States' actions in Latin America, we must also consider the rapidly shifting political, economic, and social currents within Latin America; domestic concerns; and the ideological makeup of presidential administrations.

Power and Influence

The United States obviously holds enormous power vis-à-vis its Latin American neighbors. Value judgments aside, the United States' almost unrestricted power gives it a tremendous economic, political, and military advantage. Washington is far more capable of influencing events and policies within the hemisphere than its neighbors are of influencing U.S. policy. For example, take the Clinton administration's decision in March 1995 to "decertify" Bolivia for what it deemed the country's inadequate progress in the war on drugs. As one might suspect, this decision was deeply unpopular in the South American nation. Yet Bolivia certainly could not decertify the United States in return, even if a strong majority felt that the nation was being highly hypocritical in its approach to the drug war.

Nevertheless, Washington does not necessarily use its power exclusively to promote its own national interests in Latin America. For example, ten successive presidential administrations have continued a policy aimed at ending Fidel Castro's rule in Cuba. The United States certainly has the military capacity to conquer the island and to determine an outcome favorable to its national interests. Yet it has not done so for many reasons: concern over the political fallout, fear of disproportionate civilian casualties, and belief that the military operation would serve only to embolden Castro's supporters, as in the 1961 Bay of Pigs invasion, when the defeat of the CIA-sponsored anti-Castro invasion galvanized Cuban support for Castro's regime. Even with its tremendous might, the United States faces constraints on the application of its power in the hemisphere.

Another unequal aspect of Washington's foreign policy vis-à-vis Latin America is that the United States has policy *choices*. In contrast with its hemispheric neighbors, the United States can act variably, with greater flexibility than its counterparts. Thus, to return to the Cuba example, Washington could invade the Caribbean island but could also opt just to maintain the decades-long economic embargo. On the other hand, it could opt to normalize its relationship with Havana. Again, however, just because Washington has more options does not ensure that it will adopt the most effective or beneficial policy with respect to its own interests.

Although Washington's power and choices in the hemisphere might be unparalleled, its *influence* varies greatly. Take, for instance, the case of the Grenada invasion in 1983 during the height of the Cold War. The U.S. military occupied this tiny island nation and quickly forced the end of a radical Marxist junta. By exerting its power, the United States transformed the very nature of Grenada's political, social, and economic situation in a matter of days. In what came as a shock to many observers, an overwhelming majority of Grenada's citizens responded positively to the invasion.

Jump forward to 2002, when the U.S. ambassador to Bolivia announced that Washington would consider cutting off development assistance if Bolivians elected a candidate who was soft on the drug war. Contrary to what Washington expected, this warning served to boost the electoral fortunes of the campaign's most radical anti-American candidate, Evo Morales. His strong second-place finish in 2002 was to propel him to eventual victory in 2005. In this case, the United States' power did not translate into influence. In fact, it backfired.

Rhetorical, Operational, and Intentional Policies

Another key element to a new approach for understanding U.S. policies in Latin America requires us to determine to what extent we take "rhetorical" foreign policy aims at face value. Over the past two decades, successive post–Cold War administrations have publicly championed a new era in U.S.–Latin America relations. But pronouncements, of course, are only rhetoric. That is, what governments say about a particular issue might be different from what these same governments want. For example, what are we supposed to make of an assistant secretary of state for the Western Hemisphere who explains that the United States' overriding policy concerns in a certain Latin American country are democracy and the rule of law? Similarly, should we take an American president's claim at face value when he says that his goal is to see a free and prosperous hemisphere? These questions remind us that understanding the rhetorical level of policy is but the first step in gaining an accurate understanding of policy.

One useful technique in foreign policy analysis is to separate rhetorical foreign policy from operational and intentional foreign policies. As the terms suggests, rhetorical foreign policy is what a government says publicly; operational policy is the action that the government carries out; and intentional policy is the series of objectives the decision makers are attempting to accomplish. Consider a hypothetical example in which Washington directs funding to a Latin American presidential candidate's campaign. Rhetorically, the administration states that its policy is aimed at promoting democracy and economic prosperity. So, we must ask, are Washington's democracy speeches and programs actually intended to fulfill their namesake and promote democracy? Or are the campaign funding efforts serving an ulterior purpose, such as upholding the claims an American company might have on that country's natural resources? On the operational level, we would look at how the U.S. government was actually carrying out this stated policy of campaign support. For the intentional, we would need to determine what Washington was truly trying to achieve by adopting these very rhetorical and operational policies.

Typically, there is less controversy at the rhetorical and operational levels because both of these policies can be easily monitored. Intentional foreign policy, however, is more open to interpretation and much more difficult to determine. Given the infinite number of interpretations, how can we come to definite conclusions about the United States' *intentions* in its Latin America policies?

The answer is that there will never be full agreement. Nevertheless, we can observe the interplay of rhetorical, operational, and intentional policies and ask whether Washington truly intends to put away the Big Stick in its dealings with its Latin American neighbors. The rhetoric of democracy and cooperation put forth by successive post–Cold War presidents suggests that a new era has arrived, but this alone is not sufficient. We need to examine closely the United States' operational policies and consider its often multilayered intentions before we can begin to make even the most tentative conclusions about the nature of U.S. policy in Latin America.

A New Latin America

Our focus on the changing nature of U.S. policy in Latin America since the end of the Cold War should not overshadow the profound changes that have occurred in Latin America. Unlike the dark periods of authoritarian rule and economic sclerosis that characterized the latter part of the Cold War, the past two decades have seen a profound shift toward electoral democracy and relative economic stability in Latin America. Today, military coups are the exception, not the norm; citizens routinely elect their leaders in usually transparent and peaceful elections.

Still, Latin America is rife with economic, political, and social problems. While voters can elect their leaders, the institutions of government are often weak and unaccountable; the rule of law can be elusive; and, oftentimes, leaders are either unable or unwilling to identify and solve the problems fundamental to the well-being of their nations' citizens. Furthermore, many Latin American democracies are strained by public apathy and the rise of populist authoritarian leaders. These shortcomings aside, for the first time in its history, Latin America has entered an era where democracy is, by and large, the "only game in town."

During this democratic era, other world powers have begun to exert their influence in the Western Hemisphere. China, for example, has become an increasingly important economic and military partner to many Latin American countries. This begs the question of whether increased Chinese involvement will mean a reduction in American influence.

Latin America's constantly evolving economic and political position raises the important issue of U.S.–Latin American convergence. Increasingly, the interests – and, by extension, the policies – of the United States and Latin America are coalescing, particularly when it comes to democracy and economic reform. Some observers, primarily in the Establishment school, see examples of convergence in efforts to expand free trade agreements throughout the region or the call by the Organization of American States (OAS) to make democracy the only form of legitimate government in the hemisphere. Keep in mind, though, that Anti-imperialist critics are much more likely to dismiss U.S. rhetoric and operational policies as a subtle way of allowing the United States to impose its interests and values on the region, all the while appearing as though it is acting as a partner and not an imperial power.

We must also consider that, while the United States exerts great influence in the region, Latin American countries are increasingly able to influence events in the United States. In the late 1990s, Colombia's ambassador in Washington, Luis Alberto Moreno, embarked on an exhaustive "inside the Beltway" campaign to convince members of Congress and the Clinton administration that greater support for the Colombian government was in the United States' national interest. Moreno met with church organizations, university students, and countless other groups connected to or interested in Colombia in order to sway public and private opinion toward his government's position. In the end, Moreno was successful beyond his wildest imagination: a bipartisan majority in Congress passed the Clinton administration's legislation authorizing funding for Plan Colombia.

Domestic Politics

A quick review of the two decades since the end of the Cold War reinforces the notion that domestic politics continues to influence the creation of U.S. policy in the Western Hemisphere. Indeed, headline-grabbing cases such as Cuba, Haiti, and the multicountry war on drugs would not have been so important to U.S. policymakers had there not been key domestic political considerations at stake – for example, domestic drug consumption or the impact of immigration. Such overlapping domestic and international issues are what constitutes our intermestic agenda in the post–Cold War era.

The Role of Ideology and Personality in Presidential Administrations

The United States does not act as a united, singular, or "realist" actor. The realist approach, appealing in its simplicity and frequent accuracy, is far from complete. As scholars, we too often resort to claims that the "United States is doing this" or "Washington is doing that" when a more accurate account would analyze (and disaggregate) the particular interests of involved policymakers or agencies. During crises, policymakers often are forced to make key decisions with imperfect information and in a matter of minutes or hours; in these intense moments, the policymakers' core ideologies strongly shape their decisions.

Much of this personal or individual element in policymaking often remains behind the scenes. Yet, if we ignore it – if we consider the United States to be a static actor that is not influenced by specific individuals like members of Congress or those serving in presidential administrations – we risk missing the true motivations of U.S. "policy." For example, the fact that George H. W. Bush was president in 1989 significantly influenced the decision to invade Panama and oust strongman Manuel Noriega. Although we will never know, we can seriously question whether the United States would have invaded Panama had the more dovish Democratic Party candidate Michael Dukakis won the 1988 presidential election.

At times it is still preferable to use more generic terms when describing the United States as a political actor. In fact, we will frequently rely upon these terms (i.e., "Washington" and "the United States") when doing so does not oversimplify the decision-making process. Nevertheless, the reader should be aware that using these broad terms can run the risk of generalizing what are, in reality, much more complex and nuanced policy considerations.

We should not conclude, though, that the United States lacks core interests or does not pursue policies that endure over several successive presidential administrations. On the contrary, the United States has acted cohesively and consistently on issues continuing over multiple administrations. For example, as a key U.S. policy in the region, the war on drugs has proved remarkably resilient over the course of three post–Cold War presidential administrations. To get an accurate picture, we must consider both the structural and personal elements that lead the United States to act the way that it does in its own hemisphere. With this in mind, we now move on to examine the particular natures and inclinations of these presidents and their administrations in order see how each approached Latin American policy after the Cold War.

2

Policies across Three Presidential Administrations

The two decades after the Cold War's end witnessed a fascinating series of developments in terms of U.S. policies and involvement in the Americas: a multibillion dollar program to support the Colombian government in its fight against insurgents and drug trafficking; responses to dramatic financial crises in Mexico, Brazil, and Argentina; and heated debates over illegal immigration into the United States, the overwhelming share of it from Latin America. Many elements of U.S. policies during this era were not exclusive to one presidential administration; rather, key issues in cases such as Haiti, Cuba, and the war on drugs spanned across the three post–Cold War administrations. At other times, though, a particular policy was tied inextricably to a single administration.

Accordingly, we must examine the extent to which the formulation and implementation of policy either endured or changed across these administrations. To what degree did these administrations inherit their policies from their predecessors or create them during their period in office? This effort will help us determine which aspects of U.S. policy tend to be "structural" and which result from the particular ideology or personal predilection of a specific administration.

GEORGE H. W. BUSH (1989–1993)

George Bush took office in January 1989 when the Berlin Wall was still standing. Even the most astute observers did not anticipate how abruptly and completely the Cold War would end. Almost overnight, the global ideological struggle of the Cold War was replaced by a reality that appeared more optimistic, made famous by Bush's proclamation of a "new world order."

During his one-term presidency, Bush oversaw two Latin America policies. The first, driven by the overriding priority of checking perceived Soviet and Cuban advancement, fell squarely within the global East-West clash of the Cold War. The second phase, which consisted of economic and democracy initiatives, stemmed directly from the fact that the anticommunist cause had become largely irrelevant almost overnight.

Bush was eager to make Latin America policy (and Central America policy in particular) less controversial and partisan than it had been during his predecessor's tenure in the Oval Office. To achieve these ends, Bush's top Latin America aides and diplomats made aggressive efforts to broker peace agreements and promote electoral outcomes in war-torn Central American countries such as El Salvador and Nicaragua. Within the first two years of Bush's term, Nicaragua held democratic elections and El Salvador's military and Marxist insurgents signed a UN-backed peace settlement. Some observers disputed how much the Bush administration had to do with these "wins," but they nevertheless happened on Bush's watch.

In terms of whether Bush deserved credit for these developments, conservative Establishment adherents cited Reagan's approach to the leftist revolutions in Central America, arguing that the former president's unapologetic support for anticommunist elements paved the way for these democratic transitions. Other liberal Establishment and Anti-imperialist observers contended that these political developments occurred *despite* Reagan's policies and that Bush had taken the right approach by focusing on diplomatic and not military solutions.

Panama, 1989

Peacefully quelling armed conflicts in Central America was not Bush's only major initiative in Central America; in fact, he ordered a full-scale military invasion and occupation in Panama less than a year into office. Bush inherited the Reagan administration's largely ineffective policy of economic sanctions against Panama, a strategy employed in an attempt to force dictatorial strongman Manuel Noriega from power primarily for his involvement in drug trafficking. By 1989 his regime had grown even more violent and recalcitrant. Because the U.S. government's efforts to strangle Noriega's government through economic sanctions served only to bolster the dictator's standing, the Bush administration began to consider other, more aggressive ways to deal with him. The Bush White House was dusting off the Big Stick for its first post–Cold War operation. Disgusted by images from May of that year showing democratic opposition candidates beaten and even shot by Noriega's forces (known as Dignity Battalions) and angered by the repeated harassment of American service members in the country, Bush ordered a full-scale invasion with the intent of bringing an end to Noriega's rule via "regime change."

In December 1989 roughly 20,000 American troops invaded the country in order to apprehend Noriega. Thus, although the Bush administration was generally more inclined toward negotiation and multilateralism than was his predecessor, the invasion of Panama showed that it would use force without hesitation if it believed America's security interests were at risk.

Many in the media accused Bush of attempting to erase his image as a foreign policy "wimp." Others speculated that Bush ordered the intervention as part of a complex plot to delay or even derail the planned turnover of the canal to Panamanian hands at the end of the twentieth century. Yet, while the international community overwhelmingly condemned it, the invasion proved popular among both Americans and Panamanians, the latter having grown tired of Noriega's increasingly tyrannical rule. Reports indicated that upward of 90 percent of the Panamanian population supported the military operation because it quickly removed the hated Noriega (Figure 2.1).[1]

The Panama case marks the approximate beginning of the United States' post–Cold War policies in Latin America. Bush justified the invasion with Noriega's notoriety as an unrepentant drug trafficker, one whose sordid dealings allowed greater quantities of illicit drugs to enter the United States and the hands of its youth. Security, unlike the years of the Cold War when it had been synonymous with anticommunism, had taken on new territory, including the war on drugs.

Only six years separated the invasions of Grenada and Panama; yet the issues (communism vs. drugs) that motivated them represented two distinct eras in American foreign policy toward Latin America. For some Anti-imperialists, "drugs" was simply the new "communism" that allowed the American eagle to yield its lethal talons in Panama. For others, the Panama invasion was a necessary anomaly in an otherwise increasingly peaceful, multilateral era.

The Primacy of Economics

Beyond the civil wars in Central America and the Panama invasion in 1989, Bush and his advisers set out to establish a new economic relationship

---

[1] Russell Crandall, *Gunboat Democracy: U.S. Interventions in the Dominican Republic, Grenada, and Panama* (Lanham, MD: Rowman & Littlefield, 2007), 209.

FIGURE 2.1. Joint U.S. and Panamanian military patrols walk the streets through the Chorrillo district, which had been destroyed during the U.S. invasion in December 1989. (Photo: Reuters/Corinne Dufka.)

between the United States and Latin America; economic reform and trade integration topped the administration's list of policy priorities. The 1980s were a "lost decade" for the countries of Latin America, many of which were riddled with devastating foreign debt obligations, uncontrollable inflation, and glaring budget deficits. Remarkably, though, the Bush administration's aggressive and innovative debt reduction program, known as the Brady Plan, allowed most desperate Latin American countries once again to borrow from foreign creditors, including commercial banks.

Contrary to the more suspicious stances they had taken toward Washington during much of the Cold War, some key Latin American countries now began to consider developing a closer economic relationship with the United States. In particular, Mexico, under President Carlos Salinas de Gortari, actively pursued a free trade agreement with the Bush administration. Although not ratified until after Bill Clinton assumed office, the North American Free Trade Agreement (NAFTA), which also included Canada, aligned neatly with George Bush's objective of promoting a U.S.-led economic model of trade integration in the Western Hemisphere.

About the same time that the Bush administration began negotiations over NAFTA, it also launched the Enterprise for the Americas Initiative

(EAI). This plan intended to turn the Western Hemisphere into a massive free trade zone "from Alaska to Antarctica." While there are few today who still remember the EAI, its intellectual successor – the Free Trade Area of the Americas (FTAA) – continued to be a key framework for hemispheric trade talks long after the EAI was forgotten. In this sense, the EAI can be considered the father of free trade agreements in the Western Hemisphere.

By the time Bush left office in early 1993, a new post–Cold War agenda based on economic stability and trade integration could be seen on the horizon. The new plan even had substantial bipartisan support on Capitol Hill. This shift toward a consensus over the perceived merits of economic liberalization and reform was especially appealing at the time, given communism's glaring economic failures and its subsequent implosion. To this end, NAFTA quickly became the shining model for this new liberalized approach that favored the "invisible hand" of free markets over government-led economic policies.

This new focus on practical, market solutions received relatively little opposition on Capitol Hill. Members of Congress from both sides of the aisle were tired of the rancor and mistrust that had dominated Central America policymaking in the 1980s.They were eager to adopt a new, less controversial agenda and believed that open societies and open markets were the key elements for any lasting peace and prosperity.

Beyond appealing to policymakers in Washington, notions of promoting hemispheric solidarity and prosperity through economic integration and liberalization appealed to a new generation of democratic leaders in Latin America, many of whom had suffered through devastating economic turmoil during much of the 1980s and were ready for change.

Although not nearly as paramount as economic reform and trade initiatives, democracy also emerged as an integral component of Bush's policy initiatives. While the aforementioned efforts to encourage negotiated settlements in the wars in Central America were by far the most pressing concern with respect to promoting democracy, there was also the case of Haiti, where the Bush administration worked (albeit with mixed results) to promote peaceful elections in 1990.

To a certain extent, the Bush administration's democracy agenda was a product of extremely good timing, as many countries throughout the region were experiencing transitions to democratic rule during the 1980s. By the time Bush assumed the presidency in 1989, most of the difficult transitions had already occurred. For his part, Bush pushed democracy as a core element of the United States' interests in the Western Hemisphere. In 1989, for example, Secretary of State James Baker gave a speech championing a postideological push for democracy in the region. His sentiments would be echoed by his government successors for decades to come: "We need each other now as we have never before. ... Latin America's democratic leaders are reaching out to the United States to offer a new partnership. ... I am here on behalf of a new president ... with our answer: We are reaching back to you."[2] While embarking on a trip to South America, President Bush reiterated the words of his secretary of state when he said, "all of the Americas and the Caribbean must embark on a venture for the coming century: to create the first fully democratic hemisphere in the history of mankind."[3]

Overall, while still critiqued as excessively "imperialist" for the invasion of Panama, the Bush administration was able to establish what many concluded was a new, more cooperative tone in U.S. policy in Latin America. The invasion of Panama revealed that the Big Stick was still alive and well, but less "traditional" issues such as drugs, trade, and democracy had now moved onto the agenda.

BILL CLINTON (1993–2001)

With the Cold War now clearly over and Central America's fragile peace agreements and democratic governments still holding, incoming President Bill Clinton felt no need to make the Western Hemisphere a foreign policy priority. Nor did Clinton plan many serious departures from the "prosperity and democracy" agenda established by his predecessor. Despite the fact that the White House had shifted from Republican to Democratic hands, the Clinton administration initially maintained remarkable "policy continuity" with the Bush team.

Ironically, given his administration's general disinterest in the region, one of Clinton's first big foreign policy accomplishments – the ratification of NAFTA – directly involved Latin America. The controversy over NAFTA's approval, however, was infinitely more about domestic politics and economics than about any hemispheric foreign policy concern. While President Bush had made the most substantial push for NAFTA, Congress probably would not have ratified the agreement had Clinton not attached side clauses related to the protection of labor and the environment. Nevertheless,

---

[2] Quoted in Robert Pastor, "The Bush Administration and Latin America: The Pragmatic Style and the Regionalist Option," *Journal of Interamerican Studies and World Affairs* 33, no. 3 (Fall 1991): 17.

[3] Quoted in ibid., 12; also see Richard E. Feinberg, "Regionalism and Domestic Politics: U.S.–Latin American Trade Policy in the Bush Era," *Latin American Politics and Society* 44, no. 4 (Winter 2002): 127–51.

President Clinton tirelessly defended the merits of this free trade agreement initiated and signed by his erstwhile presidential opponent.

NAFTA's ratification in 1993 appeared to be a major political victory for the new president. Yet, many of the events that transpired on Bill Clinton's watch for the next seven years made this achievement seem less important than originally expected. Indeed, by the end of his second term in 2001, Bill Clinton had intervened militarily in Haiti, committed the United States to funding a multibillion dollar assistance package for Colombia, and became involved in a variety of controversial policy initiatives toward Fidel Castro's Cuba. At the same time, though, none of this would prevent critics such as Senator Christopher Dodd from accusing the Clinton administration of "ignoring" Latin America – a critique echoed during the subsequent presidency of George W. Bush as well.

As his tenure continued, Clinton and his Latin America advisers constantly upheld the agenda first pursued under George H. W. Bush, one that committed the United States to promoting a hemisphere of democratic governments and open-market economies. Perhaps the pinnacle of this new era under Clinton was the hemisphere-wide Summit of the Americas hosted by the United States in Miami in December 1994; here, economic integration topped the agenda. However, more so than President Clinton, Latin American leaders aggressively pushed this new framework at the meeting. This last development is noteworthy because it is often assumed that Washington, exploiting the tremendous power imbalance between the United States and Latin America, historically imposes free market solutions on resistant yet helpless hemispheric governments. In contrast, the summit process proved that many (and often newly) democratically elected leaders in Latin America were even more enthusiastic about market liberalization than was the United States.

Robert Pastor, a noted scholar with deep involvement in Latin America policy, describes the United States' relationship with the region in terms of a "whirlpool." In his assessment, a disinterested Washington ignores the region until a crisis breaks out that "sucks in" the United States, only to shoot it back out when the crisis abates.[4]

The whirlpool metaphor certainly seems to apply to the Clinton administration's policies toward Latin America. Key cases such as Haiti, Colombia, and Cuba all suggest that the administration was not focusing intently on events in Latin America until situations appeared to spiral out of

---

[4] Robert Pastor, *Exiting the Whirlpool: U.S. Foreign Policy toward Latin America and the Caribbean* (Boulder, CO: Westview Press, 2001), ix.

control. Other pressing international events and crises also influenced the Clinton administration's actions in Latin America. For example, the United States' failed intervention in Somalia in 1993, in which gruesome images of the bodies of American soldiers being dragged through the streets of the capital city Mogadishu, haunted the administration and American public. A year later during the Haiti crisis, when a military junta ousted the country's democratically elected president, many policies retained symptoms of "Vietnam syndrome," the enduring Cold War fear that U.S. interventions might devolve into "quagmire" situations, from which the nation would be unable to withdraw itself.

Although the Clinton administration was hampered in the Haiti case, other policy decisions indicated a serious commitment to democracy and the rule of law in the region. To this end, the Clinton administration had lined up its rhetoric of democracy with concrete actions, oftentimes conducted in concert with other regional governments. This list of accomplishments begins with the successful Summit of the Americas process and extends to the administration's diplomatic efforts to prevent unconstitutional changes of government in Ecuador and Paraguay, promoting a lasting resolution to the border war between Peru and Ecuador in early 1995, and playing a low-profile but still constructive role in the UN-led effort that resulted in the 1994 peace accords that ended Guatemala's brutal, decades-long civil war.[5]

Interestingly, Clinton did not even visit South America until his second term of office. In particular, some of Clinton's top advisers felt that they lost a wonderful opportunity when the administration failed to follow up the tremendous momentum from the 1994 Miami summit with a visit to the region to reinforce his interest in stronger relations.[6] Yet, amazingly, Clinton's reputation in the region was quite strong, particularly when compared to those of his immediate predecessor and successor. This fact is due in large part to Clinton's inimitable charisma, which allowed him to convey to Latin Americans that he understood their fears and challenges even if he was paying them only peripheral attention in comparison to more pressing crises such as the civil war in Bosnia.

---

[5] Alexander F. Watson (Assistant Secretary of State for Inter-American Affairs, 1993–6), in an interview with the author, Washington, DC, February 16, 2007. For a comprehensive take on the Clinton administration's Latin America policy, see David Scott Palmer, *U.S. Relations with Latin America during the Clinton Years: Opportunities Lost or Opportunities Squandered?* (Gainesville: University Press of Florida, 2006).

[6] Richard E. Feinberg (Special Assistant to the President for Inter-American Affairs, 1993–6), in a telephone interview with the author March 16, 2007.

One classic example is Clinton's visit to Colombia in 2000. This visit followed on the heels of several years of bitter relations between Washington and Bogotá that had resulted from disagreements over the execution of the war on drugs. Although Clinton spent only eight hours in the coastal city of Cartagena, his charm and steel-trap mastery of the policy issues allowed him immediately to win over the hearts and minds of countless Colombians. According to one Democratic congressional aide, Clinton's Latin America policies were "ones of symbolism"; however, the source also stressed: "Symbolism was important. Given the dark period we had endured during the Cold War, this seemed good enough. We needed to celebrate Latin America's remarkable turn to democracy during these years. So, yes, some of it was 'feel good' policy. But it seemed to be more than enough at the time."[7]

Bill Clinton's presidency succeeded in maintaining and deepening the pro-democracy, pro-free-market agenda established by his predecessor. Latin America was never a priority for the Clinton White House, but many of its critical policies toward democracy promotion represented a break from the Cold War–era when such efforts were supported only to the extent that they served the broader anticommunist strategy. Yet, like Bush's invasion of Panama, Clinton's decision to send in the U.S. military into Haiti in 1994 served as a reminder that, even if the intention was largely humanitarian, the Big Stick approach to Latin America continued.

GEORGE W. BUSH (2001–)

During the 2000 presidential campaign, candidate George W. Bush criticized Bill Clinton for losing the momentum on hemispheric trade talks as well as generally neglecting Latin America. When Bush assumed office, many thought he would follow up on his campaign rhetoric by making Latin America a foreign policy priority – something that had not been done in nearly a decade.

Indeed, Bush made an early symbolic gesture toward Latin America by making Mexico the destination for his first foreign visit. He also hosted Mexican president Vicente Fox at his Texas ranch in order to promote strong Washington–Mexico City ties and to establish what he touted as "amigo diplomacy" to reinforce the image of a strong, trustful bilateral

---

[7] Daniel Restrepo (Democratic professional staff member, Committee on Foreign Affairs, House of Representatives, 1993–6), in an interview with the author, Washington, DC, May 1, 2007.

relationship. Even some of Bill Clinton's former top advisers on Latin America conceded that the Americas finally appeared to have a post–Cold War president in George W. Bush, one who would engage the region regardless of whether there was a crisis at hand.

Another indication that Bush intended to strengthen ties with the region was his attendance at the 2001 Summit of the Americas meeting in Quebec, where he and thirty-three other hemispheric heads of state adopted a "democracy clause" that committed the summit's participants to oppose any attempt to undermine constitutional democracy in the hemisphere. The summit's "democracy clause" linked free trade agreements to democracy. Soon after Quebec, the OAS codified the clause in its Inter-American Democracy Charter during a meeting in Lima, Peru, on September 11, 2001. The charter defines the core elements of democracy and lists the reasons why an OAS member country could be suspended for not adhering to its norms.[8]

Secretary of State Colin Powell was in Lima to sign the charter on the United States' behalf when Islamic terrorists launched their bloody terrorist attack on American soil. Some will surely conclude that the events of 9/11 and the Bush administration's subsequent Global War on Terror put an end to the president's more engaged stance toward the Western Hemisphere.

In addition, the perception that the Fox government and Mexican public had been belated in responding, if not outright insensitive, to the 9/11 terrorist attacks left a bitter taste in the mouths of many Bush administration officials, including that of the president. While the Mexican government condemned the attacks, no mass vigils or official ceremonies were held in Mexico in remembrance of the victims in the weeks after 9/11. As a president who placed great importance on his personal relationships with other heads of state, George Bush lost a great deal of faith in Vicente Fox following what he believed to be Mexico's lack of support for the United States. In the aftermath of 9/11, Bush was looking for unwavering allies in the war on terrorism; Fox's response to the terrorist attacks did not fit that mold, something that immediately made him suspect in the Bush White House.

In addition to the personal rift between Bush and Fox, talk of greater integration with Mexico had become a political nonstarter, given the heightened concern about terrorists crossing over America's porous southern borders. Thus, the aggressive bilateral agenda aimed at increasing economic and even labor integration that Bush and Fox pursued in the "amigo diplomacy" era effectively halted.

---

[8] Feinberg, "Regionalism and Domestic Politics," 136.

It would be fascinating to know how George W. Bush would have addressed Latin America had there not been a catastrophic terrorist attack on U.S. soil. We do know that the attacks galvanized Bush's belief that the United States should spare no expense to combat terrorist threats to the United States. As we will see, this approach eventually made its way to Latin America.

Much more so than his predecessors, Bush aggressively merged the priorities of democracy, security, and economic reform in his approach to U.S. policy in Latin America. In the eyes of his administration, each element of the policy framework was necessary because each overlapped with and reinforced the others. In a speech he gave in Washington, DC, in early 2002, nearly four months after 9/11, Bush made his view of these concomitant priorities clear: "The future of this hemisphere depends on the strength of three commitments: democracy, security, and market-based development. These commitments are inseparable, and none will be achieved by half-measures. This road will not always be easy, but it's the only road to stability and prosperity for all the people – all the people – who live in this hemisphere."[9]

While George W. Bush melded the issues of democracy, security, and market economics, his policies were still largely in keeping with those that had been established in the early 1990s. Bush's rhetoric differed relatively little from that of his two predecessors, yet his deeply ideological approach departed from theirs significantly. As was the case with Fox, Bush placed tremendous significance on his personal assessment of his Latin American counterparts. Thus, if Bush did not "like" a particular president personally, then he was inclined not to focus on the particular bilateral relationship. In what surprised many observers who assumed Bush's conservative ideology would lead him to reflexively shun leaders from the opposite ideological perspective, Bush came to like his Brazilian counterpart, Luiz Inácio Lula da Silva (or "Lula"), even though he was a committed leftist. Bush's affinity for Lula then translated into a robust agenda of U.S.-Brazilian cooperation on a variety of fronts, including energy security.

Bush's policies provide us with many opportunities to examine whether his rhetorical position accorded with his administration's actions and intentions in Latin America. In one telling example of his particular approach to the region, Bush, in his first term, appointed Otto Reich first as an aide at the National Security Council and then as assistant secretary of state for the Western Hemisphere. Reich held unimpeachable anti-Castro credentials and was clearly the preferred candidate of many in the Cuban

---

[9] President George W. Bush, "Remarks by the President to the World Affairs Council National Conference," Office of the Press Secretary, Washington, DC, January 16, 2002.

exile community based in Florida. Reich's controversial record of involvement in the Iran-Contra affair during the 1980s, however, raised more than a few eyebrows in Washington, especially among Anti-imperialist critics.

These critics immediately accused Bush of selecting a "Cold Warrior" with a sordid past of involvement in undemocratic activities aimed largely at overthrowing Castro. Reich's nomination was held up by Senate Democrats until Bush was finally able to bypass a Senate vote and appoint him during a congressional recess.

How then would Bush's Latin America team manifest its ideological predilections into policy? Like any dispute between the rhetorical and the operational-intentional aspects of foreign policy, interpretation is open to constant debate. Nevertheless, critics soon argued that the Bush administration revealed its true colors in its reaction to the failed coup in Venezuela in April 2002. To these detractors, Bush's rhetoric of democracy and rule of law were intended only if these democratic governments caved in to Washington's demands for narrowly defined economic policies or American-style democracy. Supporters countered that, though the response to the attempted coup in Caracas in April 2002 might not have been perfect, it did not betray the administration's broader and genuine commitment to democracy in the hemisphere.

Controversy continued to follow the Bush administration in the year leading up to the war in Iraq. Mexico and Chile, two of Washington's strongest allies in the region, coincidentally happened to be serving as rotating members on the UN Security Council. In March, France opposed a highly contested "second resolution" against Iraq that the Bush administration supported. It became critical to see on which side countries such as Mexico and Chile would vote.

On March 17, both Mexico and Chile announced that they would not vote for the United States' proposed ultimatum on Iraq to meet UN disarmament resolutions. Despite strong pressure from the Bush administration and the president's personal "cold shoulder" toward Vicente Fox, both countries continued to oppose the resolution in the following weeks, suggesting that Washington's *influence* in the hemisphere was less than its extraordinary power. (Other Latin American countries such as El Salvador and Colombia did express support for the Bush administration's position on Iraq.)

Another key attribute of George W. Bush's approach to the Western Hemisphere was his unapologetic belief in the necessary and justifiable nature of the United States' actions. American support for Colombia serves as a key example: when considering whether to increase its military support to Colombia to help suppress the drug trade, the Clinton administration worried whether doing so might lead to "another Vietnam." On the other hand, the Bush administration immediately sent military and social assistance for the drug and counterinsurgency efforts in Colombia. As one high-level Bush appointee at the Pentagon said in 2004, "As long as Colombian troops are doing the fighting, there isn't much else that we shouldn't help them with."[10]

George W. Bush's policies toward Latin America are the most controversial of those from the three post–Cold War presidencies. In dealing with Latin American countries, whether it involved the Iraq vote at the UN Security Council or the attempted coup in Venezuela, the Bush administration was willing to press for outcomes favorable to U.S. interests in ways that critics viewed as at least in keeping with the United States' long and controversial history of controlling Latin America.

Yet, contrary to the typical evaluation that Washington is too interventionist in Latin America, others – perhaps Bush's most caustic critics – routinely accused him of not being involved enough. According to these critics, Bush seemed to be so distracted by other international developments that he ignored the region. In fact, the Bush administration did not wield its power or expand its influence nearly as much or as aggressively as some might have predicted. For one, the United States did not invade any Latin American countries during this era. At times, as in the case of Haiti, Bush even resisted domestic and international pressure to become more directly involved.

If anything, the Bush administration's Latin America policies suggest that there are new motivations and interpretations of U.S. policy that do not fall neatly into our traditional categories.

---

[10] U.S. Department of Defense Official in a confidential interview with the author, April 4, 2004.

3

Democracy

The two decades since the end of the Cold War have seen dramatic changes in the nature of U.S. policies in Latin America. As important as it is to understand the nuances of each post–Cold War presidential administration, to evaluate these changes it is also crucial to identify the key policy "drivers" that come into play when considering a particular issue or crisis. This book divides post–Cold War issues and policies into three broad categories: democracy, economics, and security. Not all U.S. policies fit into one of these three; nevertheless, we can assume that *most* of the key policies that the United States has in regard to the region fall into one or more of these general areas.

Often we see significant overlap among the three categories. For instance, the United States has pursued a variety of policies in Haiti, ranging from supporting democratic elections in 1990 to launching a military intervention in 1994 and then supporting another military intervention and a subsequent UN peacekeeping operation in 2004. Should we place Haiti under "democracy policy" or "security policy?" The best answer, of course, is both. By employing this approach to examine the motivations and characteristics of these three areas of policy, the reader will be able to evaluate more effectively the case studies of U.S. policy contained in this book, especially because almost all of these three elements significantly overlap.

Just as scholars continue to debate the United States' impact on democracy in Latin America during the Cold War, we will debate its influence in post–Cold War episodes. There are often competing interpretations of the same events and policies, often depending on the ideological predisposition of the observer involved. For example, should a multimillion dollar grant from the U.S. government to a pro-democracy, nongovernmental organization in Venezuela be considered a form of democracy promotion, as Washington claimed, or as "neo-imperialism" as the Venezuelan leader Hugo Chávez often contended?

In the post–Cold War period, to evaluate the U.S. government's commitment to both rhetorical and operational democracy policies, we must weigh the particular circumstances of the events in question, as well as the individual decisions of the U.S. officials involved.

THE EVOLUTION OF DEMOCRACY IN THE U.S. POLICY ARSENAL

The United States' preoccupation with democracy – both rhetorically and operationally – long precedes the end of the Cold War. Indeed, democracy as a core component of U.S. policy in Latin America dates back as far as the "gunboat diplomacy" era in the early twentieth century, when presidents such as Theodore Roosevelt, William Taft, and Woodrow Wilson oversaw elections in Central American and Caribbean countries while they were under U.S. military occupation. President Wilson's oft-cited admonishment that the United States "must teach the South American republics to elect good men" reminds us that even during Washington's most imperial era in Latin America, there was still a rhetorical emphasis on democracy promotion, even if U.S. policy was often applied in a very paternalistic and shortsighted manner.

During the Cold War, U.S. officials continued to espouse the axiomatic virtues of democracy; however, the United States was willing to sacrifice democracy promotion to the more pressing priorities of security, especially where communism was concerned. Once the Cold War ended, the United States began to shift away from a more rhetorically oriented democracy policy to a more substantive policy. Indeed, freed from the constraints of the anticommunist strategy, successive post–Cold War administrations made much stronger efforts to promote democracy at the operational level of policy.

This shift in democracy policy was augmented by dramatic changes in Latin America's political landscape. By the end of the Cold War, the Western Hemisphere had become more democratic; during the late 1980s and early 1990s, countries such as Nicaragua, El Salvador, and Chile made impressive transitions to democratic rule. As democracy flourished in Latin America in the post–Cold War era, Washington had an unprecedented opportunity to match its rhetorical support for democracy with its operational and intentional policies.

With this in mind, we can ask to what extent were U.S. policies during the Cold War responsible for this subsequent wave of democracy in Latin America in the 1980s and early 1990s? Supporters of U.S. policies highlight Washington's support for the Salvadoran government in its counterinsurgency war against leftist insurgents and military or American diplomatic pressure against Chile's Pinochet regime as examples in which Washington supported long-term democratic change. In fact, defenders of Reagan often dismiss critics of his administration's regional policies during the 1980s in light of the series of democratic elections and peace agreements that followed in the 1990s.

On the other hand, critics respond that Latin America made impressive democratic gains *despite* U.S. policies and wishes. They cite controversial U.S. financial and military support for the government of El Salvador in its civil war against Marxist guerrillas and the invasion of Grenada in 1983 to shore up claims that U.S. policies in the 1980s brought more death and destruction than democracy to Latin America or, more specifically, Central America. When Washington seemed to be supporting democratic change, these critics argued, there were likely ulterior motives at work, binding the United States' policies more closely to its raw national interest. Furthermore, critics claimed that Washington supported a certain *type* of democracy in Latin America, one that appealed to U.S. corporations. In other words, Washington's desire to make the Western Hemisphere safe for democracy was more about making it safe for American-style capitalism.

Whatever might have been the motivations and consequences of U.S. policy during the 1980s, the collapse of communism and the dramatic wave of democracy in Latin America set the stage for a new era in U.S.–Latin American relations.

A NEW ERA IN DEMOCRACY POLICY

No specific date exists for when the United States' policies in Latin America shifted definitively from the Cold War to the post–Cold War era. Two important "post-modern" policies include the 1989 invasion of Panama, an invasion driven not by concerns about fighting communism but rather about apprehending a ruthless "narco-strongman" in Manuel Noriega, and the advent of the U.S.-led drug war in the Andes in the late 1980s.

The Nicaraguan presidential election in the 1990s, though, most clearly symbolizes a new era for U.S. democracy policy in the region. Led by Daniel Ortega, the Sandinista party had ruled Nicaragua since 1979, when it was part of a broader revolutionary coalition that overthrew dictator Anastasio

Somoza. From Reagan's perspective, the Sandinistas were intent on spreading their Soviet- and Cuban-backed Marxist revolution to neighboring Central American countries, namely El Salvador. For the conservative American president, this potential development had to be preempted. During the first part of the 1980s, the Reagan administration made both overt and covert attempts to fund the counterrevolutionary group known as the Contras, in hopes that they would overthrow the newly installed Sandinista government.

Despite economic subsidies from both Moscow and Havana, the Contra War, compounded by economic sanctions from Washington and poor economic management, brought the Nicaraguan economy to the brink of collapse. After a decade in power, the Sandinista regime came under increased pressure to show that it had the support of the Nicaraguan people. To this end, in 1990 Ortega called for elections in order to legitimize his government both domestically and internationally. Despite the economic hardships, Ortega and most international onlookers believed that the Sandinistas would win a free and fair election.

Leading up to its election day, Nicaragua was flooded with international observers, including former president Jimmy Carter (on whose watch the Sandinistas had seized power) and delegations from the OAS and the United Nations. Convinced that the Sandinistas would resort to fraud in order to steal the election, George H. W. Bush's administration distanced itself from the election process publicly; Vice President Dan Quayle even ventured to call the elections a "sham."[1] However, the U.S. government quietly provided millions of dollars in funding to pro-U.S. opposition candidate Violeta Chamorro and her coalition known as the Unión Nacional Opositora (UNO). In the Bush administration's calculus, democracy was important in Nicaragua but even more so if "democracy" meant a Sandinista defeat at the polls.

When election results came back indicating that Chamorro had defeated Ortega in a landslide, the White House reacted with shock and excitement – the outcome was too good to be true. To the Bush administration, Chamorro's victory demonstrated that the Nicaraguan people preferred an alternative to the Sandinista government. The Bush administration quickly endorsed the electoral results, citing the outcome as an indication not only that democracy was taking root in Central America but also that the United States was playing an integral role in this development.

---

[1] Quoted in Robert A. Pastor, "The Bush Administration and Latin America: The Pragmatic Style and the Regionalist Option," *Journal of Inter-American Studies and World Affairs* 33, no. 3 (Fall 1991): 6.

Yet, while the White House was celebrating a stunning policy victory, critics cited Washington's funding of the Chamorro campaign as evidence that Washington was meddling in order to ensure an electoral outcome in line with its own interests. In other words, critics contended that Chamorro's victory was not a step forward for Nicaraguan democracy but an indication that the United States favored democracy only when their preferred candidates won the election.

As the Nicaraguan elections indicated, U.S. "democracy policy" in the post–Cold War era was subject to controversy. The Nicaraguan election of 1990 was not the last time that critics would contest Washington's motives surrounding democracy promotion.

THE EVOLVING ROLE OF THE ORGANIZATION OF AMERICAN STATES

Any discussion of the United States' post–Cold War democracy policies would be incomplete without consideration of the role of the OAS. Created with considerable U.S support at a conference in Bogotá, Colombia, in 1948, the OAS was intended to be the post–World War II regional multilateral body that would resolve conflicts among states in the Western Hemisphere peacefully. Yet during the Cold War the OAS was largely unable to achieve greater legitimacy with regard to democracy. In fact, cases like the U.S.-led intervention in the Dominican Republic in 1965 did great damage to the organization's reputation as an impartial body. In the Dominican Republic episode, the OAS hastily approved a resolution that allowed for a multinational peacekeeping force to enter the country even though the U.S. military had already intervened, giving critics the impression that the OAS endorsed American imperialism. Further damaging the hemispheric organization's reputation as a democratic and independent institution, almost all of the OAS member states participating in the peacekeeping mission during the Dominican crisis were *not* democracies.

The post–Cold War era provided the OAS with a new context in which to demonstrate that it was no longer the "toothless" debating society it was often accused of being since its inception. For Washington, the end of communism allowed for a total reconsideration of the OAS's value as an effective forum for pressing its democracy policies. Within months of the fall of the Berlin Wall, to the surprise of many skeptics, the OAS began to push U.S.-backed initiatives that promoted the idea that democracy was the only acceptable form of government in the Western Hemisphere.

This critical development meant that the OAS was now acting as a more effective and legitimate regional body, one capable of defining the terms of democracy in the Western Hemisphere. Was the OAS's new focus on democracy due to U.S. influence or that of the Latin America nations? The answer is that, in the newly democratic Latin America, the interests of Washington and the rest of the hemisphere converged over democracy promotion.

The Santiago Resolution, passed in June 1991, was one of the first signs that the OAS was beginning to emphasize democracy in the post–Cold War era. While the OAS charter had long considered democracy to be a "goal" for the hemisphere's countries, the Santiago Resolution established the first mechanism for addressing breakdowns of democracy. Resolution 1080, which soon followed, stipulated that the OAS had to call a meeting of its Permanent Council should the "democratic process" be interrupted in the region. Over the course of the next several years, the OAS invoked Resolution 1080 in multiple settings: in the 1991 coup against Haiti's democratically elected leader, in 1992 in Peru during Alberto Fujimori's infamous *auto-golpe* (self-coup), and in 1993 in Guatemala during Jorge Serrano's copycat *auto-golpe*. The OAS's condemnation of autocratic behavior served to reinforce the growing post–Cold War consensus that democracy was the only option in the Western Hemisphere.

During all of these episodes, major questions lingered: would OAS and its multilateral, consensus-driven approach be able to handle crises of democratic breakdown? Would Washington work solely through the OAS? Or would Washington fall back on determining outcomes in its "backyard" in its more traditional, unilateral manner? The example of an attempted coup in Paraguay in 1996 reveals some of the impulses surrounding the United States' approach to democracy in the post–Cold War era.

THE COUP THAT DIDN'T HAPPEN

In April 1996 Paraguayan president Juan Carlos Wasmosy asked his army commander, General Lino César Oviedo, to step down.[2] Oviedo's refusal ignited a political crisis. Many believed it was only a matter of time before Oviedo ousted Wasmosy in a classic Latin American military coup. Yet, contrary to what likely would have occurred in previous decades in a country such as Paraguay, the anticipated coup never took place.

---

[2] Arturo Valenzuela, "Paraguay: The Coup That Didn't Happen," *Journal of Democracy* 8, no. 1 (1997): 43–55.

Most observers concluded that Oviedo backed down because of the overwhelming diplomatic pressure from the international community, particularly the United States and Brazil. Early on in the crisis, the U.S. Embassy in Asunción put out a statement that recognized President Wasmosy's constitutional right to dismiss the army commander: "Oviedo's refusal to accept the president's decision constitutes a direct challenge to the constitutional order in Paraguay and runs counter to the democratic norms accepted by the countries in the hemisphere."[3]

Soon after, the ambassadors of Argentina, Brazil, and the United States appeared at military headquarters and demanded to speak directly with Oviedo. OAS secretary-general César Gaviria telephoned President Wasmosy from Bolivia to urge him to resist any call to resign. President Clinton then called Wasmosy, as did representatives from the European Union and the Mercosur customs union, which included Argentina, Brazil, Uruguay, and Paraguay. Deputy Secretary of State Strobe Talbott represented the United States before the OAS Permanent Council while it deliberated the Paraguay crisis. He urged his fellow hemispheric countries to "take action in support of the proposition that democracy is the right of all peoples in the Americas and that the day of the dictator is over."[4]

It was also noteworthy that Mercosur became involved in the unfolding dispute. Established as a multilateral body for trade among the four countries, Mercosur's intervention into a purely political matter suggested that democracy had become an essential component of hemispheric economic integration. Along these lines, the forceful diplomacy of the Mercosur governments, especially Brazil, reinforced the fact that the United States was not alone in insisting on these new democratic standards in the region.

The Clinton administration's prompt and unyielding response to the attempted coup is an example of engaged, multilateral action that prevented what otherwise would have been one more coup in Latin America's extensive history of military coups. In the Paraguay coup at least, the Clinton administration had put away the Big Stick for a more multilateral approach. Its response also suggested that Washington was willing to play more of a supporting role, allowing the OAS, and even economic integration organizations such as Mercosur, to take the lead. Senior Clinton administration officials suggested that the region's economic interdependence and free trade agreements made old-style military coups increasingly

---

[3] Quoted in ibid., 47.
[4] Quoted in ibid., 50.

impractical.[5] According to Richard Feinberg, Clinton's senior White House adviser, "In the Western Hemisphere, free trade is the best promoter and protector of democracy. That is the lesson of last week's drama in South America, in which Paraguay's trading partners and the United States joined hands with domestic democrats to roll back a blunt attack on that nation's fledgling democracy."[6]

Elements in the Clinton administration's response to the Paraguay coup hinted at a new approach, one differing greatly from the more realist, calculating manner employed in prior eras. In this case, Washington's response was measured and engaged and its rhetorical, operational, and intentional policies all seemed to be consistent with each other.

But did the Paraguay coup represent an exception to the rule in U.S. democracy policies after the Cold War? Was the Clinton administration more multilateral and cooperative in the Paraguay case merely because of the nation's vast geographical distance from the United States and its geopolitical irrelevance? Had the coup attempt not taken place in Paraguay, but in oil-rich Venezuela, the Clinton administration's actions may have taken a very different course.

A MULTILATERAL WESTERN HEMISPHERE IN THE TWENTY-FIRST CENTURY?

By the time George W. Bush took office in January 2001, democracy was quickly becoming an ingrained part of the multilateral framework in the Americas. This new reality was manifested at the 2001 Summit of the Americas in Quebec, where the hemispheric leaders endorsed a "democracy clause" that established that "any unconstitutional alteration or interruption of the democratic order in a state of the Hemisphere constitutes an insurmountable obstacle to the participation of that state's government in the Summits of the Americas process."[7] In simple language, the "democracy clause's" insertion into the Summit of the Americas process ensured that, for better or worse, there would be a link between economic integration and democratic governance. "No democracy, no trade," the clause mandated.

---

[5] Alexander F. Watson (Assistant Secretary of State for Inter-American Affairs, 1993–6), in an interview with the author, Washington, DC, February 16, 2007.

[6] Richard Feinberg, "The Coup That Wasn't," *Washington Post*, April 30, 1996, final edition, sec. A.

[7] Quoted in Richard E. Feinberg, "Regionalism and Domestic Politics: U.S.–Latin American Trade Policy in the Bush Era," *Latin American Politics and Society* 44, no. 4 (Winter 2002): 127–51, quoted on 141.

While the summit's resolution was strong, the question remained whether the trade body would back its rhetoric with action. One outstanding question is why the conservative Bush administration decided to support these multilateral approaches to democracy in Latin America. A good part of the answer is that these processes were long developed before the Bush administration took office in 2001. Furthermore, in the pre-9/11 era there was no particular reason why a U.S. presidential administration – conservative or not – would opt to oppose such an agenda.

The OAS subsequently integrated the spirit of the summit's democracy clause into its bylaws on September 11, 2001, when it approved the Inter-American Democratic Charter. The charter states emphatically: "The peoples of the Americas have a right to democracy and their governments have an obligation to promote and defend it." The charter surpassed previous OAS democratic resolutions by including the defense of human rights and the rule of law as two necessary conditions for democracy, expanding the organization's definition of democracy beyond having a popularly elected government.[8] This historic development allowed the OAS to condemn a country's democratic practices even if the country was conducting regular "free and fair elections." The charter's key enforcement proviso was that nations must either uphold democracy or face expulsion from the OAS.

In the case of the failed coup against President Hugo Chávez in Venezuela in 2002, critics lambasted the Bush administration for being hypocritical in its response to this unconstitutional action. They claimed that the United States had failed to abide by the conditions of the charter that Powell had signed on the nation's behalf just seven months before. As one observer wrote, "The United States, alone in the Americas, supported the coup, and before then it increased its financial support of the opposition. ... So it is not surprising that the whole conflict is seen in much of Latin America as just another case of Washington trying to overthrow an independent, democratically-elected government."[9]

Critics who further accused the U.S. government – the Bush administration in particular – of hypocrisy for having blatantly unaligned rhetorical and intentional policies also pointed to Bolivia's presidential election in the summer of 2002, when the American ambassador warned the Bolivian people not to vote for the coca growers' union leader Evo Morales or else

---

[8] Organization of American States, Inter-American Democratic Charter (Lima, Peru, September 10, 2001), AG/RES. 1 (XXVIII-E/01).

[9] Mark Weisbrot, "A Split Screen in Strike-Torn Venezuela," *Washington Post*, January 12, 2003, final edition, sec. B.

risk losing U.S. foreign assistance. For Anti-imperialist critics, the Inter-American Democratic Charter might have suggested that Washington had changed its rhetorical and operational tune, but the Bush administration's behavior in Venezuela and Bolivia left no doubt in their minds that the intentional policy remained the same: hegemony in Latin America.

Other voices, while not necessarily arguing that the Bush administration's policies manifested renewed hegemonic tendencies, did criticize the administration for severely damaging successful efforts to bolster respect for democracy and the rule of law in the hemisphere. Arturo Valenzuela, a top Clinton administration official who was involved in the Paraguayan crisis in 1996, chided the Bush administration in an April 2002 opinion editorial in the *Washington Post*: "Unfortunately, the Bush administration did not seem to understand what was at stake in Venezuela. ... As a result, the United States now risks losing much of the considerable moral and political leadership it had rightly won over the last decade as the nations of the Americas sought to establish the fundamental principle that the problems of democracy are solved in democracy, not resorting to unconstitutional means."[10]

Responding to its critics, the Bush administration pointed to its backing of the democracy clause and the Inter-American Democratic Charter as clear indications of its genuine support for democracy. In 2005 Secretary of State Condoleezza Rice made a speech in Brazil where she spoke of the United States' key role and interest in the promotion of democracy:

We in the Americas have codified our commitment to democracy in the *Inter-American Democratic Charter*. And we must continue to insist that leaders who are elected democratically have a responsibility to govern democratically. ... Ladies and Gentlemen, the United States is committed to the success of democracy in Latin America. And we want to expand our cooperation with great nations like Brazil to deepen democratic reform throughout this region. ... There was a time when cynics thought the diverse people of this region were not fit for democracy, as if freedom were some prize to be won. These cynics once thought the same thing about people like me in the United States, as if freedom were not God's gift to every man and woman. These cynics are still around.[11]

In Rice's characterization, the United States is a genuine and loyal partner in the effort to deepen and expand democracy in Latin America. Critics, though, read this as simply more "hot air" from an American administration that had lost all credibility on the issue.

[10] Arturo Valenzuela, "Bush's Betrayal of Democracy," *Washington Post*, April 16, 2002, final edition, sec. A.

[11] U.S. Department of State, "Remarks by Secretary of State Condoleezza Rice at the Memorial Museum of Juscelino Kubitschek," Brasilia, Brazil, April 27, 2005.

CONCLUSION

With respect to the post–Cold War period, there will never be a consensus on the United States' democracy policies. Does Washington represent a beacon of democracy in the hemisphere, as Condoleezza Rice suggested? Or does Washington purposefully manipulate the concept of democracy in order to serve its narrow national interests?

The United States' position on democracy after the end of the Cold War often depends on the attitudes and priorities of individual policymakers acting with incomplete information on tight deadlines. It also depends on the unique economic, strategic, and political factors that surround a particular episode. That is, unlike during the Cold War, there is no longer a singular focus to guide U.S. policy. This explanation is not intended as a defense of U.S. policies. Rather, it reminds us that even on issues regarding the presence of democracy in the hemisphere – a fundamental point with which most people in Washington agree – the U.S. government usually does not act always on consensus. This said, though, the post–Cold War opened up new areas for the United States' long-standing rhetorical support for democracy to be put into greater operation.

4

Security

Even in the decades following the Cold War, Washington continued to keep security at the forefront of its Western Hemisphere policies. For our purposes, we can define security as involving military and law-enforcement-related issues. Although the start of the post–Cold War era can be traced to the 1989 U.S. invasion of Panama – a more "traditional" form of U.S. security policy in the region, given that the strategic Panama Canal was in question – subsequent years have witnessed considerable changes in this area of policy. In the post–Cold War era, particularly following the terrorist attacks on September 11, 2001, issues such as the war on drugs, international terrorism, and border security have dominated U.S. security interests in the Western Hemisphere.

The immediate post–Cold War's security climate was considerably less tense than in prior eras. New concerns such as the war on drugs quickly expanded to fill communism's void. Still, the drug war never represented the tremendous threat that communism posed for U.S. policymakers, who had just finished battling what they saw as a universally threatening ideological adversary. Domestic security issues played into the aforementioned Panama invasion or the Clinton administration's 1994 decision to intervene in Haiti; however, these paled in comparison to prior crises such as the 1962 Cuban Missile Crisis or the Reagan administration's security-driven policies in Central America in the 1980s.

THE DEMOCRATIC INTERLUDE

Given that he was in office during the majority of the post–Cold War, pre-9/11 era, Bill Clinton is associated most closely with the period we can coin the "democratic interlude." With communism out of the way, security policy during the "democratic interlude" tended to focus more on domestic-related issues such as Haitian or Cuban refugees. Unlike the nuclear showdown during the Cuban Missile Crisis in 1962 that characterized the life-or-death stakes of that era, the "democratic interlude" is perhaps best characterized by the image of a U.S. Coast Guard cutter patrolling off the shores of Florida looking for drugs or Cubans or Haitians on rafts heading for American shores.

At this time, although U.S. security policy had its share of controversial and "militarized" elements (notably, the drug war), these actions none-theless began to reflect the reality that few critical threats remained in the region. Accordingly, the Clinton administration pursued a variety of issues intended to promote the unfolding "democracy question" within the overall security agenda. Knowing full well that many Latin American militaries had sordid histories of committing human rights abuses or overthrowing dem-ocratic governments, Clinton officials promoted multilateral forums such as the Defense Ministerial of the Americas (DMA), which attempted to pro-mote military-to-military cooperation, military professionalization, and respect for democracy and the rule of law. The DMA's multilateral process reinforced the growing hemispheric consensus surrounding security issues and emphasized professional, apolitical militaries to augment the democracy agenda of other multilateral organizations such as the OAS and Summit of the Americas.

In the years following 9/11, policies such as the DMA might seem trivial, given the more immediate and potentially devastating concerns of global terrorism. Although largely deemphasized during the George W. Bush administration, the "domestic interlude" security agenda of multilateral meetings and consultation among the hemispheric nations has not vanished. On the contrary, as the continuation of the DMA indicates, these sorts of issues and procedures remain key elements of the U.S. security agenda.

SECURITY IN THE POST-9/11 ERA

On September 21, 2001, the signatories of the 1947 Rio Treaty (formally known as the Inter-American Treaty of Reciprocal Assistance) voted to invoke their agreement, making the terrorist attacks on the United States an attack against all of the American states.[1] Although the treaty had been in

---

[1] See Raúl Benítez-Manaut, *Mexico and the New Challenges of Hemispheric Security* (Washington, DC: Woodrow Wilson International Center for Scholars, Latin America Program, 2004), 191.

existence for more than half a century, such a sign of hemispheric unity was unprecedented. Interestingly, in the years leading up to the attacks, Mexico had begun advocating for the treaty's replacement with agreements solely between the Latin American countries. In Mexico's thinking, this approach would allow for more national sovereignty and flexibility because countries could simply sign bilateral agreements that appealed to them and ignore others that did not. But it also would have been far less comprehensive than the proposed hemispheric-wide approach.

In the wake of 9/11, however, most Western Hemisphere governments seemed to agree on the importance of a unified front. Yet, the invocation of the Rio Treaty was not the region's only cooperative response to the attacks and the subsequent question of how to handle the terrorism threat in the Western Hemisphere. In June 2002 the OAS adopted the Inter-American Convention against Terrorism, which left open the possibility of "greater international intervention in the event of terrorist concerns."[2] This convention was also important because, like the democracy agenda, it gave the OAS an important mandate in the hemispheric security arena.

Later on the same day as the 9/11 attacks, the OAS – and not NATO, as many would have assumed – was the first regional multilateral body to declare solidarity with the United States. The OAS, at this moment, had reached its most dynamic point since its inception in 1948. In considering the attack a violation of its collective security, the OAS's prompt and decisive reponse condemning the attacks contradicted the critics who assumed the OAS was unwilling or unable to act in any meaningful manner on issues related to security and democracy.

Witnessing the OAS's unprecedented response to 9/11 could lead one to conclude that the organization was now well poised to promote multilateral solutions to challenges posed in the post–Cold War era. But the OAS's apparent resolve did not mean that the United States was necessarily also moving toward a new, increasingly multilateral approach to support its security policies in the Western Hemisphere. Some critics quickly concluded that Washington would use 9/11 as the "new communist threat" in order justify maintaining large budget expenditures and interventionist policies in Latin America. Take, for example, the analysis of U.S. policy critics Kate Doyle and Adam Isacson during the immediate aftermath of 9/11: "For Latin America, the attack will translate into an escalation of U.S. pressure over security concerns at the

---

[2] Susan Kaufman Purcell, "U.S. Foreign Policy since September 11th and Its Impact on Latin America" (paper prepared for presentation at a conference on "Power, Asymmetry and International Security," Buenos Aires, Argentina, September 6, 2002), 15.

cost of ongoing multilateral efforts to strengthen democracy, human rights, trade and development. The administration has called on its neighbors for their unequivocal backing as the United States begins to retaliate with military force; it will strengthen ties to regional armed forces accordingly."[3]

While the Anti-imperialist School feared that Washington would respond to 9/11 by inventing new threats, others believed that this new era would provide the United States an excellent opportunity to clarify and deepen its commitment to hemispheric security issues. In 2005, while visiting President Bush on his ranch in Crawford, Texas, Colombian president Álvaro Uribe made statements that contrasted with the Anti-imperialist perspective:

As you [President Bush] have well said, both of our countries have a strategic relationship that is based on mutual trust, which is aimed at deepening democracy, at combating terrorism, and on building social cohesion. Our agenda is very important for the present and future of both of our peoples, so that Colombia can free itself from the scourge of terrorism. The greatest threat of Colombian democracy is terrorism. And our great partner in defeating terrorism has been the government and people of the United States. Allow me to say here to the rest of the world that U.S. cooperation has been exemplary. It has gone beyond rhetoric, and it has, in fact, been cooperation that has been put in practice. And all democratic countries need to know that, that cooperation should be realistic and put into practice.[4]

As indicated, there are divergent views on the motivations and application of U.S. security policies in the post–Cold War and post-9/11 era and continuing controversy surrounding U.S. security policies in Latin America. What is beyond debate, however, is that the United States' security agenda in the Western Hemisphere received renewed attention after 9/11.

WAR ON DRUGS: THE NEXT "COMMUNISM"?

When President Richard Nixon coined the term "war on drugs" in the early 1970s, he referred to a war against domestic drug production and consumption; fifteen years later, what we now know as the "war on drugs," with its supply-side focus, began in earnest. The political impetus for the drug war is traceable to the mid-1980s, when drug consumption was an overriding concern for millions of Americans. With the perceived "crack cocaine" epidemic threatening to overrun schools, ruin neighborhoods, and destroy families, Americans demanded action on the drug front. In response,

---

[3] Kate Doyle and and Adam Isacson, "A New World Order? US Military Mission Grows in Latin America," *NACLA Report on the Americas* 35, no. 3 (November–December 2001): 14–20.

[4] "President, President Uribe of Colombia Discuss Terrorism and Security," Office of the Press Secretary news release, August 4, 2005.

President George H. W. Bush labeled drugs as "the gravest domestic threat facing our nation today."

Source-Country Strategy: The Andes

During the late 1980s a bipartisan consensus in Congress emerged that any effective antidrug strategy must include a "source-country" component. Proponents claimed that any efforts to reduce the domestic demand for drugs should be coupled with steps to interdict drugs before they entered the United States and, better yet, to destroy them at their source. Proponents explained the rationale for the "source-country strategy" using a beehive analogy: it is easier to target a swarm of bees at the hive rather than after they have flown away in different directions. By 1989 the U.S. government integrated this strategy into its incipient war on drugs. In the following two decades, the source-country strategy took on a variety of policies and characteristics, but its core objective remained – to reduce the quantity of illicit drugs entering the United States.

Given that coca plants were cultivated and processed into cocaine almost exclusively in South America's Andean region, the United States chose to concentrate its efforts on eradicating source-country drug production there. In 1989 the George H. W. Bush administration unveiled the U.S.$2.2 billion Andean Initiative for Colombia, Peru, and Bolivia, with the lofty goal of reducing the production of cocaine by 60 percent. While heralded at the time as an unprecedented response to the drug problem, for some observers two decades later the plan appeared woefully naive.

At the same time the Andean Initiative took off, the U.S. Congress also mandated that the Department of Defense take the lead in directing all participating government agencies in the drug war, quadrupling the Defense Department's antidrug budget in the early 1990s. The Pentagon entered the drug war reluctantly, viewing drug work as more appropriate for police forces than for militaries. This was especially true given the Pentagon's focus in the 1980s on fighting a potential war based on the "Powell Doctrine," named after then chairman of the Joint Chiefs of Staff Colin Powell, which advocated the use of overwhelming military force to achieve clearly defined political objectives. Based on these criteria, fighting a drug war in the mountains and jungles of the Andes was about as far away from the Powell Doctrine as the United States could get.

Accustomed to receiving orders and then pursuing them until they are completed, the U.S. military soon adapted and became comfortable with its new antidrug operations in the Andes. For Anti-imperialist critics, though, the

Pentagon's newfound enthusiasm for this mission confirmed their view that the drug war was being used as an excuse for excessively large military budgets and missions: "For SOUTHCOM [The U.S. military's command center for the Caribbean, Central America, and South America], the drug war quickly became a rationale for a strong U.S. military presence in the region as well as its meal ticket at a time when defense and troops levels elsewhere in the world were higher than those for Latin America on the Pentagon's agenda."[5]

High in the Andean plains, U.S. military personnel were again training their counterpart military and police forces, though now they were chasing not communists but drug traffickers. According to a senior aide to the first President Bush, "These programs were the first effort to try coordinating military, police and alternative development efforts in order to combat drugs."[6] Colorful names such as Blast Furnace and Snow Cap belied the aggressive nature of this new security mission.

Throughout the 1990s, the U.S. government placed enormous diplomatic pressure on the Andean countries to cooperate with its vision of an appropriate response to the drug problem. The United States' vision entailed an aggressive, military-led source-country strategy. Thus, in a sense, the United States transferred the burden of violence to the Andes – and, to a lesser extent, Mexico. Although the policies might have been hatched in and funded by Washington and carried out solely for the purpose of domestic politics, it was primarily Colombian, Peruvian, and Bolivian police officers and soldiers who carried out the actual antidrug operations.

Source-Country Results

Critics argued that the U.S. military's aggressive approach to the drug war only worsened the domestic situations in the Andean countries. They believed that the tremendous pressure these countries felt to conform to Washington's wishes and the resulting destruction of their peoples' rural livelihoods due to crop eradication were only endangering these nations' already fragile democracies. Referring to many of the Andean countries' troubled political and economic systems in the early twenty-first century, one analyst wrote:

U.S. policy is not totally to blame for these crises. But a myopic focus on drug policy has clearly exacerbated existing problems and has emboldened the most

---

[5] Coletta Youngers, "Cocaine Madness: Counternarcotics and Militarization in the Andes," *NACLA Report on the Americas* 34, no. 3 (2000): 18.

[6] Rand Beers (Director for Counter-Terrorism, National Security Council, 1988–92), in an interview with the author, Washington, DC, May 2, 2007.

dangerous elements of Andean society – military, police, and intelligence services, often acting independently of civilian forces – to continue to serve as forces of repression. Nor has drug policy borne fruit at home. U.S. officials are no closer to meeting their counternarcotics objectives today than they were ten years ago, and the obstacles to drug czar General Barry McCaffrey's "drug free hemisphere" are greater than ever.[7]

Between 1981 and 2001, the United States spent U.S.$8.57 billion on international antidrug efforts, most of it going to Latin America. During this same time the total estimated "production potential" of South American cocaine increased from approximately 150 tons to 870 tons. Crop eradication efforts in Bolivia and Peru resulted in a drop of about 70 percent (110,000 hectares) of cultivated land between 1995 and 2001. During this same time, however, the amount of land being planted with coca in Colombia surged by 234 percent (or 119,000 hectares). In Colombia from 2000 to 2005, aerial eradication of coca plants increased fourfold. Yet, total coca production largely remained unchanged as cultivation was relocated to other parts of the country.

On the domestic front, the quantity of drugs entering the United States also had increased during the drug war. Many analysts assumed that a rise in the street price of illicit drugs and a decrease in their purity would reveal that drug availability in the United States was declining. This assumption is based on the classic economic laws of supply and demand: less cocaine produced (supply) would bid up the street price unless the drug's purity was sacrificed in order to keep the price at the same level. Yet, the average price of a gram of cocaine in the year 2000 was $212, only half of what it was in 1981. Amazingly, this price drop occurred even though the purity of street cocaine had become 69 percent higher.[8]

Despite specific successful aspects of the source-country strategy, including the "decapitation" of the Colombian drug kingpins and a significant reduction in coca cultivation in Bolivia and Peru in the 1990s, supporters of the U.S.-led drug war usually concede that this multibillion dollar effort has yet to meet its goal of drastically reducing the amount of illicit drugs coming out of South America. In 2006 the State Department's top official for the war on drugs remarked that "a clear cut victory" over coca was impossible; instead, "it's just a question of containing it where it

---

[7] Youngers, "Cocaine Madness," 16.

[8] "Drug Control: International Policy and Approaches," *Congressional Research Service Report* (Washington, DC: Library of Congress, February 2, 2006), 6.

breaks out."[9] Thus, two decades and billions of dollars later, even the U.S. government's leading official for the war on drugs conceded that the war cannot be won.

Supporters of the drug war make the case that, instead of compounding the problem, U.S. pressure on the drug front made Andean countries more accountable and responsible. U.S. policies, they believe, might have been controversial or even highly unpopular, but the alternative was to allow these countries to become overrun with illicit drug production and violence. They cite the fact that Peru's Alan Garcia, who at first strongly opposed the United States' more militarized approach when he was president in the 1980s, eventually became one of the drug war's most ardent supporters, although they admit that much of his backing was due to U.S. financial support for alternative crop production. Nevertheless, they note that spending billions of dollars on the alternative development programs encouraged by Latin American presidents like Garcia was an effective way to reduce coca production.

In 2004, for example, according to the U.S. Agency for International Development (USAID), there were thousands of families whose annual income increased significantly due to their participation in alternative crop programs in Bolivia's coca regions of Yungas and the Chapare. In 2007, Bolivia's main licit export to the United States was canned hearts of palm, a venture funded by U.S. alternative development assistance. From 1999 to 2006, areas in Yungas planted with hearts of palm have increased by 187 percent to 8,550 hectares, a direct result U.S. government alternative-development assistance. The U.S government also claimed that in 2004 alone, American support provided for 757 kilometers of road improvement, 19 bridges, and 331 kilometers of electrical distribution lines in the Chapare and Yungas. USAID funds also helped build coffee-processing plants and potable-water systems.[10]

Transit Countries: Mexico, Central America, and the Caribbean

It is not just the Andes that U.S. antidrug policies have targeted for the past two decades. In addition to the Andean source-country strategy, which was

---

[9] Quoted in "One Step Forward in a Quagmire," *The Economist*, March 18, 2006, North America edition. See also "The President's Drug Control Strategy," Office of National Drug Control Policy (ONDCP) (Washington, DC, February 2006).

[10] Connie Veillette, "Drug Crop Eradication and Alternative Development in the Andes," *Congressional Research Service Report* (Washington, DC: Library of Congress, November 18, 2005), 7–8. Also see U.S. Department of State, "Bolivia Program Description and Activity Data Sheets," U.S. Agency for International Development fact sheet, July 13, 2005.

initially geared almost exclusively toward eradicating coca and cocaine, Washington also adopted policies intended to interdict drugs in the countries closer to its shores and borders. This, by definition, meant policies affecting Mexico, Central America, and the Caribbean. Known as "transit countries," these nations often served as intermediary points for drugs being shipped from the Andes and into the United States.

To U.S. policymakers, Mexico has been the most critical and controversial of the "transit countries." The United States and Mexico share a 2,000-mile-long border that sees millions of pedestrians and vehicle crossings each year. When added to the widely held public perception that Mexico was riddled with drug-related violence and political corruption during the 1990s, the country created a major headache for policymakers in Washington. Many argued that it should have been Mexico and not Bolivia or Colombia that deserved drug "decertification" moniker during the last decade of the twentieth century.

A new U.S.-Mexico relationship today, however, suggests an entirely different reality. In this relationship, cooperation and trust on the drug front are replacing the mutual suspicion of years past. It remains unclear as to whether this period of U.S.-Mexico cooperation in fighting the war on drugs will last and achieve its goal of interdicting drugs and rooting out the negative side effects of the drug trade.

ANTITERRORISM SECURITY STRATEGIES

After 9/11, however, Americans would never be able to look at their borders the same way again. What used to be an afterthought for many is now seen as the last line of defense against terrorists who would like nothing more than to carry out attacks on U.S. soil. This concern about border security inevitably impacts relations with the United States' most important hemispheric partners and neighbors – Canada and Mexico.

In the immediate aftermath of the 9/11 terrorist attacks, it was unclear how the United States would alter its security approach in Latin America, especially in terms of its counterterrorism strategy. Although it later modified the term, the Bush administration labeled its response to the attacks the Global War on Terror. While the impact of this "Global War" in the Western Hemisphere remained uncertain in the wake of the attacks, it was clear that there would be new and potentially controversial developments in Latin America, especially because the region encompasses the United States' most vulnerable land border.

The U.S. government made its determination in this regard exceedingly clear in the hours and days after 9/11 when it effectively shut down the border with Canada. A crossing that normally took ten or twenty minutes now took twelve hours. By September 14 some American auto plants began to shut down because they could not receive supplies from across the border.[11] The U.S. government also ordered a "Level 1 Alert" for the borders, which entailed a "sustained intensive, antiterrorism operation."

Border Security

The attacks on 9/11 elevated the "border" to the forefront of the United States' hemispheric security policy. Back in 1994, NAFTA was supposed to break down the boundaries between the United States and Mexico by encouraging trade between the nations with respect to goods and services. In 2001, at his Mexican ranch, Vicente Fox and his American counterpart George W. Bush touted "amigo diplomacy" and discussed ways to liberalize labor flows across the border. At the meeting, the two presidents developed the Guanajuato Proposal, which called for the creation of a bilateral commission to address migration and labor issues.[12]

In 2004 Congress passed the Intelligence Reform and Terrorism Prevention Act, which stipulated that citizens of the United States, Canada, and Mexico, as well as Bermuda and the countries of the Caribbean, must have a valid passport to enter other countries in the Western Hemisphere beginning in 2007. Suddenly, crossing the border to, say, spend a week-long vacation in one of these countries became much more complicated. The predicted economic impact for the affected tourist industries was tremendous – another indication of how the border security agenda held a strong economic component.

In response to the attacks of 9/11, the United States began to see itself not as part of an integrated hemisphere but as a member of a smaller yet more cohesive region, with which it must collaborate to fight immediate security threats. Complicating this "North America" scenario is the fact that, unlike Canada, Mexico is a country that lags far behind the United States in terms of its economic and political development.

---

[11] Robert Bonner, "Securing America's Borders While Safeguarding Commerce" (Heritage Lecture No. 796, Heritage Foundation, Washington, DC, September 12, 2003).

[12] "Remarks by President George W. Bush and President Vicente Fox of Mexico in Joint Press Conference," Rancho San Cristóbal, San Cristóbal, Mexico, Office of the Press Secretary news release, February 16, 2001.

A key question over the next decade will be whether and how the United States will be able to reconcile economic integration and tight security, its two greatest post–9/11 visions for the border. These two goals often conflict with each other, and it is yet undetermined whether one will take precedence over the other. Related to this issue, of course, is the ongoing controversy over the illegal immigration of Latin Americans into the United States.

This is particularly relevant to U.S.-Mexico border considerations, given that two-thirds of the illegal immigrants come from Mexico or Central America. In 2005 George Bush attempted to address this controversial topic in a speech in Arizona, suggesting that security would be his top priority:

As a former governor, I know that enforcing the law and the border is especially important to the communities along the border. Illegal immigration puts pressure on our schools and hospitals, I understand that. I understand it strains the resources needed for law enforcement and emergency services. And the vicious human smugglers – smugglers and gangs that bring illegal immigrants across the border also bring crime to our neighborhoods and danger to the highways. Illegal immigration is a serious challenge. And our responsibility is clear: We are going to protect the border.[13]

Bush's comments reveal that, even though his administration pushed a North American agenda that attempted to focus equally on security and economic prosperity, secure borders came first.

The Tri-Border Area

Apart from the border with Mexico and Colombia, U.S. counterterrorism officials see the Tri-Border Area (TBA), the hilly and densely forested area surrounding the junction of Argentina, Paraguay, and Brazil, as the most potentially threatening area for U.S. interests in the Western Hemisphere. Part of this view stems from an ongoing debate over whether Islamic terrorist groups are active in Latin America. While the attacks of September 11, 2001, indicated the presence of active terrorist cells inside the United States and Canada, it is still unclear as to whether such groups are operating further south in the hemisphere.

For many years, U.S. and Argentine officials believed that the Islamic group Hezbollah was present in the TBA and that its primary activities included laundering illicit profits in order to fund its activities. The

---

[13] "President Discusses Border Security and Immigration Reform in Arizona," Davis-Monthan Air Force Base, Tucson, Arizona, Office of the Press Secretary news release, November 28, 2005.

Paraguayan city of Ciudad del Este has a population of only 300,000 but is home to fifty-five foreign currency exchange houses where money can be wired. U.S. officials estimate that U.S.$6 billion a year is laundered there – an amount equivalent to 50 percent of Paraguay's gross domestic product.

Hezbollah gained notoriety in South America in 1992 when it carried out a car bomb attack outside the Israeli Embassy in Buenos Aires, Argentina, killing twenty-nine people. In 1994, with assistance from Iran, Hezbollah conducted a car bomb attack against the Jewish Community Center in Buenos Aires, this time killing eighty-six. Following 9/11, U.S. Intelligence officials claimed that, in addition to Hezbollah, supporters of the Egyptian group Islamic Jihad and even Al Qaeda were active in the TBA.[14] By 2005 the U.S. Department of Defense had substantial evidence of terrorist *financing* operations in the TBA, but U.S. officials made it clear that they had not detected direct terrorist activity. According to General Bantz Craddock,

We have not detected Islamic terrorist cells in the SOUTHCOM AOR [The U.S. military's Southern Command's "area of responsibility" that covers the land mass south of Mexico] that are preparing to conduct attacks against the United States, although Islamic radicals in the region have proven their operational capability in the past. We have, however, detected a number of Islamic Radical Group facilitators that continue to participate in fundraising and logistical support activities such as money laundering, document forgery, and illicit trafficking.[15]

In conjunction with the three TBA countries, the U.S. government initiated the "three plus one" group (with the "plus one" being Washington) to discuss and monitor illegal activity in the area. As one might suspect, the U.S. government includes this area as one of the regions where it is committed to taking a multilateral approach to security in the hemisphere. In a further demonstration of growing U.S. involvement in TBA-related issues, the U.S. government signed an agreement with Paraguay that allowed American troops on Paraguayan territory for a series of joint military exercises for the implicit purpose of preventing terrorism. Unlike active Al Qaeda cells in other parts of the world, the U.S. government did not consider the TBA to be an "acute" terrorist threat. Yet it was still a major concern, and, given the importance of antiterrorism policy in the post–9/11 era, Washington monitored this issue very closely.

---

[14] Philip K. Abbott, "Terrorist Threat in the Tri-Border Area: Myth or Reality?" *Military Review* 84, no. 5 (September–October 2004): 51–55.

[15] General Bantz. J. Craddock, Commander, U.S. Southern Command, "Fiscal Year 2006 National Defense Authorization Budget Request," Testimony before the House Armed Service Committee. 109th Cong., 1st sess., Washington, DC, March 9, 2005.

ECONOMIC SECURITY: THE CHINA FACTOR

During the 1980s there was substantial concern in Washington that the Japanese economy stood poised to challenge America's for dominance in the Western Hemisphere. In the early years of the twenty-first century, however, that concern seemed almost unimaginable. Instead, new fears arose over China's entry into the Western Hemisphere. Beijing was involved primarily in economic matters, particularly in the purchase of natural resources such as copper and tin from countries such as Peru and Chile. China also demonstrated a willingness to maintain a dialogue with some of Washington's most disliked neighbors, including Hugo Chávez and Fidel Castro. Officials in Washington watched nervously in 2001 as Castro and the president of China, Jiang Zemin, met in Havana to sign a series of agreements formalizing their cooperation in technological development, education, and trade. Signifying the start of an era of unprecedented cooperation between the two nations, the accords opened the floodgates for Sino-Cuban exchanges. As a direct result, in 2006 trade between the two nations reached U.S.$1.8 billion, an increase of more than 100 percent since 2005.

China's growing footprint in Latin America had some American policymakers and politicians "seeing red." After decades of fearing communist infiltration, more conservative Establishment policymakers viewed China as the single remaining communist outpost that could challenge Washington's long-standing influence in the Western Hemisphere. In particular, those proponents believed that Beijing above all coveted the control of the Panama Canal, citing the purchase of the unloading facilities at both ends of the canal by Chinese-owned Hutchison Whampoa Ltd. as a clear signal of the nation's true intentions. Senate Majority Leader Trent Lott wrote to Defense Secretary William S. Cohen in response to the buyout: "It appears that we have given away the farm without a shot being fired."[16]

Others within the U.S. government believed that, while Washington should monitor China's activities vigilantly, China's growing involvement did not pose much of a threat to American interests. They pointed to Chinese economic investment in Latin America, which totaled nearly U.S.$22 billion in 2004, as evidence of its positive contribution to hemispheric growth. China supporters also listed the country's contribution of police

---

[16] Quoted in Rowan Scarborough, "China Company Grabs Power over Panama Canal," *Washington Times*, August 12, 1999.

officers to a UN peacekeeping operation in Haiti that same year as the type of behavior characteristic of an engaged, responsible global power.[17]

During the first decade of the twenty-first century, China expanded its involvement in Latin America into realms other than trade and investment. Of particular concern to Washington was Beijing's demonstrated eagerness to provide military training to its Latin American counterparts. Unlike the United States in Latin America, China often had a "don't ask, don't tell" policy when it came to human rights, which, for many in the Establishment school, seemed to confirm the argument that a decrease in U.S. military training might not be healthy for the overall human rights situation in the region.

Will Latin American governments attempt to leverage Chinese involvement to "balance" Washington's influence? China and Venezuela are both able to direct their influence in a way that, while still less potent than U.S. action, is changing regional dynamics. How Washington responds to this redistribution of power and influence will be a crucial elements of its Western Hemisphere security policy over the next few decades.

CONCLUSION

After observing the Bush administration's assertive, unilateral approach to the Global War on Terror, many concluded that it would further manifest itself in heavy-handed security policies in the Western Hemisphere. Recalling the president's infamous phrase regarding the war on terrorism, "You're with us or you're against us," some feared it would become the nation's mantra for the Western Hemisphere as well.

At the same time, though, the last two years of George W. Bush's term in office witnessed a noticeable downplaying of such assertive rhetoric and policies. Of particular note, Bush's March 2007 visit to Brazil, Uruguay, Colombia, Guatemala, and Mexico emphasized the social policies that the U.S. government was supporting, such as emergency medicine and microenterprise. According to one American diplomat involved in the visit, "We wanted to get Bush out of the capital cities and into the countryside, loading bags of coffee. We knew we would never win the public relations battle, but we did want to show that the President was not just about hard power."[18] Many critics were not convinced that Bush had converted to "softer" security

---

[17] Jorge I. Domínguez, "China's Relations with Latin America: Shared Gains, Asymmetric Hopes," Inter-American Dialogue Working Paper (Washington, DC, June 2006).

[18] U.S. Department of State official in a confidential interview with the author, Washington, DC, May 6, 2007.

policies toward Latin America. The president's intentions aside, U.S. officials, including General Craddock, continued to use the rhetoric of speaking enthusiastically on behalf of cooperation, leadership, and multilateralism:

U.S. Southern Command's mission is to conduct military operations and promote security cooperation to achieve U.S. strategic objectives. Our vision is that SOUTHCOM be the recognized partner of choice and center of excellence for regional security affairs within a hemisphere of escalating importance; organized to defend the homeland and deter, dissuade, and defeat transnational threats; focused on achieving regional partnerships with nations to promote commitment to democratic values, respect for human rights, territorial security and sovereignty, and collective regional security.[19]

Operationally, at least, this meant that the United States – and the Pentagon in particular – continued to battle the post–Cold War threats like the drug war, while at the same time identifying and pursuing new ones. These new concerns included drug-funded gang activity in Central America, "narcoterrorism" in the Andes, and Islamic terrorist financing in the tri-border area of Paraguay, Brazil, and Argentina.

Critics argued that the U.S. military has begun to do exactly what it should not be doing: acting as the "hands and feet" of U.S. policy in the Western Hemisphere. More specifically, they believed that U.S. policy in the region had become "securitized" or "militarized" – that U.S. security policy overwhelmed other arenas such as those of social justice and economic development. Needless to say, the controversy and disagreement over U.S. security policy in Latin America did not end with the Cold War.

INTERMEZZO: ARTICLE 98 AND THE FAILURE OF U.S. POWER IN LATIN AMERICA

In 2002 the U.S. Congress passed the American Service Members Protection Act. The legislation intended to protect American military personnel operating in foreign countries from being prosecuted under the International Criminal Court (ICC). The fear was that an American service member could be apprehended in a signatory country and then transferred to the ICC for trial. In order to protect American soldiers, the law mandated that the United States could not provide military assistance to countries that were parties to the ICC unless they signed a bilateral pact with the United States granting U.S. citizens immunity from the ICC's jurisdiction. Known as Article 98 agreements, named for the statute in the ICC treaty that allows

---

[19] Craddock, "Fiscal Year 2006 National Defense Authorization Budget Request."

for such exemptions, the United States signed nearly 100 Article 98 agreements with countries around the world.

From its onset, Article 98 proved highly unpopular in the hemisphere, as Latin American governments and citizens viewed it as a clear example of American heavy-handedness. In reference to the article, Ecuadorian president Alfredo Palacio said, "absolutely no one is going to make me cower," while Costa Rican foreign minister Roberto Tovar called the immunity proposals "offensive" and added, "one can be poor, but dignified."[20] Mexican presidential spokesman Rubén Aguilar claimed, "whether or not there will be a reduction in aid is not relevant to us, what is relevant is that our convictions and principles mean something."[21]

Over the next four years, the U.S. government cut off military training assistance to twelve Latin American countries, including Peru, Bolivia, and Brazil, otherwise critical players in U.S.–Latin American relations. Yet, contrary to what some in the Bush administration had predicted, cutting off the assistance created little incentive for the Latin American governments to sign Article 98 agreements. Instead, those countries and militaries denied aid by the United States turned to countries such as China to fill the gap. In this instance, American "sticks" failed to produce an outcome favorable to Washington. In fact, it produced an outcome explicitly unfavorable to Washington's interests.

Modifying what was now understood to have been a policy failure, in late 2006 President Bush issued a partial waiver of the application of the law, which allowed military assistance to go to eleven of the countries that had seen their aid cut. Only Hugo Chávez's Venezuela was not included on this list.

---

[20] Quoted in "Erasing the Lines: Trends in U.S. Military Programs with Latin America," Report by the Latin America Working Group Fund, Center for International Policy, and Washington Office on Latin America (Washington, DC: December 2005), 13, http://ciponline.org/facts/0512eras.pdf (accessed July 27, 2007).

[21] Adam Isacson, "The Impact on Latin America of the Servicemember's Protection Act," Testimony before the Senate Committee on Foreign Relations, Subcommittee on Western Hemisphere, Peace Corps and Narcotics Affairs, 109th Cong., 2nd sess., March 8, 2006.

5

Economics

In the midst of the Cold War, it was easy to overlook any sort of U.S. economic policy toward Latin America. Indeed, Washington's ongoing anticommunist security efforts dwarfed any concerted emphasis on economic policies, such as trade integration or free market liberalization. What is more, the period between the 1950s and late 1980s was a time when the Latin American economies "looked inward." In addition to the prevailing global realities that made domestic industrialization more necessary, the prevailing economic philosophies of the era that argued that Latin America's position on the "periphery" in the global "South" as opposed to the "core" of the industrialized "North," composed of Europe and North America, ensured that Latin America would grow poorer while its northern neighbors became richer. In economic terms, these scholars and philosophers argued, this economic relationship was a "zero-sum game" – my win is, by definition, your loss.

Thus, during these years Latin America often avoided dealing with the United States in the economic realm. Instead, Latin American governments placed trade restrictions on many goods exported to their countries from the North in the hope that they would be able to produce these goods domestically instead. With the glaring exception of Chile following the military takeover in 1973, this economic philosophy, known as import-substitution industrialization (ISI), dominated Latin America during the Cold War.

In turn, the growth of ISI meant that the United States did not pursue an active economic policy in the region. There were attempts, however, at using economic development as part of a broader political strategy of containing communism. President John F. Kennedy's Alliance for Progress was the most high-profile and concerted effort to use economic reform as a means of generating more political stability and faith in democracy – and, by extension, making sure that there were fewer willing recruits for violent Marxist revolutions.

By the late 1980s the economic scenario had changed dramatically, both globally and in the Western Hemisphere. The implosion of communism had done much to discredit the more command-oriented economic models in these countries. The "closed" economies of Eastern Europe and Latin America contrasted starkly with the dynamism of the seemingly more liberalized East Asian "tigers" such as Taiwan, South Korea, and Singapore.

With the Cold War over, the world had entered into a new era of capitalism-based globalization. Desperate for a new approach, many of the newly elected democratic leaders in Latin America were eager to embrace the invisible hand of free market economics. In fact, the often U.S.-educated, pro-free-market Latin American leaders were pushing Washington on issues such as trade integration.

Starting in the late 1990s, however, some of this initial enthusiasm for free markets and a reduction in the state's role in the economy subsided. Economic growth at times remained sluggish and the region was racked by economic crises. In response, many Latin Americans began to blame the vaunted free market policies – collectively known as the Washington Consensus – for the economic malaise that plagued their countries. At times, this malaise fomented a "populist" or leftist backlash against U.S.-supported free market policies. For example, Venezuela's Hugo Chávez ran for president in 1998 on an anti–Washington Consensus platform.

Within these constantly changing dynamics, the United States pursued economic policies such as free trade agreements and debt restructuring following the end of the Cold War. Although these pro-globalization policies at times have taken different forms, the focus on economic liberalization, more private enterprise, and less government intervention remained remarkably constant over the course of the three post–Cold War presidential administrations.

THE LOST DECADE AND A NEW ERA

The 1980s were not kind to Latin America. Starting with Mexico's economic implosion in 1982 due to an unsustainable foreign debt burden, the region experienced a series of foreign debt defaults and subsequent economic contractions and rampant inflation. After decades of relatively robust economic growth, Mexico's abrupt economic chaos was a rude awakening for many Latin American countries. The 1980s in Latin America came to be known in both the United States and Latin America as the "lost decade," a sober descriptor of the economic and, by extension, social and political turmoil that ravaged the region during these years. In most cases, defaults on foreign debt led to deep economic contractions and accompanying unemployment and despair, often testing the very social fabric of these countries. Nearly every country experienced negative economic growth; poverty rates skyrocketed; and, in some cases, hyperinflation robbed the growing numbers of poor of the meager savings that they might have accumulated. The magnitude of the crisis also helped explain why in subsequent years many of the Latin American governments reacted by adopting unprecedented free market economic policies.

The debt reduction initiative promoted by the administration of George H. W. Bush marks the beginning of the United States' post–Cold War economic policies in the Western Hemisphere. Part of the Bush administration's motivation for the plan was financial: bankrupt countries were unable to pay back the loans they owed to mainly American banks. The White House also realized the tremendous social costs that the prolonged crisis was having on the newly democratic countries in the region. Known as the Brady Plan, this policy initiative was innovative in its explicit acceptance of the argument that what Latin America needed in the late 1980s was debt relief, not just more borrowing. In addition to contributions from the International Monetary Fund (IMF) and other states such as Japan, the Bush administration provided almost U.S.$50 billion of collateral support as part of this aggressive debt reduction plan. The Brady Plan's lasting legacy is that it successfully allowed Latin American governments to reaccess the international financial markets that had stopped loaning to Latin America at the onset of the "lost decade" in 1982.

In 1990 the Bush administration launched the Enterprise for the Americas Initiative (EAI), promoting it as a hemispheric-wide attempt to support sound economic policies and integration. More telling than the launch of this now long-forgotten initiative was the reaction from Latin American leaders such as Argentine president Carlos Menem, who announced triumphantly, "We are passing though the most brilliant moment in our relations with the United States." Uruguayan president Luis Lacalle called Bush to thank him, saying "When, after years of our complaining of neglect, the most important man in the world offers his hand ... then, I think we should grab it – and the arm and the elbow and the shoulder, too." Venezuela's president Carlos Andrés Pérez called it "the most advanced proposal the United States has ever proposed for Latin America. It's revolutionary, historical."[1]

---

[1] Quoted in Robert Pastor, "The Bush Administration and Latin America: The Pragmatic Style and the Regionalist Option," *Journal of Interamerican Studies and World Affairs* 33, no. 3 (Fall 1991): 11.

Many Establishment analysts, echoing the enthusiastic Latin American governments, were convinced that a new era of cooperation, both economic and political, was in store for hemispheric relations. According to scholar Abraham Lowenthal, writing in the early 1990s,

The broad regional turn towards harmonious relations with the United States has also been unmistakable. For years many Latin Americans defined their foreign policies primarily in opposition to Washington. They denounced U.S. interventionism and exploitation, bemoaned Latin American "dependence," and blamed the United States for many of their frustrations. Restrictive policies on foreign investment, reserved markets, high tariff barriers, movements toward regional economic integration and diplomatic concentration were all forged in part as response to U.S. power. Only in the "banana republics" could a Latin American leader advocate close collaboration with Washington without political risk.[2]

From the words of these Latin American leaders, it appeared as though the Bush administration's EAI and debt relief program had ushered in a new Latin America attitude toward the United States.

THE NORTH AMERICAN FREE TRADE AGREEMENT

By the early 1990s, Latin American leaders were often the ones pushing Washington to engage issues of economic reform more seriously. The North American Free Trade Agreement (NAFTA), first conceptualized in the 1980s, required substantial pressure on the United States from its Mexican neighbors and took several years to launch. And there was no Mexican leader who was more aggressive or self-confident than Carlos Salinas de Gortari.

In a radical departure from traditional policy for a country that for more than a century had been highly suspicious of any sustained integration with the United States, President Salinas proposed the idea of a Mexico-U.S. free trade agreement in the spring of 1990. He began to pursue the arrangement after concluding that Mexico's economic future lay not in economic isolation but in deep integration with the colossus to the north. For the technocratic and U.S.-educated Salinas, Mexico needed to use the "comparative advantage" of Mexico's privileged geographic position next to the United States in order to launch it into the age of globalization. Even though it had already negotiated a trade pact with Washington, Canada soon joined the talks and the agreement became the trilateral NAFTA. The Bush administration deftly negotiated the

---

[2] Abraham F. Lowenthal, "Latin America: Ready for Partnership?" *Foreign Affairs* 72, no. 1 (1993–4): 74–92.

agreement, which was signed just before the American president left office. George H. W. Bush left the daunting task of guiding NAFTA through Congress to his Democratic successor, Bill Clinton.

During the 1992 campaign, however, it was unclear whether Clinton intended to support NAFTA, especially given that labor unions, a key electoral base, vociferously opposed the agreement. In a noted speech in October 1992, Clinton based his support for the pact on its importance to domestic policy: "In the end, whether NAFTA is a good thing for America is not a question of foreign policy. It is a question of domestic policy."[3]

After assuming the presidency, Clinton decided to make NAFTA one of his biggest foreign policy (or, in reality, domestic policy) priorities. This move surprised many observers who felt that the new Democratic president would attempt to ignore the treaty. Yet, as a "new Democrat" in the age of globalization, Clinton boldly pursued the agreement, knowing full well that the major obstacle to approving this trade agreement lay not with the opposition Republicans but rather within his own party. The "blue-green" coalition of labor and environmentalists opposed the agreement because it believed NAFTA would export jobs southward and harm the environment in both countries, even though labor and environment "side agreements" had been negotiated in order to assuage these groups. Clinton invited former presidents Bush, Carter, and Ford to the White House for the signing of the side agreements to show that NAFTA was not a narrow political or partisan concern but rather a treaty in the nation's best interest.

Perhaps the biggest breakthrough for the Clinton White House occurred when Vice President Al Gore and former presidential candidate Ross Perot debated the merits of NAFTA on the *Larry King Live* television show; millions of Americans tuned in to watch this verbal exchange between Gore and Perot. Arguing that NAFTA would harm the U.S. economy, Perot made his point metaphorically by predicting a "giant sucking sound" of American jobs heading for Mexico. Gore outdebated him, promoting the administration's claim that the trade pact would be a plus for the American economy, especially in terms of how many jobs it would provide.

The treaty was most contentious in the House of Representatives, where it passed by a narrow margin of 234–200. Clinton received the backing of 132 Republicans on the vote, but just 102 members of his own party

---

[3] Quoted in Robert A. Pastor, "The Clinton Administration and the Americas: The Postwar Rhythm and Blues," *Journal of Interamerican Studies and World Affairs* 38, no. 4 (Winter 1996–7): 100–28.

showed their support. The subsequent vote in the Senate was not as contested; the treaty passed by a vote of 61–38.

NAFTA's narrow and controversial ratification in 1993 reinforces the notion that, although successive post–Cold War presidents have lauded the virtue and need for free trade rhetorically, the issue never has been popular either with Congress or with the American public. By definition, free trade agreements sacrifice certain existing jobs in exchange for the promise of yet unknown future jobs. As a result, free trade agreements are difficult to sell politically because these potential future jobholders cannot vote in elections or write letters to their congressional representatives. Because of the opposition it generated, the free trade impulse in the United States that began with NAFTA slowed dramatically after its ratification; the agreement represented the high-water mark for the United States' liberalized trade policies during the 1990s.[4]

SUMMIT OF THE AMERICAS

The preceding Enterprise for the Americas Initiative and Capitol Hill's ratification of NAFTA convinced many Latin American governments that the time was right to push even more ambitious trade deals with the United States. Political economists would characterize this mutual goal of economic integration as convergence: both the United States and most Latin American countries saw trade integration as promoting their own economic interests.

In many ways, the Summit of the Americas inaugural meeting in Miami in 1994 highlighted the nascent faith that many U.S. and Latin American leaders began to have in free market economics as a cure for the region's many ills. While Clinton's top administration officials were at first uncertain as to what they would push for on the summit's agenda, economic policy, in particular free trade, emerged as the overriding topic.

Whether or not they showed convergence of U.S. and Latin American economic interests, the images and rhetoric from the meeting in Miami served as a powerful contrast to those of U.S.–Latin American relations during the Cold War. At least at first glance, the invisible hand appeared to replace the Big Stick as the driving factor in U.S. policy in the Western Hemisphere. Some observers noted the "spirit of Miami" was one of cooperation and mutual interest in promoting economic reform – the optimism and convergence at Miami that year made the Iran-Contra scandal, invasion of Grenada,

[4] "Ten Years of NAFTA: Free Trade on Trial," *The Economist*, December 30, 2003.

and the efforts to undermine Salvador Allende's government seem like events of an entirely different era.

For those of the Establishment school, the Miami summit was a dream come true. Four thousand VIP guests attended a multicultural extravaganza that included salsa star Tito Puente and American saxophonist Kenny G.[5] This pro-trade, pro-integration "powwow" reflected the adherents' strong belief that engagement, cooperation, and mutual gain were becoming the new hallmarks of U.S.–Latin American relations. According to one observer, "That both the United States and Latin America, after a hundred years of conflict over their respective interests, now shared the same priorities was even more to be applauded. The 'old Latin America hands' felt that the Miami summit was the best thing they had seen in years, and their enthusiasm was infectious."[6]

From the "photo ops" and lofty speeches in Miami, it seemed as though the region was in full agreement about the path forward. More Adam Smith, less Karl Marx, was the message coming from both President Clinton and his Latin American counterparts. In his opening speech to the assembled leaders at the summit, Clinton declared, "The so-called lost decade in Latin America is a fading memory. These reforms are working wonders. ... These are remarkable, hopeful times."[7] In a speech designed to set the stage for the summit, President Clinton demonstrated his view that free trade and economics were linked inextricably both to a country's well-being and to the strength of its democracy. "To grow and deepen their [emerging democracies'] legitimacy, to foster a middle class and civil culture, they need the ability to tap into a growing global economy."[8]

Yet, nine days after this historical summit, Mexico announced that it was widening the band in which it allowed its currency, the peso, to float. As every Wall Street banker working on Mexico knew instantly, this announcement meant that Mexico no longer had the foreign reserves required to keep its currency fixed to the U.S. dollar. Within a matter of days, Mexico was forced to devalue the peso, and the country appeared headed toward economic Armageddon. Despite its aggressive attempts to modernize its economic

---

[5] Paul Blustein, "NAFTA Lite?" *Washington Post*, April 15, 2001.

[6] Howard J. Wiarda, "After Miami: The Summit, the Peso Crisis, and the Future of U.S.–Latin American Relations," *Journal of Interamerican Studies and World Affairs* 37, no. 1 (Spring 1995): 52.

[7] Quoted in Moisés Naím, "Latin America the Morning After," *Foreign Affairs* 74, no. 4 (July–August 1995): 49.

[8] President William Clinton, "American Leadership and Global Change," U.S. Department of State Dispatch, March 1, 1993.

system, Mexico still had a long road to travel to achieve even a fraction of the success enjoyed by other economic powers and American trade partners like Japen and Germany.

THE FREE TRADE AREA OF THE AMERICAS

Mexico's dramatic and unexpected economic crisis starting in late 1994 sent a shockwave through the Clinton administration's Latin American economic policy agenda. Yet a key concept from the initial summit meeting endured: a commitment among the region's governments to push for a hemisphere-wide free trade agreement. Given an original deadline for the agreement's completion of January 2005, the Free Trade Area of the Americas (FTAA) was intended to be the forum through which this hemispheric integration process would take place. Unlike "subregional" trade agreements such as NAFTA, the FTAA was anticipated to be "all-inclusive" – it would obligate its members (thirty-four Western Hemisphere countries, save Cuba) to abide by one agreement.

In an approach that began under Clinton but was continued by the George W. Bush administration, the U.S. government attempted to mold the FTAA along the lines of NAFTA. That is, the hemisphere-wide comprehensive FTAA would be about eliminating tariffs on traded goods and services. In fact, some observers labeled the U.S. approach to the FTAA as "NAFTA on steroids" due to the extent to which it promoted regional economic integration.

For the Clinton administration, the FTAA represented its vision of economic integration in the Western Hemisphere in the post–Cold War era. According to one of President Clinton's top advisers, "seizing control of their own destiny, Latin American actors have successfully engaged the United States to negotiate what could amount to a strategic alliance for the twenty-first century: the FTAA."[9] The Bush administration supported the FTAA as well, although it also proceeded to sign bilateral, subregional agreements with Chile, most of Central America, Panama, Peru, and Colombia. In rhetoric similar to that of the Clinton administration, in 2002 Grant D. Aldonas, under secretary for international trade at the Department of Commerce, emphasized the stakes the Bush administration was placing on a successful FTAA:

The implementation of the FTAA is critical at this juncture in the history and development of the Western Hemisphere. We must balance the great benefits of trade with the overarching need of promoting democracy and equality among

---

[9] Richard E. Feinberg, "Regionalism and Domestic Politics: U.S.–Latin American Trade Policy in the Bush Era," *Latin American Politics and Society* 44, no. 4 (Winter 2002): 129.

peoples. It is a difficult goal, but one that we are determined to reach. The United States and all of the nations of this hemisphere will bring down barriers and rise above borders in order to realize their great potential.[10]

Some in the Anti-Imperialist school, however, were less enthralled with the FTAA process. Responding to the events that occurred during the fourth Summit of the Americas in Argentina in 2005, policy analyst Laura Carlsen wrote: "The defeat of the prospects for a hemisphere-wide agreement deals a heavy blow to Washington's commercial strategy in the region. Since its inception in 1994, the FTAA has constituted the most ambitious forum for imposing a very specific model of free trade, dictated by U.S. interests and those of its transnational companies."[11]

FTAA negotiations did not begin in earnest until 1998, at the second Summit of the Americas meeting in Santiago, Chile. Progress on an agreement proved extremely difficult, a reality that confounded both the Clinton and Bush administrations. Thus, while the United States subsequently made progress on individual free trade agreements such as the Bush administration's agreement with Chile in 2002 and Central American Free Trade Agreement (CAFTA) in 2005, the American-led vision for an FTAA floundered from the onset of negotiations.

Part of this was attributable to the actions of two hemispheric heavy-weights – Brazil and the United States – and their drastically different ideas about exactly what an FTAA should look like. In particular, Brazil was eager to see the United States liberalize its own domestic agriculture sector by cutting farm subsidies. Key Brazilian agricultural goods such as orange juice faced stiff competition in the United States because of these subsidies, which allowed American growers to sell their crops and related products at artificially low prices.[12]

With each side believing that it would gain a more favorable resolution to these trade disputes in a global forum, both the United States and Brazil wanted their respective issues to be decided through the World Trade

[10] Grant D. Aldonas, "The FTAA: Mapping the Road to Economic Growth and Development," *Economic Perspectives* 7, no. 3 (October 2002), http://usinfo.state.gov/journals/ites/1002/ijee/ftaa-aldonas.htm (accessed July 5, 2007).

[11] Laura Carlsen, "Timely Demise for Free Trade Area of the Americas," IRC Americas Program Commentary (Silver City, NM: International Relations Center, November 23, 2005).

[12] See J. F. Hornbeck, "Brazilian Trade Policy and the United States," *Congressional Research Service Report* (Washington, DC: Library of Congress, February 3, 2006); "Free Trade Area of the Americas: Missed Deadline Prompts Efforts to Restart Stalled Hemispheric Trade Negotiations," Report to the Chairman, Committee on Finance, U.S. Senate, and to the Chairman, Committee on Ways and Means, House of Representatives, United States Governmental Accountability Office, 109th Cong., 1st sess., March 18, 2005, GAO-05-166.

FIGURE 5.1. Argentine employees of a Spanish telephone company clean the street a day after rioters attacked its office during a protest against the presence of U.S. president George W. Bush at the Fourth Summit of the Americas in Mar del Plata, Argentina, on November 5, 2005. Leaders from across the Americas sought to strike a chord of unity at the summit, possibly by reviving a free trade push after street protests and a violent riot marred the first day of meetings. The graffiti reads, "Bush Go Home." (Photo: Reuters/Enrique Marcarian.)

Organization (WTO) and not as part of the FTAA, thus undermining the need for the FTAA at all. At the 2003 FTAA ministerial meeting in Miami, co-chairs Brazil and the United States agreed to a modified FTAA model. Unlike the original premise that called for a comprehensive agreement, there would now be "two tiers" whereby all members agreed to certain rules but each country could adopt selected areas. Dubbed "FTAA-lite," this compromise demonstrated that Brazil and Washington were still interested in the success of the FTAA but had highly divergent ideas of how the agreement should be realized.

During the 2005 Summit of the Americas in Mar del Plata, Argentina (Figure 5.1), the oft-delayed FTAA process donned a theatrical tinge. Indeed, it appeared that the Bush administration had little idea of how it wanted to move forward with hemispheric trade integration. Even though the FTAA had been the hallmark of the numerous Summit of the Americas–related ministerial negotiations since its inception in 1998, it was not clear even at the last hour if trade would be included on the agenda at Mar del Plata. The FTAA was placed on the agenda ultimately, but only after the Venezuelan delegation proposed that the FTAA process be ended, at which point the Bush administration joined more than two dozen other countries supporting the continuation of the FTAA process.

The FTAA survived to live another day, at least as a topic of debate. The perhaps unrealistic concept of hemispheric consensus surrounding the FTAA in 1994 was no longer the case in 2006. Consensus and convergence among hemispheric governments, which characterized the 1994 Miami summit, had been replaced just a decade later by greater contestation of the premises behind the FTAA model.

FAST-TRACK

Starting with the NAFTA debate in the early 1990s, "fast-track" remained a controversial part of hemispheric free trade agreements. Stated simply, the "fast-track" authorization allows the president to bring trade deals before Congress for an up-or-down vote and avoid the amendment process.[13] Proponents argue that this process is crucial for trade agreements as foreign governments are otherwise reluctant to see the treaties subject to amendments in the U.S. Congress. Critics, on the other hand, believe that this freedom from amendment ensures that trade agreements are inherently undemocratic. More specifically, the same "blue-green" coalition of labor and environmental groups opposed to trade deals criticized fast-track for its potential to overlook the negative side effects such as pollution.

Pressure against fast-track grew substantially in 1998, when a bill for the renewal of this negotiating authority was defeated in the House of Representatives by a vote of 243 to 180, with more than 80 percent of Democrats voting against the legislation. Needless to say, the defeat of fast-track was an embarrassment for the pro-trade President Clinton; it also reinforced the reality that free trade was a sort of political spinach – not the most popular item on the menu.

In 2002, to demonstrate his interest in reviving the trade agenda, George W. Bush declared that approving fast-track would be his "top legislative priority." Leading up to the vote, a report by the Brookings Institution labeled fast-track the "Moby Dick" of American trade politics: "presidents

---

[13] For a formal description of the fast-track process, see M. Angeles Villarreal, "Trade Integration in the Americas," *Congressional Research Service Report* (Washington, DC: Library of Congress, November 22, 2005).

have expended enormous political capital pursuing the White Whale of swift negotiating authority, and the hunt has come close to capsizing the ship of American trade policy."[14]

Unlike his predecessor, Bush was able to pass fast-track in 2002. The vote was 64–34 in the Senate and 215–212 in the House.[15] With the authority he sought, Bush then used the mechanism, now renamed the "Trade Promotion Authority," to start negotiations on the Dominican Republic–Central American Free Trade Agreement (DR-CAFTA).

DR-CAFTA

On June 30, 2005, the U.S. Senate voted 54–45 in favor of the DR-CAFTA agreement (usually referred to as solely CAFTA), which included Nicaragua, Guatemala, El Salvador, Costa Rica, Honduras, and the Dominican Republic. A month later, the legislation passed in the House of Representatives by the slimmest of margins: 217 to 215. In a demonstration of how unpopular free trade agreements had become by 2005, of the 217 votes in favor, only 15 came from Democrats, while 27 Republicans formed part of the 215 votes in opposition.[16] A decade after NAFTA, the pro-free-trade coalitions were far weaker, if not defunct. The Bush administration's hopes of keeping the hemispheric free trade agenda moving forward had narrowly escaped a crushing setback.

The debate in Washington over the CAFTA agreement resembled the bitter contest surrounding NAFTA more than a decade earlier. Once again, supporters claimed that CAFTA would be a "win-win" game in that both the United States and the Central American countries would benefit from the permanent lowering of trade restrictions. In addition, the Bush administration posited that CAFTA was not only about trade and economic issues but also about the United States' strategic interests in its own hemisphere. According to the Office of the U.S. Trade Representative,

In the 1980s, Central America was characterized by civil war, chaos, dictators, and Communist insurgencies. Today, Central America is a region of fragile democracies that need U.S. support. Elected leaders in the region are embracing freedom and economic reform, fighting corruption, strengthening the rule of law and battling crime, and supporting America in the war on terrorism. But anti-reform forces in the

---

[14] Lael Brainard and Hal Shapiro, "Fast Track Trade Promotion Authority," Brookings Policy Brief 91 (Washington, DC: Brookings Institution, December 1, 2001).

[15] Sue Kirchhoff, "Senate OK's Trade Measure: Bill Expands Power of the President in Negotiating Pacts," *Boston Globe*, August 2, 2002.

[16] See Stephen J. Norton, "CAFTA Squeaks through in House Vote," *CQ Weekly*, July 29, 2005.

region have not gone away. CAFTA is a way for America to support freedom, democracy and economic reform in our own neighborhood.[17]

Critics responded that, like NAFTA, CAFTA would promote trade for the profit of "Big Business," at the expense of workers and the environment. Perhaps the most ardent opposition came from American labor unions. Linda Chavez, a senior executive for the AFL-CIO, provided their point of view in testimony before Congress:

> Instead of improving things, CAFTA will further oppress workers, depress wages in Central America, and cost jobs in the United States. CAFTA is utterly devoid of compassion and opportunity for those who need it the most, the 37 million Central Americans struggling in poverty and the millions of hard-working immigrants in this nation most vulnerable to exploitation and lay-offs. Under CAFTA rules, multinational corporations will speed up their race to the bottom when it comes to wages and workplace protections. The deal will do nothing to pull people out of poverty in Central America, and it has the potential to plunge workers further into exploitation.[18]

Given the markedly smaller economies involved in the CAFTA accord, one might conclude that its approval in the U.S. Congress should have been much easier. With a combined gross domestic product of 0.5 percent of the United States', CAFTA was a drop in the bucket tradewise when compared to other successfully ratified agreements such as NAFTA. Yet, the climate in the United States surrounding trade issues had changed significantly in the twelve years since NAFTA was passed. In the November 2006 midterm elections, for example, a number of new Democratic candidates won office by running campaigns based on aggressive and unapologetic opposition to free trade agreements. These Democratic Party "populists" such as North Carolina representative Heath Shuler, who won a traditionally Republican district running on an antitrade platform, argued that agreements such as NAFTA and CAFTA had placed the interests of wealthy and powerful corporations before those of the American worker. CAFTA had become a part of the U.S. trade strategy in the Western Hemisphere, but the controversy surrounding free trade remained as strong as ever.

---

[17] Office of the U.S. Trade Representative, "The Case for CAFTA," Trade Policy Brief, February 2005.

[18] Linda Chavez-Thompson, Executive Vice President of the American Federation of Labor and Congress of Industrial Organization (AFL-CIO), Testimony before the House International Relations Committee, Subcommittee on the Western Hemisphere, 109th Cong., 1st sess., April 13, 2005. For more criticism of CAFTA, see "CAFTA's Missed Opportunities," *WOLA Bulletin* (Washington, DC: Washington Office on Latin America, March 2004).

INTERMEZZO: THE WASHINGTON CONSENSUS

The Washington Consensus's Legacy

If the 1980s was the "lost decade," then the 1990s was the decade of the Washington Consensus: convergence and pro-globalization were paramount. As the Miami summit's general accord over trade initiatives indicated, the Washington Consensus was not exclusively a U.S. priority or imposition. Rather, it represented a set of policy prescriptions and ideological predilections shared by politicians and policymakers in Washington as well as in capitals throughout the region. Many of these "technocratic democratic" leaders in Latin America had been educated in American universities and were unapologetic proponents of free market economic policies.

Presidents such as Salinas of Mexico, Menem of Argentina, Cardoso of Brazil, and Fujimori of Peru aggressively implemented the broad tenets of the Washington Consensus. The name was coined originally in 1990 as a term to describe what was already taking place in Latin America and not (as is frequently believed to be the case) as a recommendation or imposition of a set of policies. That said, the term Washington Consensus subsequently took on a life of its own; critics and supporters of free market economics tend to have entirely different ideas of what the Washington Consensus is and how successful it has been in Latin America. Establishment proponents tend to see the consensus as a pragmatic set of economic programs including lower inflation and trade liberalization. On the other hand, Anti-imperialist critics see it as heartless, U.S.-imposed capitalism that seeks to profit at the expense of Latin America's workers and environment.

In some ways, the United States actually played more of a secondary or indirect role in promoting free market economic policies during the 1990s. Instead, such international financial institutions as the International Monetary Fund (IMF), the World Bank, and the Inter-American Development Bank (IDB) often took responsibility for directly, though not exclusively, promoting market-friendly reforms.

The IMF's involvement began in earnest during the lost decade when it became one of the few creditors willing to loan to the region after Mexico's debt default in 1982. The inevitable quid pro quo for the new loans required the Latin American borrowers to implement severe "structural adjustment" programs intended to bring their often-unsustainable fiscal deficits into better balance.

This form of "bitter medicine" was highly controversial. Critics accused the IMF of forcing the Latin American governments to cut critical social spending programs in order to balance the budget; supporters countered that the IMF was only responding to a crisis, not creating it, and that this "conditionality" was critical in order to prevent future crises. Some observers argued that the while the IMF appeared to be independent, it was effectively controlled by the White House. The IMF's deep and controversial involvement in Latin America did not end with the debt crisis in the 1980s; rather, the institution played a critical role in devising the size and terms of a number of "bailout" loan packages following a number of crushing economic meltdowns in Mexico in 1994, Brazil in 1998, and Argentina in 2001.

As for the United States, its involvement in Latin America's repeated financial crises during the 1990s varied greatly, especially from administration to administration. The administration of George H. W. Bush was deeply involved in the debt reduction plan in the late 1980s, and the Clinton administration expended sizable political capital to bail Mexico out of its peso crisis in 1994. However, in late 2001, the administration of George W. Bush refused to get involved in what it considered a crisis of Argentina's own making. In contrast, an overwhelming majority of Argentines believed that both the IMF and the U.S. government were largely responsible for the crisis.

Wither the Washington Consensus?

During the late 1990s and early twenty-first century, the consensus that drove the aggressive free market reforms for the previous decades began to crumble. Many citizens of Latin America, after looking around at the still pervasive levels of poverty and unemployment in the region, as well as countries' continually unresponsive government institutions, blamed the Washington Consensus. Officials at the World Bank and IDB called this "reform fatigue"; the less technical term is "backlash." Officials in Washington immediately began to ask the Western Hemisphere variant of that age-old question when a country or region of the world appears to turn against U.S. interests, "Who lost Latin America?"

Many Latin American citizens responded to their frustration with the failures of free market policies by throwing their political support behind newly energized left-wing political candidates and parties that promised a gentler set of policies, ones that would not sacrifice citizens' welfare for the profits of Wall Street or narrow interests of the White House or U.S. Treasury. Such leaders, including Venezuela's Hugo Chávez and Bolivia's Evo Morales, were swept into office on the populist surge, which had been building momentum over a decade of perceived hegemonic and debilitating economic coercion from the global North.

But the rise of this "democratic left" was not uniform. There were a number of variants, such as Brazil's Lula, whose initial political rhetoric was much more populist than his ultimate policy decisions, which continued along the free market path set out by his predecessor. Yet, the voices of figures such as Chávez continued to resonate, as they urged a more radical vision of political, economic, and social order. Under the banner of this ideal, known loosely as "Bolivarianism," the nations and peoples of Latin America wondered if they could unite to promote their own economic policies and welfare – if their "liberation" would finally allow them to resist the American-led imperialism that had oppressed them for more than a century.

6

Washington, the IMF, and Financial Meltdowns in Latin America

The story of Argentina's dramatic and wrenching economic fall from "poster child" to "basket case" provides an important and fascinating look at the tremendous power and role that the International Monetary Fund (IMF), U.S. Treasury, and Wall Street banks played in the finances of many of the large Latin American economies in the post–Cold War era.

During the 1990s, Argentina had been the model for Washington Consensus–style economic reforms in Latin America. Perhaps more than any other country in the region, Argentina's economic officials dutifully implemented the free market policies such as trade liberalization that were encouraged by the U.S. government and private banks. Thus, for many officials and analysts in the U.S. Treasury, IMF, and Wall Street investment houses, Argentina's financial woes were truly unexpected. Argentina seemed to be doing everything right, they estimated. Yet, by 2001, as the country hurtled toward economic meltdown, Argentine officials assumed that, given the country's record of adhering to the mandates and suggestions given by the Washington Consensus, certainly these same institutions would come to Argentina's aid.

CASA ROSADA, BUENOS AIRES, ARGENTINA, 2001

On August 3, 2001, John Taylor, the U.S. under secretary of the treasury for international affairs, arrived in Buenos Aires to meet with President Fernando de la Rúa at the Casa Rosada, the presidential workplace. De la Rúa admitted to Taylor that the American official was "the man who holds the fate of my country in his hands."[1] Given Argentina's dire economic outlook at the time, de la Rúa did not exaggerate.

As part of a U.S.$14 billion effort to shore up Argentina's finances, in preceding years Argentina had been receiving routine loans from the IMF. By the time of the fateful meeting, the Argentine government already had received a little less than half of the loan package, roughly U.S.$6 billion. Yet, given Argentina's still-shaky finances, de la Rúa hoped that Taylor would put the U.S. government's support behind an "augmentation" of another U.S.$8 billion in addition to the already-scheduled IMF loans – and de la Rúa wanted the money as soon as possible.

During the summer of 2001, billions of dollars were leaving Argentina as residents converted their local currency, pesos, into dollars at the fixed exchange rate of 1:1. In July alone, 7 percent of all dollars left the country. This development was particularly harmful to Argentina's financial health, given that its entire economic model was predicated on a permanently fixed exchange rate with the U.S. dollar. In short, whither goes the fixed exchange rate, so goes Argentina's economic stability. In fact, following its inception in the early 1990s, the "convertibility" (or 1:1) exchange rate became so ingrained and accepted that merchants in Argentina unquestioningly would accept payment in pesos and provide change in dollars, or vice versa.

Because of the precedents in 1994 in Mexico and 1998 in Brazil, President de la Rúa expected that the IMF and U.S. government would support his request to increase the size of the "bailout" for his country. Yet both the IMF and Bush administration ultimately decided not to support the augmentation request. Then, in November 2001 the IMF ruled that it could not support even a continuation of its already agreed-upon bailout package. Argentina had been cut off.

In drastic response to the IMF's cancellation of its scheduled loan, the Argentine government announced the *corralito* (or crib, for the way that it would limit financial activity), a program that severely limited the amount of money that Argentines could take out of their savings accounts to U.S. $250 per week. In effect, the Argentine government confiscated the savings of its citizens. Within days, riots broke out across the country. Protestors chanted, "Give me pesos! Give me pesos!"[2] As the situation devolved into chaos, more than a dozen Argentines were killed.

---

[1] Quoted in Paul Blustein, *And the Money Kept Rolling In (and Out): Wall Street, the IMF, and the Bankrupting of Argentina* (New York: Public Affairs, 2006), 135.
[2] Ibid., 161.

On December 21, 2001, President de la Rúa resigned and was replaced by a succession of new heads of state (five presidents sworn in over two weeks). After the national assembly swore into office the ephemeral President Rodríguez Saá, he quickly declared a suspension of government debt, saying that the "gravest thing that has happened here is that priority has been given to foreign debt while the state has an internal obligation to its own people."[3] Saá's words indicated where most Argentines would lay the blame for their economic implosion.

In early January 2002, running out of U.S. dollar reserves that allowed them to meet the massive demand to sell pesos, the Argentine monetary authorities devalued the peso. Argentina's decade-long experiment with "convertibility" was finished. The country's new economy minister declared, "We are in a collapse. We are broke."[4]

Argentina's dramatic and precipitous financial meltdown illustrates that the international institutions and actors involved in the crisis did not act, as is often believed, as a monolith; rather, there was often considerable disagreement among the three bodies. Nor were the IMF, U.S. Treasury, and Wall Street bankers the only "actors" in U.S. economic policy toward Latin America, although they were targeted frequently as the agents of U.S. "imperialism" or "colonialism" by leaders like Hugo Chávez and Anti-imperialist observers in the United States. In the case of Argentina, for example, Italian citizens purchased a significant portion of the Argentine debt, thus also launching them into the controversy during the eventual debt refinancing negotiations.

At the same time, though, the U.S. government often played an outsized role in influencing the decisions of international financial institutions, including the IMF. The U.S. director of the IMF board exercises 18 percent of the vote, three times the voting power of any other nation. Thus, while they are not synonymous, the IMF made few major policy decisions without input from the U.S. government, particularly the U.S. Treasury. Often there was serious debate among the various U.S. government agencies regarding which policies to adopt directly or to recommend for the IMF. During the Argentine crisis, the State Department and National Security Council supported more generous loan terms for Argentina, while the Council on Economic Advisors adopted a more conservative stance.

Another key factor to consider when evaluating the U.S. government's financial policies in Latin America is the variation between presidential

---

[3] Quoted in ibid., 186.
[4] Ibid., 187.

administrations. For example, with the Brady Plan, the administration of George H. W. Bush aggressively pursued a comprehensive debt reduction package for Latin America. In the same general spirit, the Clinton administration adopted a policy strategy that generally supported large bailout packages for countries such as Mexico and Brazil. In contrast, the George W. Bush administration came into office with a predisposition against "handouts" for what it deemed irresponsible government policies.

Examining the case of the Bush administration's response to Argentina's crisis also highlights the concept of "policy blowback." In this case, given how subsequent events in Argentina unfolded, one can argue that the Bush team's policies created more enduring problems for U.S. interests than they resolved. More specifically, unlike before the crisis, Argentina is no longer Washington's staunch ally in the region. To understand how this shift in bilateral relations came about, it is important to examine the Clinton administration's responses to Mexico's financial meltdown in December 1994 and Brazil's in 1998 that preceded the Bush administration's subsequent involvement in Argentina.

MEXICO, 1994

Leading up to Mexico's financial crash in late 1994, as would be the case with Argentina some years later, both Wall Street and the U.S. government touted Mexico's market economic policies as a model for the developing world. Indeed, to many international bankers and Establishment observers, Mexico appeared to be on the verge of an economic breakthrough, one that would vault it away from economic stagnation and into the world of globalization. In this view, the historic NAFTA agreement with Canada and the United States was only the latest signal that Mexico's economy had come of age. What is more, Mexico's legions of often extremely savvy, Ivy League–trained, English-speaking "technocrats" reassured international investors and U.S. government officials that Mexico had finally left behind the economic "bad habits" of rampant inflation, anemic growth, and state ownership of industry.

Yet, 1994 was the "year of living dangerously" for the Mexican people and government, and the country's shaky finances were only the beginning of the problem. On January 1, declaring the beginning of their insurrection, the ski-mask-wearing "Zapatistas" dramatically descended on provincial towns and cities in the southern state of Chiapas. The images of impoverished Indians rising up to protest injustice – including the NAFTA agreement that went into effect on the same day – instantly became a profound embarrassment for President Carlos Salinas. As Mexico was wracked by a series of political scandals and assassinations, financial analysts began to question Mexico's supposed entrance into the elite club of industrialized economies. As Mexico's "country risk," a valuation of financial risk that includes political factors, crept upward, both domestic and international investors began, mostly quietly, to "sell" Mexico.

At this time, foreshadowing Argentina in 2001, Mexico was committed to a fixed exchange rate, at about three pesos to the U.S. dollar. Given Mexico's long history of exchange rate volatility, the fixed exchange was intended to provide both the Mexican public and foreign investors with more certainty about the currency's long-term stability. With foreign and domestic investors getting cold feet, the Mexican Central Bank needed to sell its dollar reserves to match the demand to buy dollars from both inside and outside Mexico. Had Mexico instead opted to retain its foreign reserve levels, its peso would have depreciated, or, more aptly, the dollar appreciated. However, the fixed exchange "anchored" the country's economic policy and the Mexican authorities decided that allowing it to fluctuate (in this case, certainly depreciate) was out of the question. In addition, 1994 was a presidential election year and the Institutional Revolutionary Party (PRI) had no intention of devaluing the peso before the vote on July 1.

Fearing devaluation, domestic and foreign investors began converting their peso holdings to dollars at the fixed rate, inciting a "herd mentality" sellout. "Herd mentality" occurs when large numbers of investors sell their domestic currency, based on the fact that other investors are selling. The destructive potential in this kind of market activity is rooted in the fact that, ultimately, the individual investor does not consider how his decisions will impact a country's economic position. For profit-driven investors, all that matters is what happens to the exchange rate. In Mexico, investors knew that devaluation of the peso would reduce dollar-denominated profits – their profits.

For example, consider an American firm that holds 300 pesos in profit at a time when the exchange rate is 3 pesos to U.S.$1 (3:1). Thus, after going to the Mexican Central Bank to convert the 300 pesos at the 3:1 rate, the American firm's dollar profit is $100. If there is a devaluation that suddenly bumps the exchange rate to 6 pesos to U.S.$1, then the profit of 300 pesos becomes only U.S.$50. Thus, in 1994 in Mexico, no one wanted to be stuck holding pesos following the devaluation. Paradoxically, though, the very act of one investor selling pesos for dollars makes devaluation even more likely, further prompting other investors to sell pesos. And so on.

By December, though, Mexico's peso devaluation had become inevitable. The Central Bank had bled billions of dollars of foreign reserves, down to a paltry U.S.$5 billion, as domestic and international investors were scrambling to get rid of pesos before the devaluation.[5] Yet to be seen, though, was under which presidential administration this devaluation would occur. Historically, the PRI tended to devalue the peso right as a president was leaving office, thereby allowing the incoming president to blame the economic mismanagement (and resulting ills) on his predecessor.

This time around, though, outgoing president Salinas had his eye on the head of the newly created World Trade Organization (WTO). Newly inaugurated president Ernesto Zedillo was left holding the "hot tamale" when in December 2004, the Mexican authorities allowed the peso to devalue by 13 percent. Investors, however, were unconvinced that the Mexican authorities had the foreign reserves to defend the peso even at this newly devalued rate. Furious selling of pesos continued unabated; within days the peso devalued fully as the Mexican Central Bank no longer could keep it fixed at the set rate.

THE CLINTON BAILOUT

Following Mexico's dramatic devaluation of its currency, attention quickly turned to what role, if any, the U.S. government would play in responding to the unfolding financial meltdown. Especially given that only a year earlier a seemingly confident and dynamic Mexico had entered into NAFTA, top Clinton administration officials were concerned about the broader economic ramifications (often referred to as economic "contagion") that could pull down the economy of the United States and other countries in the region.

After diagnosing Mexico's financial predicament as more a question of liquidity than solvency (think of liquidity as when you have the money to pay, but just not right now; solvency is more whether you have the money at all), the Clinton administration concluded that Mexico required a massive and immediate loan (read, "bailout") from the international community. In its estimation, this loan would fill up Mexico's foreign reserves so that it could meet its pressing obligations, avoid default, and reschedule its future debt in more favorable terms.

Yet, while preventing Mexico's domestic financial crisis from turning into a regional financial catastrophe was on the minds of the Clinton administration, sentiment within the U.S. Congress was less enthusiastic. By winning control of both houses of Congress, the Republican Party had scored a

---

[5] Sidney Weintraub, "As Mexico Imploded: Action and Inaction in the United States," *North-South Agenda Papers* 28 (July 1997): 6.

historic victory at the November 2004 midterm elections. And given that the Republicans had campaigned on a "smaller government" platform, the notion of a multibillion dollar aid package for Mexico garnered little support.

Interestingly enough, while the Republican rank and file in Congress was opposed to a bailout, the party's leadership supported the Clinton White House's plan to ensure Mexico received the loans. Following the advice of Republican leaders such as Senator Robert Dole (R-KA), the Clinton administration decided to bypass any potential congressional opposition by tapping the little-known Exchange Stabilization Fund (ESF). Established in 1934 to help stabilize the dollar's value, the ESF's funds were available to the executive branch without congressional approval.[6] The Clinton administration argued that Mexico's current crisis qualified for ESF support because Mexico's devalued currency was linked directly to the U.S. dollar.

Next, the Clinton administration leveraged the roughly U.S.$20 billion from the ESF with contributions from other international donors. Given the U.S. voting power on the board, the IMF quickly offered almost U.S.$18 billion for the package. Eventually, the package topped out at a whopping U.S.$52.8 billion. Knowing that the critics were likely to claim that the bailout served only to throw good money after bad, the Clinton administration ensured that the package included substantial "conditionality," which linked the disbursements to Mexico's adherence to an IMF-prescribed economic reform plan. In addition, the Mexican government agreed to tie its formidable oil revenues to the loans.

In hindsight, there is near consensus that the bailout was the perfect policy decision; the bailout provided a financial "life preserver" to a country nearing severe economic crisis. With the assistance, Mexico rescheduled its debt in order to address its crisis of liquidity. Only two years later, Mexico had paid back the entire loan. In fact, it repaid it early, along with billions of dollars in interest. Even more importantly, the Mexican economy rebounded from the crisis with a string of years of robust economic growth and relatively low inflation. Although an initial contagion spread throughout Latin America (known as the "tequila effect"), the broader financial fallout from Mexico's crisis was very likely contained to a greater degree than possible had there been no "rescue package."

Yet, the Clinton administration's package for Mexico might have worked *too* perfectly. When other counties such as Russia and Brazil began

---

[6] See Gary Springer and and Jorge Molina, "The Mexican Financial Crisis: Genesis, Impact, and Implications," *Journal of Interamerican Studies and World Affairs* 37, no. 2, (Summer 1995): 57–81.

to stumble in the late 1990s, the administration's "*peso crisis* response" proved to be less than adequate under different conditions.

BAILOUT NUMBER 2: BRAZIL, 1998

The successful rescue package for Mexico averted a much broader financial catastrophe. Yet by 1998 the international financial system was once again in trouble. In Asia, several economic "tigers" such as Thailand, Malaysia, and Indonesia were experiencing debilitating economic crises, often precipitated by exchange rate problems similar to Mexico's in 1994. In addition to Asia's financial turmoil, Russia devalued its currency, the ruble, despite the preemptive infusion of billions of dollars from the IMF and other donors.

Within this volatile and precarious global economic climate, Brazil appeared to be the next victim. For reasons similar to Mexico's, Brazil had predicated its macroeconomic reform program on a strongly valued currency (the *real*) linked to the U.S. dollar. But, once again, by 1998 this strategy seemed untenable as billions of dollars were flowing out of the country as investors "dumped" the currency. The Brazilian authorities responded with a series of interest rate hikes in order to increase the return on asset holdings in Brazil. In turn, administrators hoped that this would increase the demand for Brazilian currency and help reverse the massive selloff. At the same time, though, the interest rate hikes were crippling an already sluggish economy. The overriding question was how high the Brazilian Central Bank would push interest rates in order to defend its currency.

The Clinton administration and the IMF formulated their response to Brazil's dire economic situation based on the successful Mexican assistance package. The Clinton administration recognized that the contagion from a full-scale financial crisis in Brazil would be catastrophic at a time when the global economy was already under tremendous stress. According to one Wall Street analyst at the time, "There is no way that they can allow Brazil to fail."[7] Another observer commented, "The IMF's credibility, and that of its powerful backers at the U.S. Treasury, is on the line with [Brazil's] package as never before. Earlier rescue packages have drawn fire from critics for either being too protective of big-money investors or ineffective in halting panics."[8] The resulting bailout package totaled U.S.$41.5 billion

---

[7] Quoted in Louis Uchitelle, "Calculated Risks: U.S. and IMF Lead Push for Brazil Bailout Plan," *New York Times*, September 28, 1998, national edition.

[8] Quoted in Paul Blustein, "U.S., IMF Announce Plan to Avert Financial Crisis," *Washington Post*, November 14, 1998, final edition.

and was slated to be dispersed in several installments. However, there was a key distinction between the rescue packages for Mexico and Brazil that would undermine the latter's success. In the case of Mexico, the loans came *after* the devaluation and therefore were not used to prop up the fixed (and highly untenable) exchange rate. In Brazil, however, the loans were intended to fill up Brazil's reserves preemptively so that investors and speculators would not continue to make a run on the currency.

But this did not happen. Instead, the Brazilian authorities used the loans to "subsidize" the overvalued and doomed exchange rate. Speculators, seeing that the Brazilian authorities had just received an infusion of dollars into its foreign reserves, interpreted the move as a sign that the exchange rate regime could be maintained at least long enough to sell their *reals*. By the time Brazil devalued the *real* in January 1999, the country had received only U.S.$9 billion of the total package, the majority of which no longer resided in Brazil. Rather, it had been sold to investors looking to purchase dollars and sell their *reals* at the still fixed exchange rate. Even though the money had vanished, Brazil still owed the money.

In sum, the Clinton-led bailout for Brazil failed to forestall devaluation. Indeed, the discouraging results from the Russian and Brazilian packages suggested that large financial bailouts failed to prevent crises, but nonetheless sweetened the pockets of international investors.

Criticism came from both the left and right, Anti-imperialist and Establishment: conservatives tended to see the bailouts as financial welfare for irresponsible polices; on the other hand, leftist observers tended to see the IMF's conditionality as a form of financial imperialism. Whatever the case, in 2001 the incoming Bush administration adopted a more conservative approach to financial crises in Latin America.

ARGENTINA, LATE 1990S

Between 1991 and 1997, Argentina ranked at the top of Latin American economies, with an average growth rate of 6.1 percent. Following the punishing hyperinflation and generalized economic crisis of the 1980s, many Argentines were ecstatic with their country's newfound and seemingly endless economic boom. More than any other figure, "superstar" economy minister Domingo Cavallo embodied Argentina's confidence and dynamism.[9] Among

[9] For a comprehensive take on this era, see Steven Levitsky, "Argentina: From Crisis to Consolidation (and Back)," in *Constructing Democratic Governance: South America in the 1990s*, ed. Jorge Dominguez and Michael Shifter (Baltimore: Johns Hopkins University

his many talents, Cavallo was a master at selling the notion of Argentina as a stable and lucrative emerging market to the rest of the world, especially Wall Street investors. Cavallo's reputation was linked to what was at that point the novel and apparently brilliant "convertibility" exchange rate system. As Cavallo explained, because it prohibited printing money to cover debts, convertibility ensured that Argentine officials would not be able to revert to their old ways of profligate spending. Yet, what Cavallo usually neglected to mention was that, while convertibility took monetary policy decisions out of the hands of the Central Bank, it did nothing to prevent the Argentine government from *borrowing* money to meet its obligations. Because Argentina's borrowing continued to soar during the boom years of the 1990s, convertibility became like a time bomb waiting to go off. The stable exchange rate and robust economic growth suggested that Argentina was thriving, while beneath the surface the gradually accumulating debt made the inevitable crash even greater.

In hindsight, the massive overborrowing should have sounded alarms both in Argentina and abroad; yet during the boom years few analysts predicted Argentina's dramatic economic implosion. In fact, Argentina was one of the model emerging markets where stability combined with high yields to ensure dramatic profits for foreign investors. One high-level Argentine finance official found that on his trips to the United States to promote investment that "people were *desperate* to buy Argentina."[10]

From the Establishment perspective, Argentina in the 1990s epitomized all that Latin America needed to be doing in order to modernize both politically and economically. While this chapter is focused on the economic policies, it merits mentioning that Argentina's "economic miracle" was unfolding under a democratic government. In addition, the cordial bilateral relations between Bill Clinton and his Argentine counterpart, Carlos Menem, reinforced the conception that a Washington Consensus–driven convergence between U.S. and Latin American interests and policies was taking place (Figure 6.1).

By the late 1990s, the dramatic events of the Asian financial crisis, plus the Russian and Brazilian devaluations, shook the international financial system to its foundations. Triggered by a dramatic decline in Asian demand, the global prices for Argentina's commodity exports fell by 20

Press, 2003), 244–68; Carol Graham and Paul Masson, "The IMF's Dilemma in Argentina: Time for a New Approach to Lending?" Brookings Policy Brief 11 (Washington, DC: Brookings Institution, November 2002).

[10] Quoted in Blustein, *And the Money Kept Rolling In (and Out)*, 31.

FIGURE 6.1. U.S. president Bill Clinton speaks with Argentine president Carlos Menem during his visit to Washington in October 1998. (Photo: Courtesy of the William J. Clinton Presidential Library.)

percent in 1998. This was of critical concern, given that the commodity exports were a key source of desperately needed foreign reserves in order to meet its foreign debt obligations. To make matters worse, the U.S. dollar continued to appreciate during this time, which in a fixed system meant that the peso appreciated as well, causing Argentina's exports to become relatively more expensive.

Faced with this rapidly declining economic climate, the Argentine authorities covered their obligations by borrowing even more money abroad. In short, Argentina needed to float more debt at the very time when international investors did not want to hold more of its debt.

As Argentina continued to be jolted from the unstable global economic climate, a new phenomenon unfolded. *Riesgo país* (country risk) was the term used to describe the premium (usually relative to the yield on a U.S. Treasury bond) that Argentina needed to add to its borrowing in order to cover for the country's overall risk situation. Stated simply, a lower premium was good news. In the best boom years, the *riesgo país* hovered around 300 points, which meant that Argentina could sell bonds for only about 3 percent more than the U.S. Treasury bonds. After the Russian default in 1998, however, the rate shot up to 1,000, and in subsequent years, it would continue to rise. The *riesgo país* was published in newspapers; in an indication of how the entire society had become obsessed with Argentina's increasingly precarious financial standing, taxi drivers and school children could now recite it to visitors. Apart from its immediate domestic significance, the phenomenon of *riesgo país* indicated that, for better or worse, Argentina's economic fate was tied to the international economy.

By 2000 Argentina's financial condition was grave. International investors continued to sell the emerging market "asset class," which included Argentina. In addition, Argentina's now inescapably high debt levels provided an extra incentive for investors to move their money out of the country. Fearing devaluation at a time when many believed the international economy could not suffer another one, the Clinton administration supported a robust IMF package for Argentina. Known as *blindaje* (or "armor," for the protection it would provide for the Argentine economy), the IMF set aside more than U.S.$20 billion, while in return the Argentine government agreed to a series of new policies intended to rein in debt, increase government revenues, and cut government spending. In one more example of IMF-imposed conditionality, Argentina agreed to rigorous austerity measures in return for the loans intended to preserve convertibility.

THE BUSH ADMINISTRATION RESPONSE TO ARGENTINA

In 2001 the incoming Bush administration began to engage the persistent Argentine problem and, not surprisingly, expressed little desire to support continued IMF bailout packages. This ambivalence ultimately manifested itself in the policy question of whether the U.S. government would support the existing IMF program as well as any additional funds for Argentina. High-level officials such as Under Secretary of the Treasury for International Affairs John Taylor had little enthusiasm for more welfare for "deadbeat" countries. In fact, when he was still an economics professor at Stanford, Taylor had once advocated the abolition of the IMF.[11] Early into his tenure, Treasury Secretary Paul O'Neill told Congress that the IMF "had been too often associated with failure." O'Neill's April 2001 speech was broadcast repeatedly in Argentina as a sign of what many in that country believed was American indifference to the Argentina's economic ills: "As we in the finance ministries of the world talk glibly about billions of dollars of support for policies gone wrong, we need to remember that the money we

[11] Quoted in ibid., 118.

are entrusted with came from plumbers and carpenters who sent 25 percent of their U.S.$50,000 income to us for wise use."[12] Following up on O'Neill's comments and reinforcing that the Bush administration had made a dramatic shift in policy toward Argentina, several months later National Security Advisor Condoleezza Rice stated that the U.S. government had "no interest in a new support package" for Argentina.[13]

While the Bush administration's public comments suggested that there was little support for sustained IMF loans to Argentina, in private deliberations there was much more disagreement about what to do. In particular, the White House's Council of Economic Advisors supported cutting the financial cord with Argentina as a way to send a clear message about irresponsible financial behavior. On the other side, the Treasury Department, State Department, and National Security Council all supported some sort of continued program with Argentina, largely given that the perceived consequences of a meltdown were so dramatic.

Following these disputes within the "interagency" of the U.S. government, the Bush administration's actual policy toward Argentina was to defer to the IMF. Bush's White House gave little policy direction to IMF officials in terms of how they should deal with the situation. Thus, the IMF had an unusually high degree of autonomy from the U.S. government when it announced in late November 2001 that it was unable to make the scheduled U.S.$1.24 billion disbursement. Remarkably, the IMF had pulled the plug on Argentina as the Bush administration watched from the sidelines.

In December 2001, without the IMF lifeline, the Argentine government implemented the *corralito*, which drastically restricted access to bank accounts, sparking political, social, and economic chaos in Argentina. By 2002, 25 percent of the working population was unemployed; and an astonishing half of the population was living under the poverty line. Argentina's crisis affected all sectors of society, not just the poor, as is often the case. Wealthy Argentines auctioned off their Degas or Gauguin masterpieces. One middle-aged woman walked into a bank, doused herself with rubbing alcohol, and ignited herself. Buenos Aires teemed with *cartoneros* (recyclers) poring through trash in order to find food or something of value.

For many Argentines, the tragic economic implosion reinforced the impression that the IMF and Bush administration had been indifferent to the country's plight. Many Argentines asked how the international financial community could cut off the country after it had done so much to embrace

---

[12] Ibid.
[13] Quoted in "Mixed Signals," *The Economist*, August 7, 2001.

Washington Consensus policies. Did the U.S. government have any sort of obligation to provide financial assistance to Argentina? To what extent did the Bush administration's "policy of no policy" serve to diminish U.S. influence and prestige in Argentina, as well as the rest of the region?

In Argentina's ensuing presidential elections in 2003, nationalist and leftist candidate Néstor Kirchner won the election after former president Carlos Menem dramatically dropped out of the race when he realized that he was certain to lose. With Kirchner in office, any notion of friendly relations with Washington – and the Bush administration – was out of the question. Instead, Kirchner publicly and routinely denounced the IMF. Kirchner also took an unprecedented stance with the international creditors, including the IMF. According to Kirchner, Argentina would not make debt payments "at the price of hunger and exclusion of Argentines."[14]

While few analysts were surprised at Kirchner's strong language, what was more unexpected was how successful his government was in rescheduling and reducing the country's foreign debt obligations. Indeed, Kirchner went head-to-head in debt negotiations with the IMF and U.S. government and won.

CONCLUSION

The Bush administration's unwillingness to support the bailout program for Argentina largely overshadowed the fact that it was crafting substantial economic recovery programs in neighboring Uruguay and Brazil. Indeed, the U.S. Treasury supported a U.S.$15 billion package for Brazil as well as several billion for Uruguay at roughly the same time when it was cutting off Argentina. In fact, many observers concluded that the Bush administration's support for IMF loans for Uruguay is what prevented an "Argentina-like" financial crisis in that small country.

Defenders of the Bush administration's policies would contend that it was critical to differentiate between the various cases; not all countries should automatically qualify for rescue loans. In this view, Brazil's and Uruguay's "fundamentals" meant that they were more deserving of an assistance package. Officials such as John Taylor would disagree with the view that Argentina was totally abandoned, given that it did receive a portion of the bailout loans. Moreover, they would contend, U.S. government and IMF policies likely helped to ensure that "contagion" from

---

[14] Quoted in "Argentina and the IMF: The Talking Begins," *The Economist*, August 9, 2003.

Argentina's crisis made relatively little impact on the global economy. Whatever the case, one yet-unanswered question is to what extent the controversial response to the Argentine crisis diminished the U.S. government's future ability "to exercise global leadership" either on its own or through the IMF.[15]

---

[15] Quoted in Blustein, *And the Money Kept Rolling In (and Out)*, 207.

7

Colombia

The Narcotization of U.S. Policy

WASHINGTON, DC, 1994

Still a year away from winning the presidency of Colombia, candidate Ernesto Samper visited Washington and met with American officials at a hotel in order to convince them that, if elected, his government would be tough on drugs. For years, Samper had been plagued by allegations and rumors of ties to narcotraffickers and his efforts in the late 1970s to legalize marijuana. U.S. officials believed he had dirty hands. At the meeting, American diplomat Phillip McLean offered Samper some advice on what to do if his government wanted to enjoy warm relations with Washington, "I said, 'Ernesto, you have a major, major problem with the United States: you're perceived as being soft on narcotics. This is the problem and there's only one way to fix it – you have to show that you're serious about this issue and you're going to have to do something about [it].'"[1] The frankness of McLean's comments to Samper reflected the nature of U.S. policy toward Colombia in the first decade following the Cold War. U.S. policy, to put it bluntly, was "narcotized." Washington's policies – and the related bilateral relationship with Bogotá – focused on one issue: the war on drugs. During the 1990s, this "narcotization" led to the rapid deterioration of the relationship between the United States and Colombia – two longtime hemispheric allies.

---

[1] Russell Crandall. *Driven by Drugs: U.S. Policy toward Colombia* (Boulder, CO: Lynne Rienner Publishers, 2002), 102. As part of the research for this chapter, in December 2006 and February 2007, the author conducted roughly two dozen private interviews in Bogotá and Washington, DC, with U.S. and Colombian officials.

In contrast, one decade later, Colombian president Álvaro Uribe met with President George W. Bush in Crawford, Texas. Uribe was originally scheduled to meet his American counterpart at the White House in Washington; however, Bush's foreign policy aides had been working quietly for months with the hope that they could instead hold the meeting at the more intimate Crawford setting in order to reinforce Bush's personal support for Uribe and his government. While at the ranch, Uribe apparently lamented to Bush that he did not possess the military hardware needed to carry out a successful war against the country's formidable leftist insurgencies. Bush quickly asked his aides why his Colombian guest did not have what he needed.

As his unwavering support for Uribe demonstrated, Bush believed that Colombia was a key ally in the United States' global war on terrorism. Since 2002, the Bush administration had been coordinating massive military assistance and training for Colombia, not only to pursue the war on drugs (as had been the case previously) but also to help the Colombian military fight its ongoing counterinsurgency war against Marxist guerrillas. While U.S. policy in the twenty-first century still focused largely on fighting drugs, the fight against "narcoterrorists" also became a top priority.

In addition to the massive military assistance, implementation of U.S. policy in Colombia included the dispersion of U.S. Special Forces soldiers throughout the countryside, where they were embedded as trainers to their Colombia military counterparts. The U.S. government continued to send Colombia hundreds of millions of dollars' worth of aid annually, comprising military hardware and also "soft side" items, such as financial support for social programs and human rights. In the post-9/11 era, Washington's bitter relationship with Ernesto Samper's government was now firmly in the past. Colombia was once again a strong ally of the United States.

Yet, the Uribe-Bush "synergy" and resulting stronger bilateral ties did not put an end to the controversy surrounding U.S. involvement in Colombia. On the contrary, U.S. policy in Colombia remains a lightning rod for critics who claim that U.S. policies are imperialistic and destabilizing and actually make the security and human rights situation in Colombia worse, not better.

THE ROOTS OF U.S. DRUG POLICY IN COLOMBIA

Like so many key policies focused on the Western Hemisphere, U.S. policy in Colombia after the Cold War has its roots in American domestic politics. As the war on drugs became an important domestic issue during the 1990s,

Colombia, the world's largest cocaine-producing country, became a critical area for the U.S. government. Because the American public was paranoid about illicit drugs such as cocaine, national politicians faced tremendous pressure to "do something" about the drug trade. And this quickly meant going after the drug production at its source in the Andes. By the late 1990s, the drug war in the Andes was an integral part of the U.S. government's overall policy objectives in Latin America. Most members of Congress – both Republican and Democrat – were disposed to support the Clinton administration's plan known as Plan Colombia.

In military, economic, and diplomatic terms, the United States dwarfed its Colombian counterpart. This "power asymmetry" between the United States and Colombia allowed Washington to influence events in the Latin American country to a greater degree than vice versa.

While violence related to the drug trade had been on the upswing in Colombia for years, the U.S. government's perspective on the situation in Colombia changed dramatically after the August 1989 assassination of Liberal Party presidential candidate Luis Carlos Galán. American officials considered Galán a reformer and maverick against the seemingly unending "narco-kingpin" influence on Colombia's political system. Galán's violent death at a campaign rally prompted an emergency response by the George H. W. Bush administration, which sent an additional U.S.$65 million in assistance to Colombia on top of the original U.S.$10 million slated for annual aid.

A month later, the Bush administration announced the launch of the Andean Initiative, a U.S.$2.2 billion program intended to "win the war on drugs" in the Andes. This signified that the drug war in the Andes had replaced the civil wars in Central America as the U.S. government's over-riding policy concern in Latin America. Programs such as the Andean Initiative demonstrated that U.S. government concern in Latin American had moved from stopping communism to, among other things, stopping drugs.

To make gains on the drug front during the early 1990s, the U.S. and Colombian authorities began collaborating, especially on the "kingpin strategy." The U.S. government tailored its strategy in Colombia to target "drug cartels," such as that of Pablo Escobar in the provincial city of Medellín. When combined with crop eradication efforts in Bolivia and Peru, U.S. officials believed eliminating the Colombian cartels – and therefore the "human capital" underpinning the drug trade – would force the entire drug trade to collapse.

After eighteen months of intense searching and aided by U.S. counter-narcotics operatives, Colombian authorities located and killed Pablo Escobar while he was attempting to flee on foot from a rooftop in Medellín. Yet, while the strategy succeeded in killing or apprehending Colombia's drug kingpins such as Escobar, it did almost nothing to affect the broader drug war. In fact, the kingpin strategy's "success" is now credited with "atomizing" Colombia's drug production and trade into much smaller and more elusive drug trafficking entities.

WASHINGTON GOES AFTER ERNESTO SAMPER

During the aforementioned Washington hotel meeting in 1994, the Clinton administration had made clear to presidential candidate Ernesto Samper that it was concerned about his financial links to the Cali cartel. In November 1993 Robert Gelbard, former ambassador to Bolivia and the State Department's top counternarcotics official, did not mince words when he told Samper, "We have information, we believe it, and the money must stop if you want to have any kind of decent relationship with the United States."[2]

Nine months after the meeting with Gelbard in Washington, Samper was elected president of Colombia. Initially, U.S. officials only asked Samper to govern as if he had not been compromised by drug money. However, continued drug-related revelations about many of Samper's top campaign advisers led the Clinton administration to assume a much more adversarial position. In addition, hawkish U.S. Congress members such as Jesse Helms (R-NC) argued that the United States should not do business with the drug-tainted Colombian president. In a direct rebuke to the incoming Colombian president, Helms introduced an amendment to the 1994 Foreign Assistance Act that would permit U.S. aid to Colombia only if its government complied more effectively with U.S.-led antidrug policies. Gelbard quickly voiced his opposition to the move, stating "Let there be no doubt what would occur as a consequence of the actions that we are taking in the legislature. We are going to deny, to one of our critical allies in the war on drugs, access to the equipment and information that they need to continue their war on drugs."[3]

Yet, within a year, the Clinton administration assumed a stance toward Ernesto Samper similar to Helms's in 1994. As Samper's willingness to prosecute the drug war decreased, the United States applied more pressure, requiring Samper to do far more than his predecessors to demonstrate his mettle in the drug war. Already compromised severely by the drug allegations, Samper usually had no choice other than to comply. In particular, Samper pursued aggressive policies against the Cali cartel, the very organization believed to have funded his presidential campaign.

[2] Ibid., 102.
[3] Ibid., 105.

The Clinton administration faced a dilemma: how to carry out an aggressive set of counternarcotics policies while at the same time isolating the Samper government. U.S. officials developed strong relationships with certain key Colombian government officials and largely ignored Samper himself. Amazingly, by 1996 U.S. government agencies such as the State Department and Pentagon had very little contact with Ernesto Samper, preferring to work instead with trusted counterparts such as General Rosso José Serrano, the head of the national police. In this way, U.S. officials met their objectives without cooperation from Samper's office.

Ironically, the Samper government made enormous strides against drug traffickers at the very moment that the United States was ratcheting up its pressure. In 1995, in an effort led by General Serrano, the Colombian national police effectively eliminated the Cali cartel, the drug organization that had filled the vacuum following the Medellín cartel's downfall a few years earlier. U.S. officials lauded Colombia for these developments. White House drug policy adviser Lee P. Brown stated, "Colombia gets two thumbs up from me on this. ... They have made a good start."[4] Myles Frechette, the American ambassador in Bogotá, commented that "this was a triumph of the Samper administration and one that without doubt is going to improve the relation between Colombia and the United States."[5]

Soon after, though, American officials modified their response given the recent positive developments. But while they continued to credit Colombian authorities for making great gains in the drug war, they claimed that such efforts came *despite* Samper's role. According to one State Department official directly involved in the issue, "[Samper] took credit for everything, but he had no input. It was Serrano backed up by us that did the trick with Cali."[6]

A subsequent development further reinforced the extent to which Ernesto Samper had become the "enemy" in the drug war. In 1997 the Colombian congress voted against pursuing certain charges of illegal activity lodged against Samper. President Clinton's response indicated how "narcotized" the bilateral relationship had become: "[T]he United States judges its relationship between the two countries by one standard: whether they are cooperating with us in the fight against narcotics."[7] State Department spokesman Nicholas Burns emphasized that the Colombian government "has the next month or two to convince the United States that it is going to

[4] Ibid., 113.
[5] Ibid., 113.
[6] Ibid., 114.
[7] Ibid., 122.

be a more serious, more effective, more committed partner in the fight against narcotics trafficking. ... Colombia would, in effect, be a pariah state, should we choose to go down this road."[8] The Clinton administration responded by revoking Samper's visa to enter the United States, one of only a few heads of state ever to receive this dubious distinction. In a move of even greater symbolic significance, the White House "decertified" Colombia in both 1996 and 1997 for insufficient cooperation on the war on drugs.

The decertification decision, normally reserved for "rogue states" like Afghanistan, was clearly a stab at Samper. During the 1996 decertification process, Jesse Helms wrote:

No government can be completely committed to obliterating the drug cartels, drug corruption, and drug-related violence, nor effective in the achievement of these goals, if its senior officials owe fealty to drug kingpins. The Colombian government never will be dedicated to fighting drugs or drug corruption as long as Ernesto Samper is its leader, and its politicians, police, and judiciary are all guided by the money and kingpins.[9]

Robert Gelbard's testimony before Congress reflected the extent to which the Clinton administration's policy nearly converged with that of the Republican "drug hawks," who were constantly pushing for harder policies against Samper, "These [successful counternarcotics] efforts have been undercut at every turn by a government and a legislature not only plagued by corruption, but which are fostering corruption in order to protect themselves."[10]

During the Samper era, very few policy deliberations within the Clinton administration seemed to involve high-level officials. Instead of figures such as Secretary of State Warren Christopher, midlevel officials, mostly at the State Department, set policy in Colombia. However, this changed when, late into the Clinton term, top administration officials began to realize the unexpected consequences of their policy of isolation. Clinton's senior advisers concluded that U.S. drug policies were weakening the Colombian state at a time when armed groups on the right and left were stronger than ever. Indeed, both right-wing paramilitary and left-wing Marxist insurgent groups appeared to be on a rampage in the late 1990s. In addition, coca cultivation, which normally occurred in Bolivia and Peru, was now exploding in Colombia, further adding to the country's volatile mix of illegal armed groups and drug production. U.S. officials now saw Colombia as a country spiraling downward, making U.S. concern with Samper seem

[8] Ibid., 112.
[9] Ibid., 119.
[10] Ibid., 119.

like a needless obsession. Instead, Colombia was in "crisis" and in need of immediate attention.

PLAN COLOMBIA

In 1998 Samper's successor Andrés Pastrana took office. U.S. officials believed that Pastrana was the reliable and honest counterpart they needed to make a shift in policy. The changes began in earnest when in 1999 the Pastrana administration announced the creation of the U.S.$7.5 billion Plan Colombia, an unprecedented program intended to address Colombia's security situation.

While both Colombian and American officials claimed that Plan Colombia had been created in Bogotá, the program's "intellectual roots" were in Washington. Indeed, Plan Colombia was the Clinton administration's decision to "save" Colombia by instituting a massive increase in bilateral aid aimed almost exclusively at the drug war. In other words, the administration saw the solution to Colombia's myriad ills in winning the war on drugs. To achieve this objective, the new assistance to Colombia included military hardware such as helicopters that the Colombian military and national police could use to fight drugs. When the Plan Colombia–related assistance was approved by the U.S. Congress and signed by President Clinton the following year, the United States had embarked on the most costly and highest profile initiative since the war on drugs began in the Andes.

In terms of "inside the Beltway" politics, the Clinton administration's move was quite shrewd. By dramatically increasing the amount of counternarcotics assistance to Colombia, the Clinton White House took the wind out of the sails of Republican drug hawks who had been calling for a large increase for some time. Privately, staffers for leading drug hawks bitterly complained that Clinton had stolen their policy and taken subsequent credit for a renewed antidrug push in Colombia.

While demonstrating that it could be as tough as the drug hawks, the Clinton team also insulated itself from concerns about "another Vietnam" by reiterating the massive support package's singular focus on fighting drugs. Clinton made this point clear during an August 2000 visit to the coastal city of Cartagena (Figure 7.1), just a few weeks after he had signed the legislation supporting the U.S.$1.3 billion allocation for Colombia:

[A] condition of this aid is that we are not going to get into a shooting war. This is not Vietnam; neither is it Yankee imperialism. Those are the two false charges that have been hurled against Plan Colombia. You have a perfect right to question

FIGURE 7.1. U.S. president Bill Clinton pets a drug-sniffing dog, Darling, while Colombian president Andrés Pastrana (*center*) watches during a tour of a drug inspection station at Cartagena, Colombia, in August 2000. (Photo: Courtesy of the William J. Clinton Presidential Library.)

whether you think it will work or whether we've properly distributed the resources. But I can assure you that a lot of the opposition to this plan is coming from people who are afraid that it will work.[11]

Perhaps the most noteworthy element of the congressional debate in 2000 was the extent of the bipartisan support for Plan Colombia. While there were members of Congress on both sides of the aisle who attempted to cut the assistance levels drastically – for example, Representative Nancy Pelosi (D-CA) introduced an unsuccessful amendment that called for the entire proposed U.S.$1.3 billion in aid to Colombia to be shifted to domestic drug treatment programs – the core of the debate centered on the actual *type* of military assistance that would go to Colombia.

   One major argument erupted over the type of helicopter to send: either the state of the art Black Hawks, manufactured by the Sikorsky Corporation in Connecticut, or the less sophisticated "Hueys," manufactured by Bell-Textron in Texas. Interestingly, and maybe not surprisingly, Connecticut senator Christopher Dodd proposed that the Black Hawks be included in the

[11] Ibid., 157.

package. A vocal critic of the Reagan administration's policies in Central America during the 1980s and a leading dove on Latin America policy in general, the senator appeared hawkish in his support for Plan Colombia. As Dodd's support for the infusion of Black Hawks suggests, domestic political considerations were first and foremost in the minds of many members of Congress as they deliberated over the legislation.

In the House of Representatives, the final vote for support for Plan Colombia was 263–146, while in the Senate it was 95–4, indicating a resounding congressional endorsement. Not all of the assistance in the first aid package (or subsequent ones, for that matter) was military hardware. Instead, about 20 percent of the first round of assistance was intended for nonmilitary programs, such as judicial reform, human rights, and alternative crop development assistance. Collectively known as "soft side" assistance, these budget allocations allowed the Clinton administration to argue that its new policy was not solely of a military nature.

SEPTEMBER 11 AND "NARCOTERRORISM"

The Clinton administration might have created Plan Colombia, but the Bush administration became responsible for most of the program's implementation. As with the NAFTA treaty that Clinton inherited from the first Bush presidency, George W. Bush inherited Plan Colombia from Clinton. Indeed, most of the matériel mandated under Plan Colombia was delivered under the Bush administration's watch. Overall, the incoming president continued Clinton's broad outline for Plan Colombia, although Bush administration officials were less concerned about U.S. involvement in Colombia mirroring the slippery slope of Vietnam. Even before the 9/11 terrorist attacks, the Bush team was comfortable with the idea of the United States providing hardware and training not just for the drug war but also for the counterinsurgency effort.

In the first several years of the twenty-first century, the Colombian government faced a highly deteriorated security situation. Most threatening was the increasing use of terrorist-like operations by the Revolutionary Armed Forces of Colombia (FARC), including the kidnapping of several prominent political figures in 2002. After the Pastrana administration's unconditional concessions to the FARC, which included the granting of a liberated zone the size of Switzerland within the country, many Colombians concluded that the FARC had no interest in a negotiated settlement. The Colombian people were desperate for a forceful leader who would put an end to the FARC's rampage. As a result, presidential candidate Álvaro

Uribe won an unprecedented election based on a "get tough" campaign against lawlessness, especially that of the FARC.

For the hawkish Bush administration, Uribe was the right president at the right time in the right country. Washington officials had chalked up Pastrana's attempts to negotiate peace as failures, and they were eager to support the incoming Colombian president, who appeared to "get" the concept of the global war on terrorism. In fact, if anything, it was Uribe and not the Bush administration who made the most strident arguments that Colombia warranted inclusion in the United States' global war on terror.

We will never know if the Bush administration would have sought a change in the authorization of U.S. assistance to Colombia had 9/11 not occurred. However, its move to include Colombia's counterinsurgency in a predominantly antidrug war did not follow directly as a result of 9/11. Instead, many were already concluding that a tougher, military-based approach was necessary in order to deal effectively with Colombia's many glaring vacuums of security and state presence – as well as the still seemingly limitless narcotics production and export.

The aftermath of 9/11 made moving U.S. assistance and training to include the counterinsurgency issue easier, with respect to both passing a bill through Congress and garnering public approval. By August 2002 the U.S. Congress approved a change in legislation to allow U.S. assistance to Colombia to include counterinsurgency efforts in addition to the existing counternarcotics programs.

The expansion to counterinsurgency assistance reflected a new episode in U.S. policy in Colombia. The objective now was not just to eradicate drugs but also to aid the Colombian military in its efforts to battle guerrillas and right-wing paramilitaries. Unlike previous years when U.S. policy dictated a healthy distance from Colombia's civil war, in the post-9/11 era, legions of U.S. Special Forces trainers were embedded with their Colombian counterparts throughout the countryside. With these developments, Anti-imperialist critics saw the beginnings of another "Vietnam" of American soldiers coming home in body bags (Figure 7.2). For proponents of this policy, the United States was backing a key ally in its fight against narcoterrorism.

Another key development in U.S. policies in Colombia was the extent to which the bilateral relationship focused on Uribe himself, in keeping with President Bush's preference to base his foreign policy on his personal views of foreign leaders. In both Colombia and Washington, Uribe was seen as the unapologetically hawkish leader whom the country needed to restore order in the face of narcotics-driven violence. Through a series of meetings and statements, which included an unprecedented visit by the Colombian

FIGURE 7.2. Human rights activists lie on the ground in body bags during a protest against Colombia's President Álvaro Uribe outside the Center for American Progress in Washington, DC, on May 2, 2007. With support of U.S. president George W. Bush, Uribe sought to convince U.S. lawmakers to approve more military and antinarcotics aid and to back a trade deal. (Photo: Reuters/Yuri Gripas.)

president to the Crawford ranch in 2005, Bush's Colombia policy gradually came to resemble an "Uribe" policy; Uribe now had become the reason for supporting Colombia. Given that President Uribe remained widely popular in Colombia and was overwhelmingly reelected in 2006, there seemed to be little downside in so strongly and so visibly tying U.S. policy to the Colombian leader.

One should not conclude that, just because the Bush administration expanded U.S support to include the counterinsurgency, the United States had abandoned a narcotized policy in Colombia. On the contrary, the war on drugs remained an integral part of the U.S. strategy in Colombia even after 9/11. Annually, U.S.-supported antidrug efforts resulted in the eradication of more than 100,000 hectares of coca plants, a marked increase over what occurred in the 1990s. In addition, the U.S. government has spent approximately U.S.$400 million annually to fund antidrug efforts since Plan Colombia was inaugurated, including the delivery of expensive Black Hawk helicopters.

Terrorism and Colombia's precarious security situation accompanied the drug war but did not replace it. In fact, the vast majority of U.S. assistance to Colombia is still directly related to the drug war, and even the "soft side" programs intended to strengthen Colombia's democracy are tied to alternative development efforts linked to eradicating drugs.

Just as narcotization continued to be an integral part of U.S. efforts, so did the controversies in Washington over Colombian policy. Anti-imperialist critics alleged that the Bush administration had invented a new pretext (i.e., terrorism) to justify its interventionist and exploitative policies in Colombia. Others such as Senator Patrick Leahy (D-VT) were concerned that the Bush administration's unapologetic support of the Colombian military might come at the expense of the U.S. government's human rights agenda. In March 2007 Leahy held up U.S.$55 million in aid to Colombia until he received an explanation of why the State Department decided to "certify" what he believed was the country's still dire human rights situation.

CONCLUSION

U.S. policy in Colombia has evolved drastically since the Samper era. In the early 1990s U.S. assistance totaled a few million dollars annually and was slated entirely for the national police, not the military. In addition, this aid was reserved exclusively for helping the Colombian government prosecute the war on drugs. More recently, and especially after 9/11, U.S. policy assumed additional objectives, including providing U.S. training and hardware for the Colombian military's counterinsurgency war.

For the Bush administration, the expansion to the counterinsurgency war in Colombia was a necessary move to a more aggressive, military-based stance at a critical time in the Andean country's history. According to George W. Bush's top diplomat for the Western Hemisphere, Thomas Shannon,

A successful Colombia will change the face of South America. The U.S. has committed over $5 billion since 2000 to support Colombia's comprehensive approach to fighting the intertwined threats of narcotics and terrorism and improving the lives of the Colombian people. Colombia itself has paid the majority of the costs and continues to increase its defense and social spending. Challenges remain, but under President Uribe's leadership, Colombia is a success story for transformational diplomacy. For the first time in over a generation, Colombians can envisage the possibility of real peace, and the Colombian government is poised to make it a reality. We have developed a plan for U.S. support of Colombia's consolidation strategy to lock in this progress and take advantage of Colombia's new realities. The Colombian strategy puts increased emphasis on consolidating state presence through access to social services and on development through sustainable growth and trade. Our success will depend on maintaining U.S. assistance while we equip Colombia to assume responsibility for programs we are now funding.[12]

Shannon's optimistic outlook on Colombia certainly did not convince all of the Bush administration's critics with respect to the appropriate approach to Colombia. According to one Democratic Senate aide, "We've sprayed a lot of coca, but we're not doing enough to provide people with other options. I can't see how anyone could call this a success."[13] What was clear to all observers was that Colombia's history of violence, impunity, and drug trafficking ensures that the United States will be involved deeply in the country's affairs for years to come.

INTERMEZZO: ELEMENTS OF THE U.S.-LED DRUG WAR

Colombia and Extradition

Starting in the early 1990s, the U.S. government's repeated requests to extradite drug traffickers from Colombia to the United States met with tremendous opposition from successive Colombian governments. While a limited number of drug suspects were transported to the United States during this time, the procedure was banned by a clause in Colombia's new

---

[12] Thomas Shannon, Assistant Secretary of State for the Western Hemisphere, Testimony before the House Committee on Foreign Affairs, Subcommittee on the Western Hemisphere, 110th Cong., 1st sess., Washington, DC, March 1, 2007.

[13] Senior Democratic Senate aide in a confidential interview with the author, Washington, DC, May 3, 2007.

constitution in 1991. In light of the perceived setback to the war on drugs that the new legislation signified, the U.S. government intensified its pressure on its Colombian counterpart to amend the constitution to allow for retroactive extradition. American officials sought the retroactive clause because it would allow some "big fish" in Colombian jails to face further justice in the United States. In 1997, after years of intense pressure from Washington, Colombia finally amended its constitution to allow for extradition, but not with retroactivity.

After this change, the issue of extradition from Colombia typically received minimal attention in both countries. Yet, over time, drug war proponents claimed that extradition had turned out to be an unexpected silver lining in the antidrug effort. In the decades after the 1997 amendment to the constitution, more than 500 drug-related suspects were extradited to face criminal proceedings in the United States. Although this was not part of Washington's original motivation for demanding extradition, drug-related expatriation also became a critical negotiation instrument with counterinsurgency and counterparamilitary initiatives. The Colombian government leveraged the threat of extradition in its negotiations with both drug-trafficking right-wing paramilitaries and leftist guerrillas. In one instance during his first term in office (2002–6), President Álvaro Uribe convinced right-wing paramilitary fighters to agree to a highly imperfect yet critical demobilization process by convincing them to cooperate lest they end up in "gringo jail" for the rest of their lives. In a dramatic move in May 2008, Uribe extradited fourteen paramilitary leaders to the United States to face drug trafficking charges. For some paramilitary commanders at least, a "gringo" jail had become a reality.

With respect to the FARC, Colombia's oldest and largest Marxist guerrilla group, roughly fifty of its leaders have been indicted for drug charges, and two have been extradited to the United States and convicted for drug-related crimes (Figure 7.3).

Although many Colombians came to accept extradition as a legitimate and necessary part of the drug war in their country, it was brought about by U.S. pressure – or, some might say, hegemony. Whatever the case, it is worth considering whether the extradition policy was successful in the context of the United States' broader hemispheric interests. Some in the Establishment school would argue that it was Washington's unwavering stance that convinced the otherwise uncooperative Colombian government to go along with a policy that actually served Colombia's best interests. Anti-imperialist critics would contend that extradition was a gross violation of Colombia's sovereignty and reinforced the idea that the U.S. government controls the policy decisions of its "client" nations in Latin America.

FIGURE 7.3. Former FARC leader Simón Trinidad shouts "viva las FARC, viva Simón Bolívar!" as U.S. FBI agents and Colombian national police escort him to an FBI airplane in Bogotá in December 2004. Trinidad was extradited to the United States, where he faced trial for drug trafficking and kidnapping conspiracy charges. (Photo: Courtesy of U.S. Justice Department.)

Certification

Since the drug war began in earnest in the late 1980s, the "certification" process evolved as one of the U.S government's most controversial policy tools in the drug war. Mandated as part of the legislation passed with the 1988 Anti-Drug Abuse Act, the annual certification process required the U.S. president to submit a list to Congress of identified drug-producing or drug-trafficking countries. The executive branch then had several months to alert Congress as to whether these countries would receive one of the following classifications: certification, decertification, or decertification with a national security waiver. Congress then had thirty days to review the list and to determine if it wanted to add country-specific resolutions of disapproval, although these would have to survive a likely presidential veto. Decertified countries then typically received a battery of sanctions.

The Clinton administration's 1995 decertification of Bolivia served as a landmark in post–Cold War relations between the United States and its South American neighbors. For one, it indicated the creeping "narcotization" of U.S.

policy in the Andes. Bolivia's certification became the most public, albeit the most controversial, symbol that both Republicans and Democrats in Washington now considered cooperation on the drug war the basis for warm relations with the United States. Unlike the fiercely partisan and ideological debates over Haiti, drug policy enjoyed a much stronger consensus in Washington.

Even more surprising and contentious than the Bolivia instance, however, was the two-time decertification of Colombia in 1996 and 1997, when President Ernesto Samper was in office. Unlike Bolivia, which from Washington's perspective was more of a "basket case" anyway at the time, given its "narco-democracy" status, Colombia had been a strong ally historically. Yet, contrary to what U.S. officials expected, the decertification decisions against Colombia actually rallied public support around Samper, who was believed to be linked to drug money. In addition, the United States' isolation of Samper, as expressed by the decertification decisions, further weakened the Colombian state at a time when right-wing paramilitaries and Marxist guerrillas were gaining unprecedented strength.

The certification process was highly unpopular in the Latin American countries under review. Indeed, many Latin Americans viewed the procedure as a humiliating and unjustified expression of Yankee heavy-handedness for a problem (drug consumption) that resided squarely in the United States. In response to the growing bipartisan consensus in Washington that certification had created more problems that it had solved, in 2001 the U.S. Congress modified the certification procedures to eliminate some of the most controversial elements of the law, effectively ending the practice of certification. The State Department's top counternarcotics official, Rand Beers, put it mildly that year when he told Congress that the process had been "an effective, if blunt, policy instrument."[14]

On the surface, it appeared as though nothing in particular compelled the U.S. government to modify its policy of certification. Yet slightly beneath the surface was the unanticipated issue of Mexico's frustration and opposition to certification. Vicente Fox's election to the presidency in 2000 ended the Institutional Revolutionary Party's (PRI) seventy-one-year monopoly over national power in Mexico. Accordingly, many in Washington – on both sides of the aisle – wanted to foster deeper and warmer ties with this more democratic and modernizing Mexico. In short, certification had become a

---

[14] Quoted in K. Larry Storrs, "Drug Certification Requirements and Congressional Modifications in 2001," *Congressional Research Service Report* (Washington, DC: Library of Congress, January 10, 2002), 4.

perennial embarrassment for the United States' increasingly critical bilateral relationship with Mexico. Certification also repeatedly exposed the undeniable hypocrisy in U.S. policy. In a speech to a joint session of Congress a few days before 9/11, President Fox told his American hosts, "Trust requires that one partner not be judged unilaterally by the other."[15]

Although Fox's position was not unexpected, surprisingly the Bush administration and both parties in Congress agreed with him. Republicans and Democrats alike realized that Mexico was too important for the certification process to derail stronger, more institutionalized bilateral relations. According to a senior Democratic staff member on the Senate Foreign Relations committee, "The certification amendment was a cosmetic change, but it quietly ended a profoundly counterproductive annual ritual. It took the sting out. And make no mistake, without Mexico there would never have been any adjustment."[16] In a sense, Mexico's diplomatic and political standing in relation to the United States forced Washington to modify its certification process for the entire hemisphere. Late nineteenth-century Mexican dictator Porfirio Díaz is believed to have lamented, "Poor Mexico. So far from God and so close to the United States." In this case, however, Mexico's relative prosperity and proximity to the United States helped it secure benefits for Latin American countries long thought unattainable in their dealings with the United States.

---

[15] Ibid.
[16] Senior Democratic Aide to the Senate Foreign Relations Committee, in an interview with the author, Washington, DC, May 2, 2007.

8

Blowback

The Drug War in Bolivia

The story of the United States' antidrug efforts in Bolivia is a relatively uninterrupted narrative of the U.S. government's pressuring successive Bolivian governments to yield to U.S. policies. Since the late 1980s, Washington's overriding policy focus in the Andean region has been to eliminate coca production in the country. Not surprisingly, given that coca had been a traditional crop in Bolivia for centuries, and that in more recent years indigenous groups have made coca a visible part of their renewed sense of identity, the United States' approach has met with tremendous controversy and opposition.[1]

Since the drug war's inception, the U.S. government has had little difficulty requiring successive Bolivian governments to comply with all U.S. requests as part of its "zero tolerance" approach to the drug war in Bolivia. Even if the Bolivian governments had wanted to depart from the U.S.-mandated policies, there was little they could do. Yet, the relative ease Washington had in implementing its drug policies has not translated into the drug war successes that many in Washington anticipated. On the contrary, critics contend, Washington's policies have failed in the more narrow antidrug sense and have perhaps provoked a tremendous wave of societal resentment and radicalization that threatens to undermine the broader U.S. goal of promoting a stable and democratic political climate in Bolivia.

---

[1] For more on this era, see Eduardo Gamarra, "The United States and Bolivia: Fighting the Drug War," in *The United States and Latin America: The New Agenda*, ed. Victor Bulmer-Thomas and James Dunkerley (Cambridge, MA: Harvard University Press, 1999), 177–206.

The first decade of the twenty-first century witnessed the emergence of radical political parties and movements in Bolivia whose ideologies and policies were usually antithetical to those of the U.S. government. In 2005 Evo Morales's election – the culmination of the social and political mobilization of mostly indigenous Bolivians – further removed Bolivia from Washington's recommended (critics would say, imposed) agenda.

LA PAZ, 2002

In the lead up to Bolivia's 2002 presidential election, the U.S. ambassador in La Paz, Manuel Rocha, made an infamous declaration: "I want to remind the Bolivian electorate that if you elect those who want Bolivia to become a major cocaine exporter again, this will endanger the future of U.S. assistance to Bolivia."[2] Bolivians knew to whom Rocha referred: presidential candidate Evo Morales. An Aymara Indian, Morales was born in the Bolivian highlands, but in his youth migrated to the temperate region of the Chapare to seek his fortune in the region's booming coca business. Morales eventually became a vocal leader of a *cocalero* (coca grower) federation that aggressively – and at times violently – opposed the U.S.-mandated coca eradication efforts carried out by the Bolivian government. In the early 2000s, Morale's *cocalero* federations clashed repeatedly with Bolivian security forces tasked to eradicate coca.

Elected to congress in 1997 on an unapologetically pro-*cocalero* platform, by 2002 Morales had become a viable presidential candidate. At this point, he represented the *cocaleros*, as well as a broad array of recently radicalized leftist and indigenous groups. If elected, Morales vowed to end what he considered to be draconian coca eradication policies that were eliminating not just the coca plant but also Bolivia's indigenous culture.

Morales was not the favored candidate within the U.S. Embassy or the Bush administration. Yet, contrary to what Ambassador Rocha intended, Bolivian public opinion shifted in favor of Morales's candidacy. Morales only somewhat facetiously called Rocha his "best campaign chief," after gaining an estimated five percentage points in the presidential vote, which propelled him to within a few percentage points of eventual winner, staunchly pro-American Gonzalo Sánchez de Lozada.[3] Though denied the

[2] Raphael Perl, "Drug Control: International Policy and Approaches," *Congressional Research Service Issue Brief* (Washington, DC: Library of Congress, February 2, 2006).

[3] Eduardo Gamarra, "Bolivia on the Brink," *Council Special Report* 24 (Washington, DC: Council on Foreign Relations), 1–51; Evo Morales in a televised interview with Amy Goodman, Juan Gonzalez, and Margaret Prescod, *Democracy Now!*, September 22, 2006.

presidency, Morales did not abandon his political career. In fact, he spent the next four years actively fomenting a number of large and sometimes violent protests that resulted in the ouster of Sánchez de Lozada as well as his replacement, Carlos Mesa. Through his ability to oust two presidents, Morales proved that he was a force with which to be reckoned.

LA PAZ, 2005

In December 2005 Morales scored a resounding and unprecedented presidential victory, taking 53 percent of the vote. Bolivians and international observers alike waited on edge to see how Morales would tackle the major issues announced in his campaign, which included the nationalization of the hydrocarbons industry and the writing of a new, more indigenous-based constitution.

The Bush administration was concerned that Morales would unravel an almost two-decade-long effort to eliminate coca production in Bolivia, a source-country strategy effort with a price tag of hundreds of millions of – mostly U.S. – dollars. Remarkably, Morales announced that he would continue the broad outlines of the very antidrug policies that he had railed against. Suddenly, the defiant *cocalero* was upholding the need for effective antidrug efforts – with a twist. As recently as the 2005 presidential campaign, Morales had voiced the slogan, "coca sí, cocaina no," reflecting his view that his government could embrace the former without automatically condoning the latter.

Upon taking office, Morales appeared to continue most of his pro-U.S. predecessors' counternarcotics program. During the first five months of his presidency, some 1,500 hectares of coca were eradicated, a level in line with the previous years. In keeping with his pro-*cocalero* position, though, Morales appointed a former coca farmer, Felipe Cáceres as his "drug czar." In a clear indication that the United States wanted to encourage Morales to continue the antidrug efforts, the U.S. Embassy responded that Cáceres was a "great choice."[4]

Despite his willingness to follow U.S. prescriptions, Morales's perspective on the issue of coca still differed sharply from that of most drug hawks in Washington. In Morales's view – anathema to policymakers in the United

---

[4] William Francisco, Director of the Narcotic Affairs Section, U.S. Embassy in La Paz, Bolivia, quoted in Associated Press, "EEUU respalda a viceministro antidroga en Bolivia," *Terra*, January 31, 2006, http://www.terra.com/noticias/articulo/html/act330482.htm (accessed April 23, 2007).

States – coca had the potential to become a lucrative and sustainable *licit* crop. Yet the initial words and actions of both the Morales government and the Bush administration indicated that perhaps the bitter controversy and mistrust regarding anticoca efforts in the late 1990s and early 2000s had somewhat diminished.

However, the comments of Thomas Shannon, assistant secretary of state for the Western Hemisphere, in early 2006 reminded everyone that Washington still required cooperation on the drug war as a prerequisite to warm bilateral relations: "We have witnessed mixed signals from the new president. One day he says he wants to work together to fight drugs, the next day he appears in front of a banner reading, 'Long Live Coca, Death to the Yankees.' Clearly, our relationship with the new government in Bolivia is changing and will depend upon the policies they adopt on a wide range of issues, including counter-narcotics."[5] In a subtle and rhetorical use of the Big Stick, Shannon made it clear that, while there was room for negotiation and compromise, ultimately Morales was obligated to cooperate with Washington – and not the other way around.

The roots of Bolivia's recent political revolution are myriad and extremely difficult to isolate given the country's centuries-long legacy of extreme poverty, social and economic inequality, and exclusion. Yet, as Morales's meteoric political rise made clear, some of these more recent dynamics can be traced back to the U.S.-mandated forced coca eradication programs of the late 1990s. Aggressive U.S. efforts to pursue the drug agenda helped radicalize Bolivia and ushered in political leaders who were opposed to U.S. drug policies – as well as nearly every other policy with Washington's name on it. Some observers would posit that without the U.S.-led drug war, there never would have been an "Evo Morales." If ever there were a case of U.S. policy "blowback" in Latin America since the Cold War, critics would say drug policy in Bolivia is it.

At the same time, proponents of the drug war in Bolivia contend that U.S. efforts have made a marked difference in the Bolivian government's long-standing tradition of impunity and corruption. They hypothesize that, given the depth to which the political system had been corrupted by narco-traffickers' money, Bolivia was destined to become an Andean "narco-democracy" until the U.S. government effectively engaged the situation.

---

[5] Thomas Shannon, Assistant Secretary of State for the Western Hemisphere, "Counternarcotics Strategies in Latin America," Testimony before the House Committee on International Relations, Subcommittee on the Western Hemisphere, 109th Cong., 2nd sess., Washington, DC, March 30, 2006, 16.

Furthermore, proponents of the drug war count the precipitous (albeit short-lived) drop in coca cultivation in the late 1990s and concomitantly successful alternative development programs, such as the Andean Trade Preferences Act (ATPA), as clear evidence of policy successes.

DRUG WAR, PHASE ONE (1986–1997)

U.S.-led "source-country" strategies (i.e., efforts to go after coca cultivation) began in Bolivia even before the end of the Cold War. Although the U.S. military was reluctant to assume the responsibility for prosecuting the drug war due to its nonconventional nature, the Pentagon did eventually agree to spearhead these efforts. To address the "supply-side" element of coca production in Bolivia, the United States implemented a new set of crop eradication and alternative development policies designed to root out coca cultivation.

On the ground, the U.S. strategy manifested itself in military operations that almost overnight made Bolivia the first country to be on the receiving end of Washington's new policies. In particular, a landmark bilateral treaty in 1987 permitted a greater and more institutionalized U.S. military presence in the country. U.S. Special Forces soldiers now began training their Bolivian counterparts, while American counternarcotics assistance funding poured into the country. In addition to training and assistance, agents of the U.S. Drug Enforcement Agency became involved directly in drug seizures and arrests in Bolivia. Since this time in the late 1980s, U.S. strategy in Bolivia (and the Andean source countries more broadly) has been threefold: to eliminate the production of coca, to provide economic alternatives for the affected farmers or other farmers who might be considering growing coca, and to interdict cocaine that is being smuggled out of the country.

From its perspective, Washington concluded its antidrug strategy in Bolivia was working during this period based on the fact that successive Bolivian governments, albeit at times halfheartedly, agreed to the obligations that came with the counternarcotics assistance and training, knowing that refusal to cooperate would result in a cessation or sharp reduction in American aid to Bolivia. These U.S.-devised policies were also adopted into Bolivian law.[6]

Indeed, early U.S antidrug efforts in Bolivia marked the beginning of the "conditionality" question. Forceful ambassadors such as Robert Gelbard repeatedly threatened to cut off assistance if Bolivia did not cooperate on

---

[6] U.S. Department of State, "Bolivia Fact Sheet," 2007. See also Executive Office of the President, "The President's National Drug Control Strategy," Office of National Drug Control Policy, February 2006.

the drug war. In 1988 the U.S. Embassy even accused President Jaime Paz Zomora of running a "narco-democracy" and receiving campaign funds from drug traffickers.

Since this time, critics have charged that strengthening and expanding the Bolivian military's capabilities and mandate served only to weaken Bolivia's already fragile democracy. On the other hand, supporters of the policies contended that it is only Bolivia's security forces that have the wherewithal and legitimacy to fight what is at times an unsavory drug war. Overall, though, the first several years witnessed significant eradication of coca, but little progress toward reducing the amount of coca cultivated in the country in new plantings. In addition, Bolivian governments were at times lackluster in their own support for what some viewed as a "gringo obsession."

Part of the Bolivian government's initial reluctance to embrace Washington's efforts to eliminate coca from Bolivian territory was due to the coca industry's tremendous impact on the economy. Ravaged by decades of economic mismanagement and more recent years of hyperinflation, Bolivia embarked in the middle 1980s on a wrenching economic austerity program of fiscal restraint and debt restructuring. While these policies worked miracles in eliminating the country's chronic macroeconomic instability, they also contributed to considerable economic and social upheaval, especially widespread unemployment. Of particular importance were the 2,300 miners who were let go (an estimated 75 percent of the work force in the mines) when unprofitable mines were closed.

Confronted with economic misery if they remained in their highland towns located near the mines, countless Bolivians migrated to the only part of the country (the Chapare) that was undergoing an economic boom – or, more specifically, a coca boom. Unlike the Yungas region, the Chapare was never a traditional coca-growing area. Like the Sierra Nevada in the 1849 California Gold Rush, the Chapare in the late 1980s was a boom region, but this time the precious commodity was questionably legal. Indeed, coca appeared to be the perfect crop to grow given that it was hearty, provided several harvests a year, thrived in the Chapare's moist climate, seemed to always have a ready buyer, and usually occupied the entire family in its production.

By the early 1990s an estimated 6 to 13 percent of the active work force in Bolivia was believed to be involved in the cultivation of what was now mostly illegal coca. The coca trade was a key contributor (up to almost 4 percent by 1997) to Bolivia's gross domestic product.[7] Bolivia was a

---

[7] "Coca, Drugs, and Social Protest in Bolivia and Peru," Latin America Report No. 12 (Bogotá, Colombia: International Crisis Group, March 3, 2006), 5.

democracy at this time, but from the U.S. government's perspective the coca trade served to undermine the nation's very tenuous democratic institutions.

The legions of *cocaleros* in the Chapare were opposed vehemently to the U.S.-led eradication efforts implemented to counter the boom in cultivation. The farmers found it difficult to understand why the United States would want to eradicate the only crop that provided them with half a chance at more stable and prosperous lives. They harbored an equal contempt for those in the Bolivian government whom they believed were yielding weakly to Washington's demands. For the first decade of Washington's source-country strategy in Bolivia, the insatiable attraction of planting coca was colliding with the U.S. government's insistence that the Bolivian government eradicate the crop.

DRUG WAR, PHASE TWO (1997–2006)

The second decade of the U.S. drug war in Bolivia was characterized by much greater cooperation and a firm belief by successive Bolivian governments (save Evo Morales) that coca eradication was necessary. The 1997 election of Hugo Banzer as president ushered in the beginning of this new era in Bolivia's drug war. Banzer had ruled as an undemocratic "strongman" during Bolivia's economically and politically tumultuous decade of the 1970s, but this time he returned as a democrat. Starting in early 1998, Banzer's government implemented Plan Dignidad (Dignity Plan), a new anticoca program whose ambitious goal was to achieve "zero coca" in Bolivia by 2001. Dignidad increased the Bolivian military's direct role in eradicating coca, including using soldiers to uproot coca crops manually, placing the Bolivian military at the forefront of antidrug efforts. In turn, this development sparked direct confrontations with *cocaleros*, episodes whose intensity grew dramatically in ensuing years.

The Clinton administration considered Banzer's plan to be a forceful step toward the complete eradication of coca in Bolivia. The administration demonstrated its strong approval of Dignidad by providing U.S.$75 million to support complementary alternative development programs. Then, in 1998, U.S. assistance funded the creation of Joint Task Forces (JTFs), or combined Bolivian military and police units specially geared for antidrug operations. The JTFs were at once effective and controversial: both coca eradication and accusations of brutality filed against the JTFs soared during this period.[8]

---

[8] Advocacy groups such as the Washington Office on Latin America issued several reports on this topic. See "Coca and Conflict in the Chapare," *WOLA Drug War Monitor* (Washington, DC: Washington Office on Latin America, July 2002).

At the onset of Dignidad, estimated coca production in Bolivia was 45,000 hectares. Remarkably, in just a few years the forceful "zero tolerance" strategy had reduced coca cultivation in the Chapare by 90 percent. This achievement startled critics who believed that Dignidad would fail just like the previous anticoca efforts conducted since the days of Snow Cap and Blast Furnace operations in the late 1980s.

The eradication efforts had a devastating impact on the economy in the coca-growing regions, costing the Bolivian economy an estimated U.S.$700 million annually. The U.S. Agency for International Development worked aggressively to support alternative development programs in order to cushion the eradication efforts. While these programs never received the attention or elicited the controversies of forced eradication, the U.S. government poured hundreds of millions of dollars into alternative development efforts.

Although there have certainly been setbacks and frustrations, the programs met some successes as well. In fact, by 2003 more than 25,000 Bolivian families in the Chapare had received development assistance in return for not growing coca. By 2002 the legal agricultural products leaving the Chapare exceeded U.S.$25 million, a drastic increase over just a few years earlier. In 2006, due to alternative development efforts, the Chapare's principal export was hearts of palm, not coca.[9]

Yet, despite the millions of dollars in funding for alternative development, forced eradication still delivered a tremendous economic blow to the coca farmers. Frustration and violence continued to simmer. Starting in September 2001, organized *cocaleros* began protesting in order to demand that they be legally permitted to grow one *cato* (1,600 square meters or roughly half the size of a football field). Tensions between protestors and Bolivian security forces quickly increased; during one clash protesting *cocaleros* were shot, further heightening animosities between the two groups.

In the following weeks and months, *cocaleros* staged a number of protests, which included blocking the highway between the provincial cities of Santa Cruz and Cochabamba, the principal artery through the Chapare. The administration of president Jorge Quiroga (Banzer had died from cancer and had been replaced by Vice President Quiroga) responded by transferring 2,000 soldiers to the region and establishing road checkpoints. By the end of November, there were between 4,000 and 4,500 security forces in the region. Quiroga's deployment was met with more protests – and more deaths.

---

[9] U.S. Department of State, "Alternative Development in Bolivia," USAID data sheet, 2005.

At the height of the crisis, U.S. ambassador Rocha reminded the Bolivian government of the consequences it would face if it responded to the protests by somehow backtracking on the zero tolerance coca policies. According to Rocha, "[i]f a time comes in which this commitment no longer exists, be assured, our aid will be different. The funds are there because of the commitment and without it, the aid will diminish."[10]

In January 2002 the coca clashes went from bad to worse when the Bolivian government enforced a law that prohibited the drying, transport, and sale of coca leaf in the Chapare and closed more than a dozen markets where coca was openly sold. Incensed, *cocaleros* reacted by targeting Bolivian security forces and their compounds, even setting fire to two dozen government vehicles. As the dust settled, four security officers were found dead, their heads bashed in by rocks. Bolivian public sentiment began to turn against the *cocaleros* as some now began to see them less as victims and more as radical vigilantes. While these clashes were still raging, the Bolivian congress voted to remove member Evo Morales, who still retained his affiliation as a key leader of the *cocalero* movement. The move was intended to make Morales eligible for prosecution on criminal charges related to the coca protests, but the effort served only to increase his visibility.

By February the Quiroga government and the coca leaders had reached agreements under which the *cocaleros* would cease with road blocks and the government would suspend the anticoca transporting law for three months. Quiroga's administration also promised to carry out an investigation into the alleged abuses committed by the security forces. Some *cocaleros* were released from captivity. Contrary to what many observers expected, these agreements ushered in a period of reduced violence and protest in the Chapare, largely because "zero tolerance" effectively had been abandoned. Less violent clashes did continue, but in 2004 Chapare coca leaders signed an agreement with the government that allowed for the cultivation of one *cato* per family. Any production over this amount was subject to eradication.

POLICY BLOWBACK

Easily lost amid the violence and controversy of the "coca clashes" in the Chapare since Plan Dignidad began was the emergence of new *cocalero*-based political movements. In particular, the Movimiento al Socialismo (Movement toward Socialism, MAS) organized itself in the late 1990s and

[10] Quoted in "Coca and Conflict in the Chapare," 8.

FIGURE 8.1. Cuban president Fidel Castro (*center*), Bolivian president Evo Morales (*right*), and Venezuelan president Hugo Chávez (*left*) wave to a crowd during a meeting of the three leaders in Havana, Cuba, on April 30, 2006. (Photo: Polaris Images/Jose Goitia.)

quickly grew to dominate politics in the Chapare.[11] As the party's name suggests, the members of MAS were the antithesis of pro–Washington Consensus, pro-U.S. politicians. Rather, influenced by Fidel Castro's and Hugo Chávez's leftist, nationalist "Bolivarian" rhetoric, the MAS called for radical changes to Bolivia's political, economic, and social structures, including the Bolivian state's control over economic resources and industry (Figure 8.1). Needless to say, the MAS opposed U.S.-mandated anticoca programs.

By 2002 the MAS had evolved from a coca growers' party into a more broad-based movement that included all sorts of social groups. Its politicians were now as likely to rail against the proposed plan for a natural gas pipeline through Chile as they were forced eradication. Born in the fires of the coca clashes, the MAS was now a viable and radical national political movement whose presidential candidate won in a historical landslide in 2006.

---

[11] Linda Farthing and and Benjamin Kohl, "Conflicting Agendas: The Politics of Development Aid in Drug-Producing Areas," *Development Policy Review* 23, no. 2 (March 2005): 183–98.

For many decades, the United States got what it wanted from the Bolivian government. All three post–Cold War administrations placed the same unyielding diplomatic conditions on La Paz, illustrating the depth to which a militarized drug war had become an institutionalized component of U.S. policy in Latin America – and in the Andes in particular. Yet, as the meteoric rise of Evo Morales suggested, the short-term victories the United States gained over the narcotics trade (or, as critics would contend, over the Bolivian government) throughout the 1980s and 1990s resulted in a long-term defeat for U.S. interests.

"Coca Sí, Cocaina No?"

As we have discussed, presidential candidate Evo Morales promised that as president he would end the controversial practice of the forced eradication of coca. Calling his policy "coca si, cocaina no," Morales contended that there was no reason why Bolivia could not cultivate copious amounts of what would become coca, but still successfully combat narcotics trafficking. As one might expect, U.S. officials were alarmed that Morales's moves might push the country toward a twenty-first century "narco-democracy."

Morales's policies suggested that he was attempting to maintain the status quo on interdiction, alternative development, and even eradication, but hoped to change the government's approach to coca cultivation. In fact, in his first year in office, cocaine confiscations increased from 11.5 to 14 metric tons, although it was not fully clear if this was due to greater vigilance or increased cocaine production.[12]

Not one to shy away from controversy, Morales soon made waves when he formalized the 2004 agreement allowing each family in the Chapare to dedicate one *cato* to coca cultivation, effectively legalizing 8,000 hectares of coca in the Chapare. The "one *cato*" policy also encouraged an influx of new *cocaleros* into the region. Not surprisingly, the United Nations reported in June 2006 that coca production had shot up 19 percent in the Chapare, the largest factor in the 8 percent increase in coca production throughout Bolivia that year.[13]

The key question surrounding this marked growth became, What was happening to all the excess coca? UN and U.S. officials agreed that the

---

[12] See "Bolivia: Monitoreo de Cultivos de coca," Report by the UN Office on Drugs and Crime (UNODC), June 2006; "Informe de la Junta Internacional de Fiscalización de Estupefacientes," Report by UNODC, 2007.

[13] "Coca Cultivation in the Andean Region: A Survey of Bolivia, Colombia, Ecuador and Peru," Report by UNODC, June 2007, 17.

12,000 legal hectares in the Yungas already more than covered the total domestic demand for cultural use. Using the cultivation statistics from 2007, if one took a conservative estimate of Bolivia's coca production (26,000 hectares) and subtracted a generous number for domestic legal demand (10,000 hectares), there were still 16,000 hectares "unaccounted for" in Bolivia.

As one can see, the estimated domestic demand for coca was critical in order to gauge how much of the crop should be grown. The European Commission offered the Bolivian government €1million to conduct a study, but the Morales government dragged its feet. Some observers believed this was due to Morales's fear that the study would reveal far less domestic demand for coca than his administration suggested.

In 2006 total eradication declined to 5,000 hectares, the lowest level in ten years and the minimum level that Morales had negotiated with the U.S. government. Foreign diplomats privately contended that Morales was underestimating the critical importance of forced eradication. According to a senior U.S. counternarcotics official, "The whole idea is to get people to switch to, say, hearts of palm. But these crops can never compete with coca because the narcos will pay top dollar for it. Folks only switch when there is the threat of losing their entire coca crop."[14]

Industrialize It!

Evo Morales contended that the solution to "excess coca" was not to limit its cultivation but rather to greatly increase the crop's licit uses. The Bolivian government's term for this was "industrialization." Morales floated ideas about using coca for toothpaste, hemorrhoid cream, flour, and even wine. Most experts outside the government remained dubious about industrialization's prospects. According to one analyst, "The coca flour costs three times as much as normal flour and it tastes like shit." Another asked, "Why can't Evo understand that people like to drink wine made from grapes, not coca?"[15] In a twist of regional geopolitical intrigue, Venezuelan president Hugo Chávez spent U.S.$1 million to fund two coca "refineries" in Bolivia and promised to buy all of its products. The Morales administration also touted the possibility of sending 500,000 tons of coca leaf to China for

[14] U.S. counternarcotics official in a confidential interview with the author, La Paz, Bolivia, May 9, 2007.
[15] Ramiro Orias, Bolivian political analyst, in an interview with the author, La Paz, Bolivia, May 10, 2007.

medicinal uses. Needless to say, the U.S. government did not foresee any of these developments when it implemented its source-country strategy two decades earlier.

REGIONAL CONCERNS

Toward the end of the first decade of the twenty-first century, almost no Bolivian cocaine was reaching the United States. Instead, it was destined for Brazil, Argentina, and Europe. This reality had European and Latin American governments concerned that the increased coca in Bolivia was translating into increased cocaine consumption in their countries. Already, Brazil had become the second-largest consumer of cocaine in the world after the United States.

Accordingly, both the Europeans and neighboring Latin governments made it clear that they doubted industrialization as a panacea for excess production. Interestingly, this put these governments in greater alignment with Washington's long-standing antidrug policies. According to an American diplomat in La Paz, "the Brazilians are now saying what we've been saying for years."[16]

During these years, Bolivia itself also experienced a noticeable increase in the consumption of coca paste (the intermediate product in cocaine production) and cocaine. In 2007 around 1,400 Bolivians were jailed on drug-trafficking charges across the globe. At one point, Spanish authorities at Madrid's airport detained a five-year-old Bolivian boy who was carrying 5.5 kilograms of cocaine in his toys. For critics such as the U.S. government, these realities belied the Morales government's contention that it could permit unlimited coca production without provoking any negative developments.

While the U.S. Embassy in La Paz was eager to demonstrate patience toward Morales's yet-evolving coca policies, some U.S. officials in Washington and members of Congress saw Morales's moves as the first step toward Bolivia once again becoming a "narco-democracy." In the fall of 2006, the State Department's Western Hemisphere bureau won a fierce bureaucratic fight in order to keep Bolivia from being listed as "uncooperative" in the drug war, a ruling that could have resulted in the cessation of economic assistance. Those who successfully opposed the listing argued that patience and flexibility, not the Big Stick, would ultimately be more effective in getting Morales to

---

[16] U.S. Department of State official in a confidential interview with the author, La Paz, Bolivia, May 9, 2007.

cooperate on the drug front. On the other end, those who urged for decertification contended that Washington should not reward Morales's "bad behavior."[17] However, other critics argued that a better policy would be to ignore Morales's moves because the Bolivian cocaine was not coming to the United States. Although Morales's routine denunciations of "American imperialism" certainly did not help the case of those in the U.S. government who were urging patience and engagement with his government, in this instance, at least, the Big Stick had lost a bureaucratic fight.

U.S. officials privately acknowledged that U.S. leverage in Bolivia was far weaker than in previous years. Few disputed the fact that Morales was attempting strategically to realign Bolivia away from its traditional orbit around Washington and toward greater cooperation with Venezuela and Cuba. Thus, unlike years past when the threat of cuts in development assistance resulted in Bolivia's total compliance with Washington's wishes, now Morales had far more options. According to one American diplomat, "What is to prevent Evo from saying, 'Forget it. Take your toys and go home'?"[18] In an interesting twist of regional geopolitical intrigue, Hugo Chávez made it clear that he was ready and willing to step in if the gringos packed up and left.

INTERMEZZO: THE ANDEAN TRADE PREFERENCES AND DRUG ERADICATION ACT

At the onset of the supply-side drug war in the Andes, the U.S. Congress passed the Andean Trade Preferences Act (ATPA) in 1991, which provided essentially tariff-free access to U.S. markets for 50 percent of imports from Bolivia, Colombia, Ecuador, and Peru. The ATPA was a policy tool designed to promote the production and export of licit products in the Andes so that illicit production (i.e., drugs) became less appealing. Ideally, for example, if the United States lowered tariffs on fresh-cut flowers from Colombia, Colombian workers could grow and sell flowers, in lieu of planting coca crops.

Once instated, the ATPA stimulated the export sectors in the participating Andean countries to a remarkable extent. For example, in 2005 Peru exported U.S.$5.1 billion to the United States, U.S.$2.3 billion of which

---

[17] Senior House Republican aide in a confidential interview with the author, Washington, DC, May 2, 2007.

[18] U.S. Department of State official in a confidential interview with the author, Washington, DC, May 2, 2007. Many of these points were first made in Russell Crandall, "Blow Hard: Evo Morales' Drug Problem," *American Interest*, Winter 2008, 21–5.

resulted from ATPA preferences.[19] Since ATPA's inception, numerous rural towns in Peru experienced unprecedented levels of high employment due to the export boom of many nontraditional products, such as exotic fruits and vegetables, that qualify under ATPA. In this sense, ATPA might be seen as a success; however, the ATPA has not succeeded in moving farmers away from cultivating illicit crops such as coca or poppy – its intended purpose.

In 2002 Congress reauthorized the act, expanded the number of approved tariff-free goods, and changed the official name to the ATPDEA, adding Drug Eradication to the title. Reflecting how much these Andean economies had come to rely on this preferential access to lucrative U.S. markets, Colombian ambassador to Washington Luis Alberto Moreno called this reauthorization "the most important message we have received in a long time."[20]

While hard-edged antidrug policies such as forced eradication of coca certainly had not disappeared, it is important to realize the extent to which seemingly minor issues such as ATPDEA were actually integral to U.S. relations with the region. Given that thousands of long-elusive, relatively well-paying jobs in the Andean countries were hanging in the balance, the U.S. Congress's periodic reauthorization of ATPDEA quickly became a front-page issue in the affected countries. Moreover, the respective Andean governments invested enormous political capital in order to convince U.S. politicians that reauthorization was the appropriate position even though the policy had not succeeded in noticeably reducing illicit crop production. In fact, the program developed a policy identity of its own, apart from the U.S. drug war in the Andes.

An issue such as the ATPDEA also reveals the intermestic nature of many of the United States' major policies in the Americas. For example, during its original approval phase in 1991, U.S. flower producers feared that the reduced tariffs would undercut their domestic prices. Amazingly, flower producers in California became key actors in the congressional debate over what needed to be done to stem illicit crop production in the Andes. Ultimately, though, ATPA was approved, and, as a consequence, the United States' domestic flower industry struggled mightily against intense competition from Andean producers. While U.S. policy during the Cold War era was primarily about security and anticommunism, in the post–Cold War

---

[19] Everett Eissenstat, Assistant U.S. Trade Representative, Americas, Office of the U.S. Trade Representative, Testimony before the House Ways and Means Committee, 109th Cong., 2nd sess., July 12, 2006. See also *Andean Trade Promotion and Drug Eradication Act*, HR 3009, 107th Cong., 1st sess., November 14, 2001.

[20] Quoted in Joseph Schatz, "Bush Wins Key Victory before Recess: Fast-Track Trade Negotiating Authority," *CQ Weekly*, August 3, 2002.

era the United States' actions in Latin America have changed to reflect the globalized world, in which domestic and foreign producers alike can act as equal players in an increasingly interconnected and competitive environment.

After taking office in early 2006, Bolivian president Evo Morales was unexpectedly cooperative with the long-standing U.S. demands of the drug war. Despite his willingness to seek common ground on the antinarcotics front, Morales rarely bypassed opportunities to bash the Bush administration, including a widely covered address to the UN General Assembly in 2006, in which he said, "I want to say with great respect to the government of the United States, we are not going to change anything. We don't need blackmail and threats. The so-called certification or decertification in the fight against narco-trafficking is simply an instrument of recolonialisation or colonialisation of the Andean countries that is unacceptable, that cannot be permitted."[21] While many in Washington saw this statement as antithetical to the Bush administration's drug war goals – source-country coca eradication in particular – Morales caught many U.S. policymakers off guard when around this same time he reached out to Washington for support on trade issues, especially the ATPDEA. Although Morales's moves may be seen as contradictory or, at worst, opportunistic, his actions illustrate the increased "interdependence" that characterized U.S.–Latin American relations since the Cold War. In this case, both countries needed to cooperate in order to reach common objectives, a reality that rarely surfaced during the Cold War.

In late 2006 the ATPDEA was in danger of not being reauthorized by the U.S. Congress. Of particular note, Congress mandated that all countries eligible for ATPDEA had to eventually sign free trade agreements with the United States. Given that Bolivia, unlike Peru and Colombia, had not pursued such a trade pact, the Morales government realized it could become left behind very quickly in terms of access to the enormous and increasingly critical U.S. markets. Indeed, like its other Andean neighbors, Bolivia had taken advantage of the ATPDEA in order to boost exports, which in turn provided employment opportunities for thousands of historically marginalized Bolivians, the natural political base for Morales. Thus, losing ATPDEA status threatened to close off a fountain of steady employment that many desperate Bolivians had come to rely upon. At the same time, though, Morales had based an element of his political credibility on standing up to

---

[21] Evo Morales, "We Need Partners Not Bosses," Address to the United Nations General Assembly, September 22, 2006.

the "gringos," so it was not clear if his heart was really in the effort to reauthorize ATPDEA.

In keeping with the often counterintuitive nature of U.S.–Latin American relations in the post–Cold War era, Morales responded to this dilemma both by pursuing an extension of ATPDEA for Bolivia by sending high-level ministers to Washington to lobby for Bolivia's plight and by continuing his routine denouncements of American imperialism.

While Morales' ministers were working furiously in order to garner support for ATPDEA renewal on Capitol Hill, key Republican congressmen were arguing that reinstating the trade preference would serve only to reward Bolivia's recalcitrance.[22] If the whole idea of ATPDEA, they argued, was to help Andean countries move away from the drug trade, why should the U.S. government support the Morales government that was openly bashing U.S. antidrug policies in Bolivia? In late June 2007 Congress approved an eight-month extension for ATPDEA, a decision that was warmly welcomed by the Morales government in La Paz.

One must wonder what Morales's stance toward Washington would have been had he not inherited the ATPDEA. It is not a stretch to conclude that his position would have been less cooperative. In sum, Morales's response to the ATPDEA is another indication of how, in the era of globalization, a multiplicity of interests – trade and financial ties not the least of them – can unite the "strange bedfellows" that so often surprise us in U.S.–Latin American relations.

---

[22] Senior Republican aide, U.S. House of Representatives, in a confidential interview with the author, Washington, DC, May 2, 2007.

9

The United States versus Hugo Chávez

During the Cold War and earlier periods, the military coup was an integral part of Latin America's political landscape. Since the end of the Cold War, constitutional rule has become the norm. However, the events in Caracas, Venezuela, in April 2002 marked a break in that trend. Venezuelan military officers and other citizens resented what they viewed as President Hugo Chávez's socialist and arbitrary policies and attempted to oust Chávez through a military coup. And the U.S. government, the rhetorical champion of democracy in Latin America since the Cold War, played an ambiguous, controversial role in the unfolding events.

CARACAS, VENEZUELA, APRIL 2002

In early April 2002, newly installed American ambassador Charles Shapiro dined with dozens of Venezuela's economic elites at a breakfast hosted in his honor by media magnet Gustavo Cisneros. While the political climate had been tense in Caracas in recent days and weeks, there had been no open moves against the populist and polarizing president Hugo Chávez. Accounts describe how the breakfast gathering was interrupted by the simultaneous ring of numerous cellular phones, bringing news of the apparent shooting of unarmed protestors at a massive anti-Chávez rally in the city. Informed of the events, Ambassador Shapiro immediately announced to some of his fellow guests that the U.S. Embassy would not tolerate a coup against Chávez.[1]

---

[1] At the present time, we only have a murky picture of the events surrounding the April coup in Venezuela. This is equally true for the Bush administration's response to the attempted coup. For more on the events of April 2002, see Dan Erickson, "Castro's Chávez Strategy,"

In the heat of the moment, the message from the American ambassador was unequivocal. Over the prior year, however, other U.S. officials had been meeting with the Venezuelans who would be involved in a coup against Chávez soon after this breakfast concluded. While it is still unclear what U.S. officials actually said to these Venezuelans in the months leading up to the coup, subsequent public interviews with the policymakers involved suggest that the Bush administration was urging them to walk a fine line between upholding constitutional procedures and doing everything short of starting a coup in order to oust Chávez. According to one U.S. official, "Our message was very clear: there are constitutional processes. We did not even wink at anyone. We were not discouraging people. ... We were sending informal, subtle signals that we don't like this guy. We didn't say, 'No, don't you dare,' and we weren't advocates saying, 'Here's some arms, we'll help you overthrow this guy.' We were not doing that."[2]

Whatever the signals, the coup plotters received from the United States, members of Venezuela's military and political opposition had worked for more than a year to remove Chávez, preferring constitutional means, but never ruling out a coup. While it was loathe to admit it, the Bush administration's response (or lack thereof) to the coup became as newsworthy as the coup itself. The impact of the officials' fateful decisions on U.S.–Latin American relations continues to this day.

CHÁVEZ AND WASHINGTON

In the immediate post–Cold War years, Venezuela barely registered for U.S. policymakers because the country appeared relatively stable politically and a reliable source of foreign oil. Chávez's rise to power changed the relationship dramatically. A former army paratrooper and leader of a failed coup attempt in 1992, Hugo Chávez assumed office in 1999, and his tenure

---

Inter-American Dialogue Working Paper (Washington, DC, December 2005); Mary Crane, "U.S.-Venezuela Relations," *CFR Backgrounder* (Washington, DC: Council on Foreign Relations, May 18, 2005); Simon Romero, "Venezuela's Rag-tag Reserves Are Marching as to War," *New York Times*, June 11, 2006; Javier Corrales, "The Logic of Extremism: How Chávez Gains by Giving So Much to Cuba," Inter-American Dialogue Working Paper (Washington, DC, December 2005); Richard Lapper, "Living with Hugo: U.S. Policy toward Hugo Chávez's Venezuela," *Council Special Report*, 20 (Washington DC: Council on Foreign Relations, November 2006); "Venezuela: Hugo Chávez's Revolution." Latin America Report No. 19 (Washington, DC: International Crisis Group, February 22, 2007).

[2] Quoted in Christopher Marquis, "Bush Officials Met with Venezuelans Who Ousted Leader," *New York Times*, April 20, 2002. See also Larry Rohter, "Venezuela's Two Fateful Days," *New York Times*, April 20, 2002.

has been extremely controversial ever since. Pursuing what he called a "Bolivarian Revolution," Chávez spent the first few years of his presidency working aggressively (and mostly democratically) to change the "rules of the game" of Venezuelan society to reflect his leftist "Bolivarian" vision of greater state control over the political and economic institutions. Most striking was his immediate push to draft a radically different "Bolivarian" constitution in 1999, which the electorate approved in that same year.

Chávez's political, social, and economic agenda was (almost literally) fueled by a dramatic increase in the Venezuelan government's oil revenues: in 1999, the government was earning roughly U.S.$8 billion from oil; in 2006, with the price of oil trading around $50 a barrel, these revenues had risen to around U.S.$85 billion, almost a tenfold increase.

Thus, the Hugo Chávez who took office was just a shadow of the Hugo Chávez who governed Venezuela five or ten years later. Ironically, the United States' insatiable demand for oil kept oil prices high. Moreover, despite the sharply deteriorated bilateral relationship between Caracas and Washington, the United States continued to purchase the overwhelming majority of Venezuela's oil. In this instance, at least, the economic interdependence between the two countries appeared to overshadow sharp ideological differences between the two governments.

Upon taking office, Chavez attempted to steer Venezuela's foreign policy far away from Washington's orbit, at least rhetorically. For example, he praised leaders such as Iraq's Saddam Hussein and Cuba's Fidel Castro for their defiance of Washington's mandates. Historically, Washington and Caracas enjoyed a generally warm bilateral relationship, due in large part to the symbiotic oil dependency between the United States (high demand) and Venezuela (high supply). During the oil boom years of the 1970s, Venezuela embarked on more of an independent foreign policy vis-à-vis Washington, but this change did not alter the underlying fundamentals of the relationship. Unlike his predecessors, Chávez has not only worked to cool the bilateral relationship but also made anti-Americanism the hallmark of his foreign policy rhetoric.

In his September 2006 speech to the UN General Assembly, President Chávez held up a copy of globally recognized, left-wing American academic Noam Chomsky's book (*Hegemony or Survival: America's Quest for Global Dominance*) and told the audience full of diplomats and heads of states that "the devil [George W. Bush] came here yesterday. It still smells of sulfur today. . . . He came here talking as if he were the owner of the world." For anyone who had been following Chávez actions over preceding years, his comments about Bush were nothing new. Chávez had previously called Bush a "donkey," "drunkard," and "coward" among other less-than-flattering terms.

While it usually tried to ignore him, the Bush administration periodically made public its own views regarding Chávez. Over her tenure as secretary of state, Condoleezza Rice called Chavez a "negative force" in the hemisphere, criticized his ties to Cuba, and claimed that he was pursuing a "Latin American brand of populism that has taken countries down the drain."[3]

Name calling aside, many of Chávez's more concrete actions raised alarm in Washington. In 2006 Chávez formed a 100,000-member civilian militia for "civil defense" that he planned to increase up to 1.5 million. In a series of deals with the Russian government around the same time, Chávez purchased attack helicopters and tens of thousands of Kalashnikov machine guns. Chávez claimed that these sorts of acquisitions were necessary because the Bush administration refused to replace the Venezuelan military's aging F-16 fighters. He stated repeatedly that this unprecedented military buildup was necessary in order to protect Venezuela from the inevitable American "invasion." U.S. officials worried aloud whether some of this matériel might have ended up in the hands of Colombian guerrillas or be used by Chávez's political supporters to repress civilian opponents.

By far, Chávez's most significant diplomatic relationship was with Cuba. Based upon an agreement (dubbed "oil for services") that both governments signed in 2000, Venezuela supplied the island nation with close to 100,000 barrels of oil per day. The estimated value of this "gift" to Cuba was between U.S.$6 billion and $8 billion over a fifteen-year period. Similar to what it did with Soviet oil during the Cold War, the Cuban government reexported the surplus oil after it had met its domestic demands, providing Havana with badly needed foreign exchange.

In return, Cuba sent between 30,000 and 50,000 technical specialists to Venezuela. A large share of this force consisted of medical doctors but also included teachers and coaches, as well as security, intelligence, and military advisers. Of particular note, given that they were extremely familiar with Russian technology and equipment, the Cuban military advisers were a critical component in the Venezuelan government's efforts to overhaul its military.

In addition to his intimate diplomatic and economic relationship with Havana, Chávez worked tirelessly to increase his influence both regionally and globally. Leftist figures and political parties and organizations around the world became recipients of Chávez's oil-driven largesse. Chávez spent an estimated U.S.$16–25 billion on foreign aid between 1999 and 2006.

[3] "US Warns against Chávez danger," *BBC News*, February 17, 2006.

In 2005 the Venezuelan government announced its intention to purchase billions of dollars of Argentina's national debt, a move that allowed Argentina's president Néstor Kirchner to end the country's stormy relationship with the IMF. Buoyed by his willingness to write checks, Chávez and Latin American governments such as Uruguay, Brazil, and Argentina agreed to found a South American cable television station, as a counter to the "imperialist CNN." Chávez was also instrumental in the founding of Petrocaribe, an oil consortium consisting of Caribbean countries, including Cuba.

For Hugo Chávez, these policies were logical steps in the consolidation and expansion of his "Bolivarian Revolution." But for Washington, and especially the conservative Bush administration, they were signs of a growing threat south of the border.

CHÁVEZ AS A "THREAT"

Some of the most difficult and heated debates over the U.S. government's Latin American policy since 1999 revolved around the question, Does Hugo Chávez represent a "threat" to the national security of the United States? The answer to this question is subjective and varies with the ideological or bureaucratic disposition of the person making the analysis. For example, if U.S. intelligence officers report that Chávez is secretly funding a fellow leftist government in Latin America, does this represent clear evidence of Chávez as a threat or just the routine diplomatic dealings that many governments undertake? The various answers to these sorts of questions helped determine how the U.S. government ultimately responded to Chávez.

While never thrilled with Chávez's bluster, between 1999 and early 2001 the Clinton administration's Latin America officials (as well as the U.S. government's intelligence community) tended to see Chávez's fiery rhetoric as just that – rhetoric. And that Venezuelan leader actually was quite reluctant to carry out the radical agenda his words promised. "Watch what Chávez's does, not what he says," was an oft-repeated phrase at the time in U.S. government circles. Accordingly, the Clinton team avoided conflict with Chávez by allowing him to denounce the United States while keeping an eye on his relatively conventional oil policies.

However, the U.S. relationship with Venezuela changed when the Bush administration took office in early 2001. In short, things got personal. Bush's top diplomat for the Western Hemisphere, Otto Reich, was a former ambassador to Caracas and held a deep personal dislike for the leftist, pro-Castro Chávez. Thus, when officials such as Reich saw the same intelligence reports as their predecessors, they often reached wildly different conclusions as to what the reports represented and what to do about them. In this sense, the remarkable events surrounding the coup attempt against Chávez in Caracas in April 2002 are also an example of the varying *interpretations* of intelligence reports.

ANATOMY OF A COUP

In December 2001 both Venezuelan labor union leaders (especially oil workers) and business leaders declared a one-day strike. The surprisingly diverse political opposition viewed Chavez's economic policies as increasingly draconian and attempted to use protest as a way to counter Chávez's policies. In early 2002, as demonstrations gained traction and grew to involve hundreds of thousands of protestors, Chávez's once soaring public approval ratings sagged to around a third of the population. It is important to keep in mind, though, that these remaining Chávez supporters (many of them self-described *chavistas*) were fiercely loyal to the one president whom they believed had their long-neglected interests at heart. Early in April, during his weekly television show Chávez announced the removal of a group of senior managers at Petróleos de Venezuela, S.A. (Petroleum of Venezuela, Inc., PDVSA), the state-controlled oil company, further flaming indignation that he was politicizing the entity. Chávez's announcement sparked a new oil workers' strike that crippled oil exports; massive protests in Caracas soon followed. With the threat of violence high, the country was on edge.

With the strike in full swing, the Venezuelan media provided wide coverage of what many reporters considered a sort of "people power" (referring to the peaceful protests against Philippine strongman Ferdinand Marcos in the mid 1980s) movement. On Thursday, April 11, as a horde of protestors shook the streets of Caracas, pro-Chávez snipers fired down on the demonstrators. Some reports indicated that Chávez had not only given these orders, but also requested that the Venezuelan military use its tanks in order to crush the protest. While details of these specific events are still unclear, at least eleven protestors were killed.

One of the first indications that Hugo Chávez was in trouble came when high-level military officers refused his orders to send in the tanks. According to one general, "the result would have been a disaster."[4] Subsequently, a

---

[4] Quoted in Richard Lapper and Andy Webb-Vidal, "End of Autocratic Regime: Militaristic President Falls Victim to Military Revolt," *Financial Times* (London), April 13, 2002.

group of ten high-ranking officers refused to recognize Chávez's authority as president. Then army commander Efraín Vasquez Velasco announced publicly that Chávez had resigned. In reality, though, Chávez did not resign outright but rather agreed to "abandon his functions," a move that should have transferred power to the National Assembly. Instead, the next day the coup plotters hastily swore in Pedro Carmona, head of the business group Fedecamaras, who announced the creation of a provisional government. Chávez, whose fate supposedly had been sealed, was whisked away from the presidential palace to a series of military installations over the next day and a half. During the ceremony, members of the country's business and economic organizations toasted Chávez's removal with eighteen-year-old Scotch.

At this point, the "coup" still enjoyed widespread support from a broad and united front of anti-Chávez business and labor leaders. However, in a move that immediately doomed his fate because it revealed his undemocratic intentions, Carmona quickly suspended the National Assembly and constitutional court. Carmona's aggressive proclamation startled many within the anti-Chávez movement and suggested that Carmona may have not have been very interested in the demands of other anti-Chávez groups, such as petroleum labor unions. In addition, pro-coup PDVSA managers ordered a halt to oil shipments to Cuba, citing the fact that Havana had fallen behind in its payments, indicating the strong ideological current to the anti-Chávez operation.

Suddenly, it appeared to even strident anti-Chávez elements that the nature of the coup had changed. For example, long-standing Chávez critic, Venezuelan journalist Teodoro Petkoff, began to sound the alarm that the more broad-based coup had been hijacked by rightist factions. "This is a classic coup. . . . There is no letter of resignation for Chávez. We do not see it anywhere."[5]

Carmona further damaged his already tenuous standing by appointing several navy officers to key positions within his new cabinet, including the minister of defense. The larger and much more influential Venezuelan army resented being upstaged by the smaller navy, a development that cost Carmona crucial military support. In addition, while the coup had widespread support within the high-level ranks of the military, most middle-level officers (who tended to be more directly influential with rank-and-file troops) remained loyal to Chávez. In particular, the powerful presidential guard stuck with Chávez and eventually played a critical role in his return to power hours later.

---

[5] Quoted in Juan Forero, "A Chávez Comeback More Stunning Than His Fall," *New York Times*, April 13, 2002.

The Venezuelan media, driven by a fierce ideological opposition to Chávez's Bolivarian Revolution, which they believed was turning the country into another Cuba, abandoned any semblance of balanced reporting and instead provided a highly biased account of the events over this long weekend. More specifically, the media refused to report the fact that Carmona's support was slipping and failed to cover the pro-Chávez protests in the capital. At Carmona's swearing in, one media magnate was reported to have told the new "president" that "we can't guarantee you the loyalty of the army, but we can promise you the support of the media."[6]

By Saturday morning, less than thirty-six hours after Chávez's "resignation," a countercoup was underway. Indignant with the biased coverage, pro-Chávez protestors began attacking media outlets. Meanwhile, various Latin American governments were making it known that they did not support the coup. American ambassador Shapiro had breakfast with Carmona and told him that he should reconsider his decision to close the National Assembly given that it was so blatantly unconstitutional.

Perhaps the most critical element in Chávez's return to power was a photocopied letter from still-imprisoned Chávez that was distributed throughout the capital. A sympathetic corporal assigned to guard Chávez hid the note in the trash and then faxed it to pro-Chávez forces. In the letter, Chávez contested the generals' assertion by stating, "I, Hugo Chávez ... have not relinquished the power legitimately given to me by the people."[7] The circulation of the note reinforced the view that, though he was ousted initially for his purportedly undemocratic orders to fire on the protestors, Chávez – not the coup leaders – was the one adhering to the constitutional principles.

By Saturday evening, under pressure from protestors and the U.S. government, a desperate Carmona announced that the National Assembly had been reinstated. The assembly immediately met and swore in Chávez's former deputy president Diosdado Cabello as president. Cabello announced that he would hold the post until Chávez returned. The coup was finished. At ten o'clock, Carmona resigned. Almost five hours later, released from an island military facility, Chávez returned to the presidential palace triumphant and accompanied by the presidential guard. By sunrise Sunday morning, tens of thousands of *chavistas* had taken to the streets of Caracas to celebrate the return of their *comandante*, looting hundreds of stores along their way.

---

[6] Quoted in "Coup and Counter Coup," *The Economist*, April 12, 2002.
[7] Quoted in Lapper and Webb-Vidal, "End of Autocratic Regime."

THE BUSH ADMINISTRATION'S RESPONSE TO THE COUP

No available evidence suggests that the U.S. government (and the Bush administration in particular) was directly behind the planning or implementation of the coup against Chávez. From what we do know, though, perhaps a more accurate explanation is that the U.S. government had very little knowledge of what was occurring in Venezuela during these eventful days. The April 2002 coup in Caracas was not a "classic" Cold War–style, CIA-hatched plot, as in Guatemala in 1954 or more indirectly in Chile in the early 1970s. On the contrary, the coup against Chávez was Venezuelan-crafted and Venezuelan-perpetrated.

Leading up to the coup, the Bush administration attempted to pursue a fine-line strategy of tacitly encouraging efforts to remove Chávez but only through constitutional means. Thus, whether coincidental or not, when the coup actually took place, coup plotters were adamant that Chávez had "resigned," which would have made his departure constitutional. In this sense, the Bush administration responded to the coup in a manner that reinforced what they wanted the public to believe about the coup, as opposed to what ultimately appeared to have taken place.

Whatever the final reality, unlike the OAS that quickly condemned the unconstitutional ouster during a security meeting in Costa Rica, White House spokesman Ari Fleischer told the media that "the [Chávez] government has suppressed what was a peaceful demonstration of the people, which led very quickly to a combustible situation in which Chavez resigned." The White House also labeled Chávez's ouster "a victory for democracy."[8]

On Friday, when Carmona still appeared to be firmly in control, Assistant Secretary of State Otto Reich summoned several Latin American ambassadors to his Foggy Bottom office to discuss the evolving situation. The Brazilian ambassador apparently stated to Reich that the Brazilian government could not condone this break in democratic rule in Venezuela. According to some of the participating ambassadors, Reich reportedly told them that Chávez's removal was not a rupture of democratic rule and that the provisional government needed the support of its Latin American neighbors.

By Saturday, reports from Caracas were clearly indicating that the new regime was in trouble, a development that exposed the Bush administration's awkward position. The Bush administration signed an OAS resolution rejecting the coup, but this was hardly convincing, given that the coup had already effectively failed. Bush's officials now began to make

[8] Quoted in Marquis, "Bush Officials Met with Venezuelans."

statements distancing the administration from the coup. Secretary of State Colin Powell, for one, commented that a violent overthrow of a Latin American government is against U.S. interests and values. After Chávez had returned, National Security Advisor Condoleezza Rice backed away from supporting Chávez's removal but also claimed that Chávez had brought the entire episode upon himself: "I hope Hugo Chávez takes the message that his people sent him: That his own policies are not working for the Venezuelan people, that he has dealt with them in a high-handed fashion."[9]

The Bush team's response to the coup reinforced a common criticism of the U.S. government's broader view of democracy in Latin America: when push came to shove, the United States cared about democracy in the region only when it involved a leader who fell in line with U.S. interests. At the height of irony, the coup appeared to damage the OAS's recently approved Inter-American Democratic Charter, an agreement that Washington had originally strongly supported and Chávez opposed.

A key counterfactual related to these events is how a different American administration might have responded to the coup. Arturo Valenzuela, a top Clinton administration aide, left no room for misinterpretation in his assessment of the damage caused by the Bush administration's clumsy response: "I think it's a very negative development for the principle of constitutional government in Latin America. I think it's going to come back and haunt all of us."[10]

Considering how a different administration might have acted reinforces the fact that particular policymakers, with their divergent interests and attitudes, do matter. Officials such as Otto Reich had a predisposition to take a harder stance toward Chávez, even if this meant coming very close to outright support for an unconstitutional coup. In addition, there were numerous U.S. officials also involved in formulating the U.S. government's response to the coup who were furious with what they saw as a hypocritical and cynical way that Bush's high-level political appointees acted during these fateful days.[11]

RELATIONS FOLLOWING THE ATTEMPTED COUP

In the weeks and months following the failed coup, Hugo Chávez's popularity surged nearly ten percentage points. If anything, the ouster had

---

[9] Quoted in Deborah McGregor, "Washington Issues Warning to President," *Financial Times*, April 15, 2002.
[10] Quoted in Marquis, "Bush Officials Met with Venezuelans."
[11] Rand Beers (Senior Director, National Security Council, 2002), in an interview with the author, May 2, 2007.

reinforced his image as the champion of the poor and dispossessed, one willing to stand up to a rancid Venezuelan oligarchy aligned with the imperial United States. At least initially, Chávez adopted a conciliatory stance toward his domestic political opposition. In one statement right after his return, Chávez told the Venezuelan people, "I call on all the local authorities and my followers not to fall into the temptation to use the extreme actions which other sectors fell into. ... We must respect dignity, there must be no retaliation, no witch-hunt, there will be no disrespect for freedoms."[12] However, by 2004, Chávez was attempting to prosecute suspected *golpistas* (coup plotters), including a noted human rights activist.

Though embarrassed by the coup episode, the Bush administration continued to take a relatively low-profile approach toward Chávez in the ensuing years. In an aphorism that suggested Chávez's rhetoric was far more stinging than his actual policies, the Clinton era's "Watch what Chávez does, not what he says" became the Bush administration's de facto postcoup policy.

By 2004 the administration had turned its eyes toward a national referendum on Chávez's rule slated for August. Because many observers believed that Chávez would lose the vote and thus assumed that a fair vote would conclude with a defeat for Chávez, the Bush administration's new strategy for Venezuela became the referendum itself. Thus, the administration was left flat-footed when international observers from the nonprofit Carter Center and European Union endorsed the pro-Chávez electoral commission's announcement that Chávez had won the vote decisively with 58 percent of the vote. Chávez's electoral success (he also triumphed in the December 2006 presidential election with a percentage similar to the 2004 referendum) made it extremely difficult for Washington to claim that he is an illegitimate president.

After the failed referendum strategy, the Bush administration continued to view the Chávez government as a serious threat. It moved to block Venezuela's acquisition of military aircraft from Spain and Brazil by denying export license for the transfer of U.S.-manufactured components for the planes. Chávez responded to Washington's decision by stating he would instead go to Beijing and Moscow for military hardware. To apply subtle pressure, or as Chávez would have it, in an act of provocation, the U.S. military deployed 6,500 personnel for two months of naval exercises in the Caribbean.

Nearing the end of the first decade of the twenty-first century, the U.S. government continued to maintain an ambivalent and contradictory set

---

[12] Quoted in Lapper and Webb-Vidal, "End of Autocratic Regime."

of policies toward the mercurial Chávez government. On one hand, oil purchases continued unabated. On the other, the Bush administration announced in 2006 that it was assigning a high-level intelligence official to cover Venezuela, a clear reflection of a deteriorating bilateral relationship. In February 2006 Chávez kicked out a U.S. military attaché for alleged spying on the Venezuelan government. In retaliation, the Bush administration ordered a Venezuelan Embassy official in Washington to leave the United States.

Discussions of the U.S. government's policies toward Venezuela in the post–Cold War era must also consider the motivations behind, as well as the impact of, U.S. funding to support Venezuela's democratic institutions and civil society. Hugo Chávez routinely railed against the United States' financing of Venezuelan nongovernmental organizations involved in election monitoring and other activities as a form of "democratic imperialism," whereby Washington pretends to be supporting democracy as a cover for its anti-Chávez intentions. The U.S. government contended that the reality is just the opposite: these efforts were about Venezuela's democracy, not any particular winner or loser.

The answers to these questions get at the heart of U.S. policy strategies and objectives in the post–Cold War era. For example, if the U.S. government-funded National Endowment for Democracy provides a grant to Súmate, a Venezuelan electoral organization largely seen as critical of Chávez, should we consider it enlightened U.S. policy or neo-imperialism? Needless to say, the answers to these sorts of questions are hotly disputed.

CONCLUSION

The U.S. government's involvement in "Caracas 2002," while certainly not on the scale of "Guatemala 1954" or "Chile 1973," is sure to remain controversial for decades to come. We do know that the Bush administration was eager to see Hugo Chávez removed from office, and while the extent of the Bush administration's involvement in the actual coup remains in dispute, the Bush White House at least initially condoned an undemocratic transfer of power in Latin America.

Does the Bush's administration's response to the coup represent a return to the Big Stick? Critics of the Bush administration would contend that there is no clearer example of the United States exercising its power to overthrow an inconvenient government in Venezuela. At the same time, however, we must also consider the fact that the coup against Hugo Chávez failed. That is, if the Big Stick is so powerful, why was it unable to prevent

Chávez from returning to power? Part of the answer to this question is that, in this newly democratic post–Cold War era, the international and regional climate surrounding democratic and constitutional rule has changed. And, as we have discussed, Washington promoted many of these new norms in an attempt to check the machinations of undemocratic actors in the region. In April 2002, however, these norms appeared to check the machinations of the Bush administration.

INTERMEZZO: "MONTE-CHINO"

For most of the 1980s and early 1990s, Peru was an economic and political disaster. Threatened by the pernicious Sendero Luminoso (Shining Path) guerrilla insurgency, successive Peruvian governments neared collapse. In turn, Peruvians became increasingly disgusted with the ruling political class. Responding to this antiestablishment sentiment, in early April 1992 Peruvian President Alberto Fujimori closed down the country's congress and declared a state of emergency. Quickly dubbed an *auto-golpe* (self-coup), Fujimori defended his undemocratic action by arguing that the level of corruption and incompetence within Peru's legislature required such drastic measures. To back up his position, Fujimori pointed to public opinion polls showing a startling 80 percent of Peruvians approved his *auto-golpe*.

In prior eras, Fujimori's move might have seemed normal given the reality of Latin American politics; by 1992, however, blatantly undemocratic and unconstitutional behavior had become less common. To a great extent, the boundaries of acceptable political behavior had gradually but substantively shifted from the preceding decades of the 1970s and 1980s, when militaries or other undemocratic regimes routinely held power, to the 1990s, when democracy was the norm.

Along with most other Latin American governments, the administration of George H. W. Bush responded to the *auto-golpe* in no uncertain terms. Speaking at a special session of the OAS, Secretary of State James Baker stated:

The actions taken by President Fujimori, whatever the justification given, are unjustified. They represent an assault on democracy that cannot and will not be supported by the United States of America. . . . This Organization of American States is founded on one unswerving principle: Representative democracy is the key to peace, it is the key to economic opportunity, and it is the key to legitimacy in this hemisphere.[13]

---

[13] Quoted in Eduardo Forrero Costa, "Peru's Presidential Coup," *Journal of Democracy* 4, no. 1 (January 1993): 35.

FIGURE 9.1. Peru's former President Alberto Fujimori waves to crowds during a military parade celebrating Peruvian Independence in Lima, Peru, July 29, 1995. (Photo: Marcelo Salinas.)

The OAS backed up Baker's condemnation by adopting a resolution condemning the situation in Peru. In fact, this prompt and categorical opposition to Fujimori's actions played the key role in forcing Fujimori to promise to restore democracy by holding new elections in short order.

Did the Bush administration's reaction to *auto-golpe* represent the beginning of a new era in U.S. policy toward Latin America? During the Cold War, critics often accused Washington of either actively fomenting military coups or, at the very least, turning a blind eye to plotters as democratic governments were overthrown. As an old policy joke goes, "There were no coups in an unnamed Latin America country today. The U.S. Embassy must have been closed." Yet, at first glance in Peru, the U.S. government appeared to be working to make the coup less likely. In this case at least, evidence suggests that the coup came under such considerable external criticism because the U.S. Embassy was in fact "open."

Following the *auto-golpe*, Alberto Fujimori remained as president while a new constitution was written and approved. In 1995 Fujimori was reelected in what most international observers considered a fair election. Thus, Fujimori restored his democratic credentials that had evaporated internationally following the *auto-golpe* (Figure 9.1).

For most of the 1990s, however, the U.S. government's main policy concern in Peru was not the quality of democracy but rather the production of drugs. Like its neighbors Bolivia and Colombia, Peru's Andes lay at the geographic heart of Washington's "source-country" counternarcotics strategy.

More specifically, in order to implement "source country strategies," a variety of U.S. government agencies worked to develop strong relationships with their Peruvian counterparts. More than anyone else, Fujimori's chief intelligence official, Vladimiro Montesinos, became the "go to guy" for everything related to drugs; Montesinos was a key player in the aggressive programs to reduce Peru's coca production and to stop drug flights through the "air bridge" into Colombia. Similar to Panamanian strongman Manuel Noriega during the 1970s and 1980s, Montesinos was on the CIA's payroll for many years.[14]

At the same time as he was a reliable ally in the fight against drugs, Montesinos was active in the efforts to keep Fujimori in power. Following the 1995 election, Fujimori's government increasingly became involved in illicit activities, especially the blackmailing of prominent Peruvian political figures. Ultimately known by Peruvians as "Monte-Chino" ("Monte" for Montesinos and "Chino" for Fujimori – the term Peruvians use to refer to people of Asian descent), the president and his intelligence chief did everything in their power to elevate Fujimori's stature at the expense of his political rivals.

The Monte-Chino phenomenon undermined Peru's democracy, as the U.S. government simultaneously relied on this same government to execute U.S. drug policies. Some agencies such as the CIA and U.S. Drug Enforcement Agency (DEA) were instinctively more willing to overlook Montesinos's illegal behavior, given that he proved reliable in the antidrug effort. In fact, U.S. drug officials continued to collaborate with Montesinos even after evidence appeared that linked him to shady dealings. On the other hand, the State Department was much more critical of the Fujimori government's actions. Perhaps most alarming to certain U.S. officials was that "their man" Montesinos was reported to be the mastermind behind a plot to divert thousands of weapons intended for the Peruvian military to Colombia guerrillas.

By 2000 the Monte-Chino efforts become a widespread scandal when Montesinos was caught on video bribing a member of the Peruvian congress.

---

[14] David Scott Palmer, *U.S. Relations with Latin America during the Clinton Years* (Gainesville: University Press of Florida, 2006), 66. See also Cynthia McClintock, *The United States and Peru: Cooperation, at a Cost* (London: Routledge, 2002).

This dramatic footage proved to be the end for the Monte-Chino conspiracy. In response, Fujimori quickly distanced himself from Montesinos, attempting to demonstrate that his "Rasputin" was more a rogue official acting outside of the president's control. But the damage was done. Within months, Montesinos fled the country and was arrested (with support from U.S. authorities) in Venezuela. Fujimori resigned by fax while in Japan and subsequently remained in self-exile in the country of his ancestors.

During the Fujimori era, U.S. policy comprised multiple policies toward Peru. These often-conflicting approaches revealed an ongoing dilemma in the U.S. government's (and, at the time, Clinton administration's) approach to Peru: should policy prioritize supporting constitutional democracy at the potential cost of the war on drugs? Or vice versa? What were the United States' interests in Peru at the time? And how do you draw conclusions about the nature of "U.S. policy" when the key U.S. agencies involved are pursuing divergent policies?

10

The United States versus Daniel Ortega

With Marshall Worsham

In June 2005, just a year out from a historic national election in Nicaragua, President Enrique Bolaños made a trip to the United States to promote Nicaragua's interest in the Central American Free Trade Agreement (CAFTA), which was scheduled for a congressional vote later that summer. As Representative Clay Shaw (R-FL) reported after a discussion with the Central American leader, "Bolaños offered a stark commentary on the importance of CAFTA's passage, emphasizing that no one would love to see CAFTA's defeat more than former strongman Daniel Ortega. But Nicaragua and Central America have moved past the days of Ortega."[1] Yet, barely a year after Bolaños's visit, in a remarkable – and somewhat counterintuitive – electoral mandate, Nicaragua chose Daniel Ortega for the presidency. This popular decision forced Nicaragua and the United States to reconsider Shaw's statement: had Nicaragua and the United States indeed moved on? While this question still remains, it seemed that even if Ortega himself had returned, the hemisphere-wide controversy that surrounded his radical brand of socialism in the late 1970s and 1980s had not.

NICARAGUA IN THE COLD WAR

The fact that the United States devoted relatively little attention to Ortega's reelection in 2006 (compared to a similar race in 1990) might allow one to forget about the Nicaraguan leader's troubled past. Indeed, during the

---

[1] Representative Clay Shaw, "CAFTA Will Allow Our Workers and Farmers to Remain Competitive," *The Hill*, June 29, 2005.

final years of the Cold War, Ortega and Nicaragua were the focal point of some of the United States' most critical and contentious hemispheric policies.

Ortega first ascended to leadership in Nicaragua in 1979, after his Sandinista National Liberation Front (FSLN) emerged as the dominant political party in a bloody revolution that ousted the country's repressive dictator, Anastasio Somoza. Although President Jimmy Carter at first accepted the Sandinista movement and its revolutionary economic and social policies, by 1981 the Reagan administration had condemned the regime. Given Reagan's overwhelming preoccupation with eliminating communism, his administration did not support Ortega's politics, which included agrarian reforms, socialization of health care, and nationalization of foreign-owned companies. Nor did it tolerate the FSLN's partnership with Cuba and the Soviet Union, or its declared opposition to what many Nicaraguans considered a terrible legacy of U.S. economic and political imperialism. As Ortega's anti-U.S. rhetoric intensified – one of his advisers included in the Sandinista national anthem, "We fight against the Yanqui, enemy of humanity" – many in Washington began to see the continuing revolution in Nicaragua as more dangerous and volatile than even Cuban communism.[2] The radicalization of Nicaragua posed a distinct "new" threat; whereas Castro was a fairly predictable nemesis by the early 1980s, Nicaragua still had the potential to erupt, which could set off a "domino effect" of communist takeovers in the region.

Attempting to pressure the Sandinista regime into collapse, the U.S. Congress authorized the Department of Defense and the CIA to fund a guerrilla war led by a group of Nicaraguan exiles based in El Salvador. The *contrarevolucionarios* (Contras) received more than U.S.$72 million between 1981 and 1984. When Congress withdrew its support for the controversial program with the passage of the Boland Amendment, the Reagan administration provided funding through clandestine arms sales to Iran. The so-called Iran-Contra affair helped fund the destructive insurgency for several additional years. The death toll, which included large numbers of civilian casualties, totaled more than 30,000. The Iran-Contra affair was indicative of the foreign policy mentality of the time: in order to control the growth of communism, the United States' other policy priorities – such as adhering to the rule of law – might have to take a back seat.

---

[2] Quoted in Robert Pastor, *The United States and Nicaragua: Not Condemned to Repetition*, 2nd ed. (Boulder, CO: Westview Press, 2002), 120.

THE 1990 ELECTION

While the Contra War raged through the 1980s, the Sandinista party held several dubious national elections, stacking all three branches of government with party affiliates. Yet, leading up to 1990, the Ortega administration acquiesced to multilateral pressure to hold a fair and internationally observed election. Violeta Chamorro emerged as Ortega's key competitor, leading a coalition party known as the National Opposition Union (UNO), which, to Ortega's discredit, represented a constituency from extreme conservatives to card-carrying Communists.

As the elections approached, most opinion polls placed Ortega ahead by a margin of at least 15 percent; contrary to the U.S. position, public sentiment in Nicaragua still tended toward the Sandinistas. Yet, as one congressional report indicated, "At the same time, three polls conducted by foreign firms showed Mrs. Chamorro ahead, but were largely discounted by U.S. analysts."[3]

While publicly voicing its support for the democratic process, Congress authorized U.S.$7 million to be distributed to Chamorro's campaign through organizations such as the Center for Democracy, Freedom House, and the National Endowment for Democracy.[4] Then, during the elections, the Bush administration sponsored an international team, the "Council of Freely-Elected Heads of Government," led by former president Jimmy Carter to observe the elections. His organization made up only 78 of the more than 2,500 international monitors in the country. In his welcome address in Managua, Carter explained, "We come here at the invitation of the Nicaraguan government, the opposition, and the Supreme Electoral Council, and we arrive with profound respect and appreciation for Nicaragua to decide on its own future. We have come to support the people of this courageous country who want to vote to build a democracy."[5] As it turned out, the elections exceeded U.S. expectations. Chamorro won a 55 percent majority vote from 1.5 million of Nicaragua's 1.7 million registered voters.

---

[3] Nina M. Serafino, "Nicaraguan Elections and Transition: Issues for U.S. Policy," *Congressional Research Service Report* (Washington, DC: Library of Congress, March 26, 1990), 2.

[4] United States General Accounting Office, National Security and International Affairs Division, "Assistance to Promote Democracy and National Reconciliation in Nicaragua," *GAO Report to Congressional Requesters*, 101st Cong., 2nd sess., GAO/NSIAD-90-245, Washington, DC, September 24, 1990, 10.

[5] Hon. Jimmy Carter, Chairman, Council of Freely-Elected Heads of Government, "Arrival Statement, Managua, February 23, 1990," in *Observing Nicaragua's Elections, 1989–1990* (Atlanta: Carter Center of Emory University, May 1990), 99.

Yet the Bush administration received heavy criticism for its actions. Many Anti-imperialists questioned the legitimacy of the administration's pro-democracy rhetoric.[6] Moreover, with the fall of the Soviet Union just a year earlier, many wondered if the Sandinista party posed as significant a threat as it once did. Indeed, Sandinismo seemed a small and insignificant force in the hemisphere now that its ideological foundations had crumbled. For these critics, the Chamorro campaign finance scheme, like the intervention in Panama that year, was a case of the United States wielding its disproportionate regional influence to secure outcomes to its liking.

Defenders of the Bush administration, on the other hand, cited this as a praiseworthy development in hemispheric relations. For them, the elections in Nicaragua stood as a prime example of what the United States *should* be doing in Latin America. Instead of funding *contras* to fight wars, the United States was now funding legitimate political parties to compete in the ballot box – parties that otherwise might not have had an opportunity to compete with the dominant Sandinistas. Moreover, the U.S. government was coordinating with other hemispheric powers to loosen the single-party ascendancy in Nicaragua, in hopes that this might contribute to the evolution of regional democracy.

In a speech delivered the day after the election results were announced, President Bush took advantage of Chamorro's election to express a new-found optimism for the state of democracy in the hemisphere:

> Any friend of democracy can take heart in the fact that Violeta Chamorro won the election. And the election process, by all accounts free and fair, is a credit to the people of Nicaragua, who chose to determine their ... nation's future at the ballot box. And that is a victory for democracy. ... Yesterday's election moves us one step closer to the day when every nation in this hemisphere is a democracy.[7]

Yet, as Washington would quickly realize, the biggest challenges for Nicaragua still remained. Chamorro's most pressing task was to arrange a transfer of power from the FSLN to the UNO. Under the 1979 constitution, the FSLN still controlled the military and police, and party leaders demanded to retain control over many governmental positions. But Chamorro proved a dynamic leader, attempting to build a coalition among the fractious political groups that still existed in the country. Perhaps most significantly, though, she liberalized the Nicaraguan economy, reprivatizing public lands

---

[6] See, for example, William M. Leogrande, "From Reagan to Bush: The Transition in U.S. Policy toward Central America," *Journal of Latin American Studies* 22, no. 3 (October 1990): 595–621.

[7] Associated Press, "Bush's Remarks on Nicaragua," *New York Times*, February 26, 1990.

and working with the IMF and World Bank to negotiate a structural read-justment program.

Meanwhile, on March 13, 1990, President Bush lifted trade barriers against Nicaragua and agreed to donate U.S.$21 million in humanitarian assistance. For many observers, this constituted a remarkable change in U.S.-Nicaraguan relations. The United States finally seemed to be doing something "constructive" for its Latin American neighbor. Yet, others saw the admin-istration's actions as an example of the United States supporting democracy only when it aligned with U.S. interests. Had Ortega won the election, this dramatic turnaround in U.S. policy may never have occurred.

ORTEGA IN THE 1990S

Despite Nicaragua's democratic advancements in the 1990s, the following decade was a trying one for the Central American republic – and Daniel Ortega's questionable conduct was by no means an exception. As his administration left office, he redistributed property and assets confiscated during the Contra War to his political cronies in what international media dubbed the *piñata*, in reference to the popular children's game in which a paper doll is beaten until it bursts, releasing candy and other treats. This devastating land grab, combined with grave economic problems carried over from the Sandinista years, caused a widespread loss of faith in the central government. Moreover, Violeta Chamorro and her successor, Arnoldo Alemán, frequently "looked the other way" when it came to workers' rights, in order to encourage international investment. Nicaragua was already the second poorest country in the hemisphere (over Haiti), and although it experienced some positive GDP growth in the early 1990s, it had little to show for it in terms of development. The Chamorro adminis-tration also struggled to eliminate a debilitating external debt.

Many critics argued that during this time the United States was ignoring Nicaragua. While the Bush and Clinton administrations supported nomi-nally democratic regimes, they overlooked the fact that the Nicaraguan government was not representing its people's interests. Indeed, the United States seemed to pay little attention in the late 1990s as President Alemán embezzled "at least $100 million during his six years in office, channeling public money through Panama, Miami and Luxembourg into his personal accounts, private property and luxurious excesses."[8] Furthermore, the

---

[8] Kevin Sullivan, "Former President's 'Hidden Treasure' Appalls Nicaragua; Successor Pursues Corruption Charges," *Washington Post*, September 12, 2002.

United States' relatively passive support for the democratic process may have undermined the evolution of democratic stability in the long run, because it allowed corrupt administrations to continue wrecking Nicaragua's economy, thus weakening public confidence in the federal structure.

On the other hand, though, one could argue that the United States did all that it should have during this time, as it provided $U.S.1.2 billion in humanitarian, development, and democracy-focused assistance. Moreover, the reality of democratic transitions is that there are obstacles along the way. The problems that Nicaragua encountered during the 1990s may have been unavoidable, or at least expected.

Ortega continued to campaign unsuccessfully for the presidency throughout the 1990s. He received a serious blow to his credibility when his stepdaughter, Zoilámerica Narváez Murillo, filed charges against him for molestation that took place in the 1980s. While it helped to prevent Ortega from being elected, it also fragmented the Sandinista party, as prominent figures in parliament attempted to distance themselves from him.

CHANGES IN THE TWENTY-FIRST CENTURY?

If the United States had ignored Nicaragua in the 1990s, it was certainly not the case during the first decade of the twenty-first century. The administration of the recently inaugurated George W. Bush directed a surprising amount of attention toward the 2001 presidential elections in Nicaragua. Although he had expressed support for the nation's fledgling democracy, since the terrorist attacks of September 11, 2001, Bush undeniably focused more of his attention on security than had either of the previous post–Cold War presidents. In Bush's estimation, Ortega posed a security threat. During his first presidency, Ortega had maintained links to Qaddafi in Libya and Castro in Cuba, and his past tendency to deny human rights "for the greater good of the revolution" had the potential to create a dangerous climate for terrorism. As one administration official explained, "I would be dishonest if I did not acknowledge that the possibility of a Sandinista victory is disconcerting to the U.S. government. ... We cannot forget that during the 1979–1990 Sandinista era, Nicaragua became a haven for violent political extremists from the Middle East, Europe, and Latin America."[9]

---

[9] John Keane, acting Deputy Secretary for Western Hemisphere Affairs, quoted in Mary Jordan, "Foes Attempt to Link Ortega to Terrorism in Nicaragua Vote," *Washington Post*, October 28, 2001.

Many observers, particularly in the Anti-imperialist camp, saw Bush's opposition to Ortega as a reassertion of Cold War–style conservatism. They noted that several administration officials had also worked on the Reagan team, helping to orchestrate the Contra War.[10] In short, many believed that the Bush administration still thought of Ortega and Nicaragua in Cold War terms without giving consideration to the substantial changes that had taken place in Nicaragua in the post–Cold War period. Nevertheless, Bush indicated that he would cut U.S. aid to Nicaragua if Ortega took the presidency.

In 2001 the Nicaraguan people elected Liberal Party candidate Enrique Bolaños.[11] The new president immediately launched a campaign to expose the corruption in the administration of his predecessor and party member Arnoldo Alemán. He finally had the ex-president arrested in September 2002 for embezzlement. In response, Alemán and Ortega formed a "pact" to undermine Bolaños's government. The agreement essentially gave Ortega's and Alemán's political parties (the FSLN and Liberal Constitutionalist Party, respectively) extralegal control of the country, through which they allocated top governmental posts to members of the FSLN and PLC and ensured Ortega and Alemán seats in the National Assembly. Using this accord, the pair stalled federal lawsuits against Alemán and drew on Sandinista-era legislation that granted legal immunity to public officials to keep Alemán and his allies out of prison. They also made plans to rewrite the constitution, placing nearly all control over Nicaragua in the hands of the parliament. As one observer in the United States described, "The pact between the Frente Sandinista's leader, Daniel Ortega, and the convicted former President Arnoldo Alemán and his minions is a naked quid pro quo: the Sandinistas get to fill key positions in order to control pivotal public institutions, and Alemán goes free, out of jail, thanks to dubious legal grounds."[12] Ultimately, the U.S. government sent a delegation led by Secretary of State Colin Powell to facilitate a dialogue among Bolaños, Ortega, and Alemán in 2005, but the talks yielded little result. Moreover, Ortega began holding negotiations with Hugo Chávez, scoring an agreement in which Venezuela would provide subsidized oil to Sandinista-controlled regions of the country.

---

[10] John Otis, "U.S. Playing Favorites in Nicaraguan Election," *Houston Chronicle*, August 20, 2006.

[11] Mary Jordan, "Sandinista Loses Nicaraguan Vote; Businessman Defeats Ortega Handily," *Washington Post*, November 6, 2001.

[12] Jaime Daremblum, Senior Fellow, the Hudson Institute, "Democracy in Latin America," Testimony before the House Committee on International Relations, Subcommittee on the Western Hemisphere, 109th Cong., 1st sess., September 28, 2005.

When Ortega announced his intention to run for president again in 2006, the U.S. government made its rhetorical opposition clear. Paul Trivelli, U.S. ambassador to Nicaragua, indicated that the United States would have to "reevaluate" its relations with Nicaragua if Ortega won.[13] Then, in October 2005, the House of Representatives passed a resolution stating, "It should be the policy of the United States to actively support the aspirations of the democratic political forces in Nicaragua for a full restoration of democracy and the rule of law in Nicaragua, headed by leaders who are committed to democracy and who deserve the trust of the Nicaraguan people."[14] In other words, not Ortega.

The Bush administration placed a great deal of faith in opposition parties, such as the Nicaraguan Liberal Alliance led by Eduardo Montealegre and the Sandinista Renovation Movement (MRS) led by Edmundo Jarquín. Despite criticism from Anti-imperialists who argued that the administration was again trying to secure an electoral outcome favorable to U.S. interests, Assistant Secretary of State Tom Shannon stated, "We see ourselves pushing the democratic process. It's all about creating political systems that are open, transparent, and inclusive."[15] Administration supporters also cited the fact that the U.S. Agency for International Development had begun a large-scale initiative in Nicaragua for election promotion and monitoring.[16]

ORTEGA RETURNS: THE END OF SANDINISMO OR A NEW FSLN?

When the election results came out on November 7, 2006, Ortega had won with 38 percent of the vote, a lower margin than he had received in his previous three bids for the presidency (Figure 10.1). While the Bush administration expressed its dismay, it nevertheless accepted the legitimate mandate. Deciding ultimately to "watch what he does, not what he says," the United States reaffirmed its policy priorities in Nicaragua: ensuring the balance of power between executive, legislative, and judicial branches and promoting economic liberalization.

---

[13] Marcela Sanchez, "Where Fear Tactics Failed: Washington's Misreading of Nicaragua," editorial, *Washington Post*, November 10, 2006.

[14] House Committee on International Relations, *Encouraging the U.S. Government to Actively Support the Democratic Political and Social Forces in Nicaragua*, 109th Congress, 1st sess., HR 252, October 7, 2005, U.S. Government Printing Office, Section 1E.

[15] Otis, "U.S. Playing Favorites."

[16] Ibid.

FIGURE 10.1. Daniel Ortega (*center*), candidate of the Frente Sandinista, waves to supporters during a campaign rally in Matagalpa, northern Nicaragua, in July 2006. Ortega, a former guerrilla leader who served as president of Nicaragua's revolutionary government in the 1980s, was elected president on November 5, 2006. (Photo: Marcelo Salinas.)

Following his return to power in Nicaragua, Ortega pursued a rather unexpected set of policies. He aligned with Hugo Chávez and the Bolivarian movement, receiving a debt relief and development assistance package from Caracas totaling more than U.S.$300 million. He also courted Iran's Mahmoud Ahmadinejad for a technology- and energy-sharing deal. Yet, rhetorically, he did not distance himself from Washington to the extent that the other populist leaders in Latin America did during the first decade of the twenty-first century. In fact, he even expressed his full support for the Bush administration's Central American Free Trade Agreement (CAFTA), despite criticism among his domestic supporters that he was supporting the "Yanqui imperialists." Ortega also adhered closely to Bolaños's liberal economic policies and drafted a proposal for a new debt-relief program under the IMF.

Since his 2006 election, Ortega has proved difficult for policymakers and scholars to "classify." On one hand, he seemed to occupy a place among the rising Latin American left. But, as one scholar argued, his reelection to the presidency "should not be viewed in the same light as the advent of Hugo Chávez, Evo Morales, and [Ecuadorian president] Rafael Correa."[17] Ortega, carrying barely 35 percent of the vote, lacked the popular mandate that has kept other populist leaders in power. Moreover, his contemporary economic and social policies, which by most measures could be considered *neoliberal*, were markedly different from the ones he espoused two decades ago.

This leaves us with a puzzling question: How *should* we view Daniel Ortega? Moreover, how should we view U.S. policy toward Ortega in the post–Cold War era? As we have seen, both Ortega's and Bush's concerns for Nicaragua have moved far beyond communism. Ortega's economic policies may have reflected a true commitment on his part to relieve poverty and to develop his country. On the other hand, they may simply have been his desperate attempts to maintain control over a population whose majority does not support him. When Ortega took office, Nicaragua was plagued by the same problems it had experienced for decades. The country's per capita GDP in 2006 was U.S.$3,100, but it was distributed such that 45 percent of the population subsisted on less than U.S.$1 a day. This represented a 3.7 percent growth from 2005, wholly insufficient for Nicaragua's growing population.[18] To make matters worse, the legislature and judicial system were held back by debilitating corruption, and the rule of law was still encumbered with dubious political agreements such as the notorious Ortega–Alemán pact.

While it remains to be seen whether Ortega has the capacity to deal effectively with Nicaragua's problems, his presidency provided a fascinating insight into the vigorous changes that Latin America has experienced since the end of the Cold War. The evolution of his leadership has followed a pattern that may best be described as fragmentation. Where Ortega was once the "radical leftist enemy," he is now at once a Bolivarian-style leftist, a CAFTA supporter, a neoliberal, an anti-imperialist, a partisan crony, a security concern, and a Bush administration antagonist. No matter what guise Ortega chooses to assume at any given moment, the United States will continue to base its policy decisions on the ever-evolving state of affairs.

[17] Marifeli Pérez-Stable, "The President of Some Nicaraguans," *Miami Herald*, June 21, 2007.
[18] *World Development Indicators, 2006*, CD-ROM (Washington, DC: World Bank, 2006).

Brazil

Ally or Rival?

With Britta Crandall

As various chapters in this volume reveal, the United States rarely maintains a singular, overarching policy toward its individual Latin American neighbors or the region as a whole. Indeed, the multiplicity of considerations and interests that influence a single bilateral relationship often result in highly dynamic, if not outright contradictory policies. While the variety of interests driving U.S. policy in Latin America is not exclusive to the post–Cold War era, the number of concerns that the United States faces has proliferated significantly since the beginning of the George H. W. Bush administration. U.S. policy in Brazil is no exception.

Several factors account for what many observers consider the United States' apathy and neglect toward its southern neighbor. One is quite simple: Portuguese. Brazil is a hemispheric outlier in that it is one of the few countries whose official language is neither English nor Spanish. Clifford Sobel, confirmed as U.S. ambassador to Brazil in July 2006, began his first speech in Brasilia stating "Eu não falo português muito bem ainda. Por favor, vamos falar em inglês agora [I still do not speak Portuguese very well. Please, let us speak in English now]."[1] Secretary of State Warren Christopher's visit to Brazil in 1996 was the first visit by an American secretary of state in eight years. And, the George W. Bush administration took nearly eighteen months to fill the position of U.S. ambassador to Brazil when Anthony Harrington left in February 2001.

The United States' lack of familiarity with Brazil, as well as Brazilians' general sentiment that the United States has "missed" its tremendous

---

[1] Statement by Ambassador Clifford Sobel, address in Brasilia International Airport, August 1, 2006.

importance as a nation, indicate just how complicated, and often conflicted, the U.S.-Brazilian relationship has been. Throughout the first three post–Cold War administrations, many in Washington felt that the United States and Brazil held "incompatible" foreign policies. Rubens Barbosa, previously the Brazilian ambassador in Washington from 1999 to 2004, posited that U.S. policymakers often think only in terms of "Big Ones" – states whose economic and political climates present national security threats to the United States. During his tenure, Barbosa challenged the United States to include Brazil as a priority "for reasons that are based on opportunities rather than threats."[2]

Brazil's foreign policy is oriented predominantly toward economic development, which, while certainly a part of Washington's policy "toolbox," often takes a back seat to other interests, especially in operational policy. In April 1985 President José Sarney stated that Brazil's fundamental foreign policy goals were the "return to development and higher employment."[3] In a November 2005 meeting with President Bush, President Luiz Inácio Lula da Silva (or "Lula") stated that Brazil's "foreign policy is not just about projecting Brazil into the rest of the world; it is also a fundamental element for our nation's project of development."[4]

Setting aside the compatibility of U.S.-Brazilian interests, U.S. policy toward Brazil is often overlooked when studying U.S.–Latin American relations. Brazil is not a particularly "sexy" or controversial topic: Brazil has sidestepped many of the crises that tormented Latin America, and, simply put, tariffs on Brazilian ethanol and frozen orange juice have a tough time competing with Colombian "narcoterrorists" and Hugo Chávez for the attention of scholars and journalists. Although often overlooked, Brazil still forms a critical element of U.S. policy interests in the region.

Reflecting the complexity and often confusing nature of this relationship, the U.S. Congress held a hearing in July 2000 entitled, "The U.S. and Brazil: Strategic Partners or Regional Competitors?" The consensus from the

---

[2] Rubens Barbosa, "The U.S. and Brazil: Strategic Partners or Regional Competitors?" Testimony before the House Committee on International Relations, Subcommittee on Western Hemisphere Affairs, 106th Cong., 2nd sess., July 26, 2000.

[3] Olavo Egydio Setubal, "Brazil's Foreign Policy in the New Republic," in *Brazil's Economic and Political Future*, ed. Julian M. Chacel, Pamela S. Falk, and David V. Fleischer (Boulder, CO: Westview Press, 1988), 241.

[4] President Luiz Inácio Lula da Silva, "Remarks Following Discussions with President Luiz Inácio Lula da Silva of Brazil in Brasilia," Office of the Press Secretary, Washington, DC, November 6, 2005.

panelists was that Brazil is at once an ally and a rival. Examples of cooperation abound, including the 2000 agreement that allows U.S. companies to launch satellites from Brazil's Alcântara Space Center and the 2007 agreement to promote the production of ethanol. However, equally abundant are examples of indifference and even acrimony. Brazilian and U.S. trade negotiators blamed each other for the failure of the latest Doha Round of the World Trade Organization in July 2006, and Brazil has openly disagreed with U.S. policy toward most Latin American countries including Cuba, Venezuela, Colombia, and Peru.

Both countries are electoral democracies, members of the United Nations, World Trade Organization, Organization of American States, and the International Monetary Fund and are committed to nonproliferation, market-led economies, and the social welfare of their citizens. Brazil and the United States are two of the largest democracies in the world, hold aspirations for international leadership, and have multiethnic societies that experience similar racial and social pressures. As Brazilian president Fernando Henrique Cardoso reflected in 2006, "you have to look at the structure of American society in order to understand Brazilian society."[5] The two countries, however, have developed quite different worldviews, resulting in countless instances of policy disagreements on issues ranging from the Amazon conservation to trade quotas.

In order to better understand U.S. policy toward Brazil since the Cold War and the dynamics that drive the bilateral relationship, it is helpful to distinguish two of the most important elements of the relationship: economic and commercial issues, and military and security issues.

ECONOMIC RELATIONS

Brazil comprises one-third of Latin American territory; its population makes up 49 percent of all of South America; and it has the eighth-largest economy in the world. Not surprisingly, U.S. policy toward Brazil in the post–Cold War era has been dominated by economic and commercial matters. However, while trade tensions seem to dominate the bilateral relationship, a strong sense of friendship and cooperation at the presidential level has added a counterintuitive element to these disputes since the end of the Cold War.

[5] Fernando Henrique Cardoso, speech at Johns Hopkins University–SAIS, Baltimore, March 29, 2006.

President George H. W. Bush

When the first Bush administration took office in 1989, Brazil's democratic transition was more than three years old and the country had just emerged from a debilitating debt crisis. Although the stage was set for a productive bilateral relationship based on political openness and economic stability, U.S. trade complaints with Brazil quickly came to dominate and sour the bilateral relationship. President Bush named Brazil an "unfair trader" in May 1989 due principally to the license requirements it placed on imports and quantitative import restrictions. Bush threatened trade retaliation under the "Super 301" clause of the United States' 1988 Trade Act if changes were not addressed quickly, a demand that offended the Brazilians. In a move that was condemned internationally as not only ineffective but also hypocritical, in June of that year Bush extended steel import quotas against twenty-nine countries, including Brazil.[6]

Many of these tensions subsided with the visit of President-elect Fernando Collor de Mello to Washington in January 1990. Emphasizing his personal interest in the Bush administration's trade concerns, he committed to change Brazil's interventionist state model, to lower import restrictions on U.S. information technology products, and to open up the Brazilian economy to increased foreign investment. Subsequently, Brazil was dropped from this "hit list" of unfair traders in April 1990. Furthermore, Congress lifted several trade sanctions in June 1990 and released ninety categories of Brazilian products for inclusion in the General System of Preferences (GSP), which allowed for tariff-free entry into the United States. Although Collor's pro-market strategy was relatively short-lived as corruption allegations forced his resignation in December 1992, his economic policies removed a source of contention between the two countries.

Individual trade disputes between the United States and Brazil were muted by Bush's launching of the Enterprise for the Americas Initiative (EAI) in June 1990. On top of its remarkable trade potential, the EAI also spelled out provisions aiming to reduce the official debt owed to the United States by the less-developed countries of Latin America, especially encouraging foreign investment. While the program appeased many Latin American governments, it faced serious criticism at home and abroad. Political scientist William Perry noted that the EAI was "not an altruistic or superficial gesture, but was intended to lock democracy and liberal economic practices into the Americas as a whole – considerably enhancing the U.S. trade position and

---

[6] Quoted in Associated Press, "Bush Extends Steel Import Quotas," July 25, 1989.

heading off political, security, and social problems that might arise to bedevil U.S. society in the future."[7] Just shy of "gunboat diplomacy"–era imperialism, many critics insisted, the EAI was an example of the United States using its economic might to secure its other interests in the hemisphere.

Latin American countries, though, seemed unconcerned about the merits of U.S. altruism, focusing instead on the possibilities for increased access to the U.S. market. Describing the Latin response to Bush's 1990 trip to Latin America to promote the EAI, the *Financial Times* reported, "Leaders in the region are convinced that Mr. Bush's presence symbolizes the beginning of a new era. ... They believe mutual antagonisms over security interests have faded away with the end of the Cold War, while cooperation has been enhanced with the region-wide consensus on market-oriented economic policies."[8]

Reflecting this sense of optimism and cooperation, in a widely heralded announcement on June 19, 1991, President Bush presented his "Rose Garden Agreement," which represented the United States' first regional pact since it announced the EAI one year prior. The United States and the four Mercosur customs union countries – Brazil, Argentina, Paraguay, and Uruguay – signed the agreement. The grouping later became known as the "four plus one" and became the precedent for the Free Trade Area of the Americas (FTAA).

Soon after the signing of the Rose Garden Agreement, two very different negotiation strategies began to emerge between the United States and Brazil. The Bush administration preferred to expand NAFTA by conducting bilateral negotiations one country at a time, whereas Brazil wanted to strengthen existing trade blocs, namely Mercosur, and to negotiate among these blocs. Meanwhile, individual trade frictions between the United States and Brazil had far from disappeared: Brazil desired to sell more shoes and orange juice to the United States while protecting its auto industry; and the United States wanted the opposite – to increase sales of autos and auto parts to Brazil, while protecting domestic orange growers and shoe manufacturers.[9]

These trade clashes were offset somewhat by robust bilateral ties between Brazil and the United States at the executive level, driven in part by the personal relationship between Bush and Collor. The two presidents had

---

[7] William Perry, "Brazil: Too Important to Ignore," *Policy Papers on the Americas*, vol. VII, study 3 (Washington, DC: Center for Strategic and International Studies Americas Program), July 15, 1996.

[8] "Bush Visit Seen as Beginning of a New Era," *Financial Times*, December 3, 1990.

[9] For a helpful summary of these issues, see Howard LaFranchi, "Cars vs. Juice: US and Brazil Find Talk Easier Than Trade," *Christian Science Monitor*, March 7, 1997.

a strong personal affinity and respect for one another; President Bush in particular was impressed by Collor's swift and determined efforts to reform the Brazilian economy. In a 1990 visit to Brazil, Bush stated, "Brazil today is poised to enter the 21st century as a leader among nations. ... I am here to tell you that you are not only on the right path, but the United States wants you to succeed and supports your efforts every step of the way."[10] In June 1991 President Bush welcomed President Collor to the White House, describing him as a "bold, active president" and declaring that the U.S.-Brazilian "relationship has never been better."[11] It seemed difficult to take these praises at face value, given the tension that surrounded the trade issue. Thus, as the sharp distinction between rhetoric and operation indicated, U.S. policy toward Brazil during this time was hardly consistent, a fact that may have directed Washington's attention away from other serious concerns in the country, such as the Collor administration's scheme to secure its ascendancy in an arguably undemocratic "dynasty" system.[12]

President Bill Clinton

President Clinton continued his predecessor's push toward hemispheric trade integration, a goal established at the December 1994 Summit of the Americas. Although the prospect of further reducing trade barriers was received coolly by the Itamar Franco administration, Fernando Henrique Cardoso increased cooperation on trade when he became president in January 1995. Not unlike Collor and his initial flurry of economic reforms five years prior, Cardoso aggressively pursued economic liberalization, including privatization and fiscal austerity. And this time, the administration obtained the support of the Brazilian Congress, which Collor had needed but never received. Legislators passed constitutional reforms paving the way for increased foreign investment and also opened up the government-run petroleum and telecommunications industries to private-sector competition. Prompted in part by pressure from the United States to protect

---

[10] President George H. W. Bush, "The US and Brazil: Fulfilling a Common Destiny," U.S. Department of State Dispatch, December 10, 1990.

[11] President George H. W. Bush, "U.S.-Brazil: Roots of Friendship," U.S. Department of State Dispatch, June 18, 1991.

[12] David Fleischer, "Political Corruption and Campaign Financing: Brazil's Slow Shift towards Anti-Corruption Laws" (paper prepared for presentation at the DEM35 Panel "Corruption in Latin America II: An Overview of the Practical Measures to Curb Corruption," XX International Congress of the Latin American Studies Association [LASA], Guadalajara, México, April 17–19, 1997), 6.

intellectual property rights – an issue important to Washington, given that the U.S. corporations are eager to protect their patents – the Brazilian Congress also passed a patent protection law in March 1996.

President Cardoso visited Washington in April 1995, initiating what became a personal friendship with President Clinton and a growing sign of post–Cold War policy convergence between the two hemispheric giants. The two leaders were both intellectuals and saw the futures of the United States and Brazil moving together in mutually beneficial paths. Said Clinton in a news conference with Cardoso, "With our two nations cooperating as never before, we stand at a moment of unparalleled opportunity. In the months and years ahead, I look forward to working with President Cardoso to forge an even stronger partnership between our nations and our peoples."[13]

Cardoso echoed Clinton's optimism stating that he came to Washington "convinced that the time has come for us to elevate bilateral relations to a new level. ... A long friendship unites our two countries. It is a friendship based on a history of shared values and joint undertakings"[14] Secretary of State Warren Christopher continued to extol Brazil's importance as an ally, calling Brazil "a natural partner of the United States" and stating that "perhaps we have not been as close to one another as we should have been, but that is changing. Now we have the chance to combine our strength and form a strategic partnership."[15] Indeed, it appeared that after Brazil's long struggle with military rule, debt, and hyperinflation, the United States was finally ready to make Brazil a more equal partner on economic and security issues. In spite of the rhetorical enthusiasm on both sides, however, this equal partnership never formed. Instead, the growing power asymmetry between the two countries complicated the idea of Brazil as an equal partner.

Still, President Clinton made it abundantly clear that it was in the United States' national interest to have an economically stable and growing Brazil. Speaking in Brasilia, Clinton asserted how important it was that the people of Brazil understand that,

just as with the trade issue and Mercosur, the United States would never knowingly make any suggestion that would undermine the growth of Brazil or any other country. It is not in our interest. ... We can only maintain our own standard of living if you grow. President Cardoso said two years ago when he visited me at the

---

[13] "Mending Ties, U.S. Praises Brazil Leader," *New York Times*, April 21, 1995.

[14] Fernando Henrique Cardoso, "A History of Friendship," *Presidents & Prime Ministers* 4, no. 4 (July–August 1995): 26.

[15] Secretary of State Warren Christopher, "Shaping a New World: U.S. and Brazilian Leadership in a Democratic, Prosperous Hemisphere," U.S. Department of State Dispatch, March 4, 1996.

White House – and I quote – "The vocation of Brazil and the United States is to stand together." I believe we stand together today as never before.[16]

True to Clinton's words, the United States played an integral role in facilitating the IMF's U.S.$41.5 billion rescue package for Brazil in 1998, and Clinton made it almost his personal crusade to shore up international support for the emerging-market crisis. The cash infusion ultimately failed to stabilize the *real*, and Cardoso was forced to float the battered currency in January 1999. However, in sharp contrast to Argentina's subsequent economic crisis, which the IMF initially brushed aside, the U.S. government and IMF's quick response to Brazil's financial turbulence reflected a degree of faith in Brazil's economic fundamentals.

Indeed, the United States' support for Brazil in 1998 was not unlike Clinton's rapid deployment of U.S. dollars for Mexico in 1994. In both cases, the United States tapped the Treasury Department's special discretionary fund (the Exchange Stabilization Fund) – $12 billion in Mexico's case, $5 billion for Brazil. The United States' response not only signaled President Clinton's and Treasury Secretary Robert Rubin's commitment to stemming financial contagion but also revealed the importance the United States placed on the stability of Brazil. Furthermore, Cardoso saw Clinton as his main ally in his quest for international aid, to such a degree that he worried that Clinton's personal political crisis and subsequent loss of political capital during this time would hurt the viability of the proposed IMF rescue package.[17]

Yet again, trade tensions flared toward the end of Clinton's presidency, after he increased tariffs on rolled steel imports and extended the tariff on orange juice after it was set to expire in 2000. Additionally, Clinton's failure to obtain fast-track authority in 2000 reflected a lack of congressional support for the FTAA and further complicated the odds of any successful FTAA negotiations.

President George W. Bush

The same bilateral disagreements on trade that had plagued George W. Bush's predecessors continued into his administration. Yet, amazingly, so did the amicable personal relationship between the executives of each country.

---

[16] President William Clinton, "The President's News Conference with President Cardoso in Brasilia," *Weekly Compilation of Presidential Documents* 33, no. 42 (October 20, 1997): 1555–1610.

[17] "Brazilian Government Worried about Clinton Factor," *Gazeta Mercantil*, September 18, 1998.

Speaking as the voice of the less-developed world, President Lula – elected on a leftist platform in 2002 – called for the lowering of U.S. trade barriers and subsidies, specifically on steel and agricultural products. For its part, the Bush administration insisted that Brazil liberalize its service-sector and government procurement policies, as well as address its weaknesses in the enforcement of intellectual property rights.

In spite of Bush's ability to secure Trade Promotion Authority (successor to fast-track) in 2002, these disagreements contributed to the failure of the September 2003 WTO meeting in Cancún, Mexico. Negotiations ended prematurely when the U.S. and Brazilian trade negotiators, Robert Zoellick and Celso Amorim respectively, reached a deadlock over the issue of subsidies. They both blamed each other's inflexibility for the failed negotiations. When the two countries chaired FTAA negotiation in 2003–4, the process further exposed their different strategies.

FTAA discussions ended again in another failure during the November 2005 Summit of the Americas in Mar del Plata, leaving the FTAA talks effectively dead. All countries save Venezuela supported the overall goal of expanding free trade, but they were unable to reach an agreement on how to get there. The U.S. and Brazilian delegations refused to budge on their respective trade demands and thus decided to wait to address their disagreements under a multilateral rubric. Brazil was holding out any FTAA agreement until the United States agreed to address its agricultural subsidies, which the Bush administration claimed it could consider changing only in global negotiations that include the European Union (EU) and Japan. In his visit to Brazil in 2005, Bush put the onus on Western Europe, saying "the United States will reduce subsidies and tariffs [on agriculture], so long as we get the same treatment from trading partners such as Europe."[18] But most European states were similarly unwilling to concede on trade issues, and so the goal of a multilateral accord by 2005, set out in the 1994 Miami summit, remained unmet.

Given the competing claims of the United States and Brazil and the many ways to manipulate tariff statistics to obtain the desired results, it is hard to get a clear picture on the trade issue. Analysts report that Brazilian tariffs against U.S. exports were generally higher than U.S. tariffs against Brazilian exports. At the same time, however, a Brazilian Embassy report claimed that U.S. tariffs on Brazil's top exports averaged 45.6 percent in 2002 whereas Brazil's tariff on top U.S. exports was only 14.3 percent. While this

---

[18] President George W. Bush, "Remarks Following Discussions with President Luiz Inácio Lula da Silva of Brazil in Brasilia," Office of the Press Secretary, November 6, 2005.

was technically correct, the embassy's calculation included a 350 percent tariff on tobacco imported from Brazil exceeding a specific quota amount. But this tariff had never been imposed because Brazil had never come close to filling the quota. Such misleading indicators appeared on both sides, further complicating the policy debate.

U.S. sources – on and off the record – often depicted Brazil as a "recalcitrant negotiator," and several members of the U.S. Congress allegedly asserted that "Brazil is the most difficult country in the hemisphere in getting on with the free-trade negotiations."[19] Moreover, Celso Amorim, Brazil's foreign minister, consistently claimed that Washington never intended to make significant cuts in agricultural or export subsidies, writing in an opinion-editorial that "the adjective 'free' should also be taken with a grain of salt. ... On non-tariff barriers, for example, there is a well-known lack of willingness by the United States to discuss antidumping measures."[20]

The constant complaints between the two countries on trade issues overshadowed the fact that both Brazil and the United States had a significant stake in an eventual FTAA. Since the end of the Cold War, both Republican and Democratic presidents were at least rhetorically pro–free trade, extolling the potential of reduced barriers to increase U.S. trade and production and ultimately the productivity and income of U.S. workers. On the other side, Brazil also needed the vast U.S. market to absorb its growing export sector. As one trade expert described, "the U.S. market is *the* economic reason for participating in at FTAA."[21]

In order to reconcile the importance of FTAA for both countries with the ongoing battle to reach an accord, one must turn to each country's domestic politics. As we have seen in most cases of U.S.-Brazilian relations, words are easier than actions, especially with the issue of trade liberalization. Given the often intermestic nature of international trade, both countries' trade policies are beholden to domestic interests, and because no strong constituency in either country enthusiastically backs hemispheric free trade, both countries' international trade agendas are saddled all the more by intractable disagreements.

The George W. Bush administration was no exception to the historical pattern of combative discourse on trade and commercial issues, which

[19] Sidney Weintraub, "Brazil–U.S. Economic Relations," *Issues in International Political Economy* 16 (Washington, DC: Center for Strategic and International Studies, April 2001): 1.

[20] "Brazilian Foreign Minister Celso Amorim Dispels FTAA Myths," *Financial Times*, August 24, 2003.

[21] Jeffrey J. Schott, "U.S.-Brazil Trade Relations in a New Era," transcript of speech, http://www.iie.com/publications/papers/paper.cfm?ResearchID=270 (accessed March 31, 2008).

FIGURE 11.1. U.S. president George W. Bush walks with Brazilian president Luiz Inácio Lula da Silva past a military honor guard after his arrival at Camp David in Maryland, March 31, 2007. (Photo: Reuters/Jason Reed.)

contrasted with official statements of flattery, respect, and deep friendship between the two countries. This has held true even with the most unlikely of bedfellows – Presidents Bush and Lula (Figure 11.1). Apart from the specifics of the trade debate, it is critical to understand the somewhat counterintuitive nature of Bush's relationship with his Brazilian counterpart. Much to the surprise of many in Washington, who feared long-time leftist politician Lula would espouse a populist agenda upon his election in 2002, as president, Lula continued Cardoso's fiscal austerity policies. Bush's official and private statements about the Brazilian chief exuded praise, respect, and deep friendship. He said in June 2003, "On a personal perspective, I am very impressed by the vision of the President of Brazil. He not only has a tremendous heart, but he has got the abilities to encourage prosperity and to end hunger."[22] Lula even received praise from then Treasury Secretary John Snow and head of the IMF Horst Köhler for his handling of the macroeconomy.

---

[22] "Bush Praises Brazil's Lula," *BBC News*, June 20, 2003.

From the Establishment perspective, Lula showed pragmatism and an understanding of the importance of the United States to Brazil. As he stated in March 2007, "We must remember that the United States continues to be our main individual partner from the standpoint of trade and is the biggest individual investor in Brazil. So we have a historical relationship. We want to preserve it and we want to improve it, but without abandoning our greater commitment, which is to the entire process of strengthening Mercosur."[23] Lula reasserted Brazil's priority of deepening regional ties through trading blocs but placed this goal within the context of maintaining the historical friendship with the United States.

In spite of the hot-button trade conflicts, as well as Bush's growing unpopularity in Latin America, the U.S. president's 2007 goodwill visit to the region went reasonably well. This was especially surprising given that the trip followed the release of two State Department reports criticizing Brazil's record on human rights and the drug trade, citing a laundry list of abuses including torture of detainees by police, violence and sexual abuse against children, trafficking in persons, and general impunity for crimes committed.[24]

Interestingly enough, it was this same annual report that contributed to an all-time low point in bilateral relations in the 1970s. Yet, unlike the first time, this most recent report was a barely blip on the bilateral radar screen. It received little media attention in either country, and neither Bush nor Lula brought it up during their meetings.

Bush's willingness to sideline such sensitive issues for the sake of mutual cooperation leads to fascinating questions about the convergence of U.S. and Brazilian interests. Many Establishment observers saw the two presidents' public amicability as a sign that the two countries were beginning to cooperate on historically contentious trade matters. However, many observers in the Anti-imperialist school argued that Bush and Lula were not cooperating on many of the big issues but pretending the issues were not there. From this perspective, many began to believe that the only reason the two seemed to be collaborating was because the United States had scaled back the pressure it had previously exerted on Brazil to concede on trade reforms.

Ethanol remained a trade issue that overlapped economics and national security, and one that possibly held the most potential as a source of cooperation between Brazil and the United States. The United States and

[23] "Lula Discusses Brazil-U.S. Ethanol Agreement," *BBC Monitoring International Reports*, March 17, 2007.
[24] U.S. Department of State, "2006 Country Reports on Human Rights Practices – Brazil," Bureau of Democracy, Human Rights, and Labor Data Sheet, March 6, 2007.

Brazil are the largest producers of ethanol in the world (U.S. ethanol is corn-based whereas Brazil's ethanol is produced from sugarcane); however, Brazil has become a global leader on the issue, having developed the industry over the past twenty years to the point that half of Brazilian automobiles are "biofuel" compatible.

Brazil reached out to countries such as Indonesia to provide technical assistance in developing their ethanol industry and the United States has shown increased interest, albeit belatedly, in cooperating as well. Presidents Bush and Lula signed an agreement in 2007 declaring the two countries' intention to increase production. And while rarely mentioned in policy speeches by President Bush during the first several years of his presidency, his "softer" policy toward Latin America that emerged in 2007 emphasized alternative energy as a national priority. Lula was even invited to Camp David – a rarity for Latin American leaders – at the end of March 2007 to discuss ways to deepen the bilateral relationship and increase cooperation.

In sum, trade was the most visible issue between the United States and Brazil, and most likely will continue to cause friction in the near future. The fanfare surrounding the Rose Garden Agreement in the immediate post–Cold War era faded over the subsequent two decades. Although the EAI did not result in substantive changes over the subsequent fifteen years, and few of its goals were put into practice, the initiative did set the stage for the ongoing efforts toward hemispheric free trade. The EAI also denoted a shift from a U.S.-Brazil relationship focusing on security and a zero-sum game, to one of cooperation and mutually beneficial growth.

THE NUCLEAR AND SECURITY AGENDA

From the turn of the century until the 1970s, the United States and Brazil had what was described as a "special relationship." Brazil was the United States' closest ally in the region, and the United States in turn provided Brazil with economic and military aid. The relationship between the two countries' militaries was particularly strong. This "unwritten alliance" began to unravel, however, with Brazil's rapid economic growth in the 1960s and early 1970s. When Brazil's longtime quest for *grandeza* (greatness) finally seemed in reach, a more independent foreign policy naturally ensued. Brazil distanced itself from any automatic alignment with Washington; conflicts over trade, human rights, and nuclear weapons soon dominated the bilateral agenda.

Brazil's nuclear ambitions were perhaps the greatest source of worry for the United States in the late 1960s and 1970s. Increased military prowess certainly looked to be in Brazil's trajectory during this time. At this time,

Brazil refused to adhere to the Nuclear Nonproliferation Treaty, believing it legitimated an unacceptable division between militarily nuclear and nonnuclear countries. Brazil also refused to sign the Treaty of Tlatelolco, the nuclear-free treaty of Latin America, and completed a multibillion-dollar agreement with West Germany in 1976 to receive nuclear fuel enrichment equipment in exchange for uranium. Indeed, many scholars assumed that Brazil aspired to hold a position not only of economic prestige but also of military power.[25] Yet, although Brazil was a major arms exporter in the 1980s, selling to more than thirty countries, including Iraq and Saudi Arabia, it spent relatively little on its own military. Amid slow world growth and protected foreign markets, arms sales were no more than a pragmatic way to improve Brazil's trade balance and to earn foreign exchange.

By the end of the Cold War, Brazil was beginning to shift away from its defensive stance on arms freezing. President Collor renounced the previous decades' nuclear aims when he publicly closed the country's nuclear reactors in 1990. Instead, Collor began a policy of allying with the United States while promoting Brazil's role as a serious global political actor. In October 1995, due in part to continuous pressure from the United States, Brazil was accepted as a member of the Missile Technology Control Regime – an institution established to limit the proliferation of ballistic missile capabilities. Following these steps, the United States and Brazil reached an agreement on peaceful nuclear cooperation in 1996 that allowed Brazil to purchase nuclear materials from the United States. This same year, Brazil also signed a space cooperation agreement with the Clinton administration allowing for American companies to launch satellites from Brazil's Alcântara Space Center in the northeastern state of Maranhão.

Many observers have offered convincing explanations for this bilateral policy shift toward greater cooperation. From the Anti-imperialist side, it was a case of the United States attempting to assert its superiority in the region. During the Cold War, the United States did not want its neighbors to have nuclear capabilities unless it retained ultimate control over them. In other words, the United States denied Latin America access to nuclear energy and weapons to ensure that it did not have any strategic competition. At best, it was an instance of unabashed paternalism, the United States judging that it was in the entire hemisphere's best interest not to allow atomic power to spread.

From the Establishment perspective, though, the United States' change in policy had nothing to do with hegemony and everything to do with the

---

[25] Riordan Roett, "Brazil Ascendant: International Relations and Geopolitics in the Late 20th Century," *Journal of International Affairs* 29, no. 2 (1975): 139–54.

national security threats associated with communism in the 1960s. Then, it was a top priority for the United States to stop nuclear proliferation to protect its own people, but once the Cold War had ended, it became a less significant issue. An interesting counterfactual to consider is how the United States might have responded if Brazil had pursued nuclear capabilities in the post–Cold War era through a source in Europe or Asia. Had the United States tried to stop Brazil from doing so, it might have given more support to the Anti-imperialist argument: even when the risks were markedly lower, the United States still would not give up its hemispheric control of the nuclear issue.

Finally and most notably, the Brazilian congress ratified the Nuclear Nonproliferation Treaty in 1998, revealing Brazil's definitive rejection of the development of military power. Brazil instead emphasized its role as a conflict mediator between the developing and developed worlds. It also asserted global leadership through its soft-power attributes exemplified by Brazil's sizable population, its economic strength, and its potential for diplomacy.[26] Indeed, in the power dynamics between Brazil and the United States – due to Brazil's dramatic shift in strategies – cooperation replaced confrontation.

The nuclear tensions that characterized U.S.-Brazil relations during the latter part of the Cold War all but disappeared by the late 1990s. During President Clinton's visit in 1997, he was asked if the United States, as the world's only superpower, was threatened by Brazil. Clinton responded by affirming that he supported "the emergence of countries to a greater role of influence and responsibility, as long as they shared our [U.S.] basic values – not agreeing with us on everything, but sharing our basic values."[27] With the memory of a potentially bellicose Brazil with nuclear aspirations ancient history, Clinton made it clear that the United States supported the growth and strengthening of Brazil.

Reflecting this tone of cooperation, Brazil was the first country to show solidarity with the United States immediately following the September 11 attacks by leading the effort within the OAS to invoke the Rio Treaty – the regional mutual defense agreement in North America. And when Secretary of State Colin Powell met with Lula in October 2004 in Brasilia, Powell confirmed that he was open to considering Brazil's permanent membership on the United Nations Security Council, especially in light of Brazil's contributions to the peacekeeping mission in Haiti. Powell went on to state that

---

[26] See Maria Regina Soares de Lima and Monica Hirst, "Brazil as an Intermediate State and Regional Power: Action, Choice and Responsibilities," *International Affairs* 82, no. 1 (2006): 21.

[27] Clinton, "The President's News Conference with President Cardoso."

the United States "understands that Brazil has no interest in a nuclear weapon, no desire and no plans, no programs, no intention of moving toward a nuclear weapon."[28]

CONCLUSION

Historically, a crucial question surrounding U.S. policy toward Brazil has been how the United States would respond to a stronger, more assertive Brazil. Would it indeed embrace this development, as Washington so often promises to do? Or would it suddenly react with alarm to this newly rising hemispheric competitor? Whatever the case, Brazil always believed in its entitlement to a more influential global role, an identity that was manifested in several foreign policy endeavors. Most notably, Brazil has been a leader in the creation of the "Group of Twenty" (G-20), a coalition within the World Trade Organization formed to serve as an alternative to the Western-oriented Group of Seven (G-7) and to promote trade reforms necessary for Third World economic growth. The G-20 has opposed the United States on almost every issue, be it free trade or patents.

Separately, Lula's Brazil increased ties with Arab and African countries; continued lobbying efforts to become a permanent member of the UN Security Council; pushed for Brazilians to head the WTO and the Inter-American Development Bank; and became a member of the IBSA initiative – a group of countries comprising India, Brazil, and South Africa cooperating to promote trade and development. As one commentator noted in 2004, "Brazil has long been a gentle and introverted giant, content to be a bystander on the world stage. Now that is changing."[29]

Since the end of the Cold War, both Republican and Democratic administrations have supported openly Brazil's "ascendancy," emphasizing that in spite of chronic trade disagreements, the United States and Brazil are fundamentally compatible countries. As President George W. Bush asserted during his 2005 visit to Brasilia, "As the largest democracy in South America, Brazil is a leader, and today, Brazil is exercising its leadership across the globe. ... Brazil aspires to set an example for the continent by building a just social order where the blessings of liberty are enjoyed by every citizen of this great nation."[30] Karen Hughes, under secretary of state

---

[28] "Warming to Brazil, Powell Says Its Nuclear Program Isn't a Concern," *New York Times*, October 6, 2004.
[29] "A Giant Stirs in Brasilia," *The Economist*, June 12, 2004, 34.
[30] "President Bush Discusses Democracy in the Western Hemisphere," Blue Tree Park Hotel, Brasilia, Brazil, Office of the Press Secretary news release, November 6, 2005.

for public diplomacy and public affairs, furthered this sentiment by pledging the United States' support of Brazil's "emergence" and its desire to help "Brazil continue its remarkable transformation."[31]

It did not appear that Brazil's growing political and economic clout would necessarily lead to conflict between the United States and Brazil. Far from it, recent years indicate that Brazil's proximity to *grandeza* may have actually paved the way for improved relations between the two countries. No longer saddled with hyperinflation, a colossal international debt burden, or a repressive military regime, Brazil has become a respected and serious global power – one that has proved to be an important regional ally for the United States. With its growing confidence, Brazil can now partner with the United States on previously contentious issues such as the environment and disarmament, and perhaps even trade.

The question for this era, then, is to what degree the United States will take advantage of this relatively new stability to engage its southern neighbor. Similarly, to what extent *must* the United States bend to Brazil's own wishes? For decades, onlookers have claimed that Brazil's "voice will be impossible to tune out" and that the United States will be forced to deal with the southern giant.[32] Has this day arrived at last?

---

[31] "U.S., Brazil Share Strong Relationship, State's Hughes Says: Calls for Collaboration to Bring Benefits of Democracy to Region," *Washington File*, March 13, 2006.

[32] See Ian Katz and John Templeman, "Power Shift in Latin America: Brazil Starts to Flex Its Muscle," *Business Week*, October 13, 1997, 29.

Castro and Cuba

A Timeless Relationship

With Marshall Worsham

Following the announcement in 1991 that the Soviet Union would withdraw its financial and military support from Cuba, the Americas stood poised to watch the hemisphere's most enduring communist regime finally topple. Fidel Castro had subjected Cuba to a closed and repressive administration for more than forty years, and it appeared that once the imploding superpower that had fueled the nation's socialist machine said *adios*, Cuba would collapse under its own economic weaknesses. In response to these developments, President George H. W. Bush announced, "Today we are closer than ever to our goal of returning freedom to Cuba. The Russian Government has announced that economic relations with Cuba will be on a hard currency basis. Also, Russia is withdrawing the former Soviet brigade and announced that as of January 1, 1992, it was ending all subsidies to Cuba. Castro is on his own."[1]

In hindsight, Castro's future in Cuba was not as grim as Bush had indicated. Although the Soviets did depart Cuba later that year, the Castro regime demonstrated remarkable resilience, still retaining its control over the island nation more than fifteen years later.

In July 2006 a surprising incident directed the world's attention back to Cuba. Following intestinal surgery, Fidel Castro announced that he was transferring executive responsibility temporarily to Raúl Castro, his younger brother and minister of defense. Once again, many observers were certain that this major disruption of leadership, the first since 1959, signaled the end of the Castro regime. Yet, this time, President George W. Bush

---

[1] President George H. W. Bush, "Statement on Actions to Support Democracy in Cuba," U.S. Department of State Dispatch, April 18, 1992.

assumed a dramatically different attitude than his father had. In an on-the-air address to the American people, he affirmed: "At this time of uncertainty in Cuba, one thing is clear: The United States is absolutely committed to supporting the Cuban people's aspirations for democracy and freedom. We have repeatedly said that the Cuban people deserve to live in freedom. I encourage all democratic nations to unite in support of the right of the Cuban people to define a democratic future for their country."[2]

President Bush's rhetoric in 2006 lacked the unequivocal judgment of his father. Instead of heralding Cuba's entrance into a new era of liberty, the Bush administration emphasized that as long as Castro was ceding power to someone within the regime, Washington would not change its policies toward Cuba. This chapter examines the reasons why U.S. policy toward Cuba has remained relatively constant throughout the three contemporary U.S. presidential administrations. It also addresses the long-standing issue of mutual hostility between the United States and Cuba, in contrast to the more congenial relations between the United States and nations that have liberalized their economies and sought to establish democratic governments.

CUBA AS AN ANALYTICAL MODEL

U.S. policy toward Cuba – namely, the comprehensive restrictions on travel and trade – remained relatively constant during and after the Cold War. Therefore, Cuba policy is a "constant" that allows us to examine whether U.S. decision makers' motivations and aspirations for the region have changed in the contemporary era. As we have already seen, Washington substituted its Cold War security concern with a wide array of factors in its Latin American policy considerations, and Cuba was no exception. For example, when President Clinton permitted American companies to export agricultural and medical goods to Cuba just before he left office in 2000, his sole concern was not to stem the rising tide of communism; rather, he considered international issues such as increased competition from European businesses operating in Cuba since the 1990s, as well as domestic concerns such as the personal interests of Cuban American refugees and the commercial interests of farmers in the American Midwest.

Acknowledging these multiple interests is not to say that security is no longer a key concern for decision makers in Washington, but neither does it permit the polarized viewpoint that the only thing driving U.S. foreign

---

[2] President George W. Bush, "Statement on Cuba," U.S. Department of State Dispatch, August 3, 2006.

policy even during the Cold War was the security threat associated with the existence of a Soviet satellite in the middle of a major shipping lane just ninety miles off the coast of Florida. What it reveals is that, although operational policy toward Cuba has remained relatively constant, the issues surrounding U.S.-Cuban relations have become vastly more complicated.

Because Cuba policy in operation has adhered so rigidly to Cold War methods, this reality enables us to observe how public discourse about the bilateral relationship has changed and to explore whether the arguments made for and against Cuba policy seem to be the same as the old Cold War criticisms, or if they have changed to meet shifting regional dynamics.

CUBA AND THE COLD WAR

As the first communist state in Latin America, Cuba had an extremely close economic, political, and ideological relationship with the Soviet Union throughout the Cold War. Yet, interestingly, when Fidel Castro first rose to power, he did not align himself with Cuba's fledgling Communist Party; in fact, initially more of a nationalist than an outright communist, Castro's initial political ambitions may have been decidedly less radical, a question that is still hotly disputed. The island nation's revolutionary roots go back to 1953, when Castro staged an attack on the Moncada military barracks in Santiago de Cuba. His rebel organization, called the 26th of July Movement for the date of the Moncada attack, consisted of 150 mostly young, radical militants, who had been trained to instigate a large-scale guerrilla war that would destabilize the government of dictator Fulgencio Batista. Castro intended to seize weapons from the Moncada arsenal to arm his insurrection. However, the 26th of July Movement failed thoroughly, and almost two-thirds of the revolutionary force was captured or killed. Castro himself fled to the mountains outside of Santiago, but he was arrested within a week and went to trial in September. In his defense, he delivered a powerful argument, which was published subsequently as the momentous "History Will Absolve Me" speech:

The nation's future and the solutions to its problems, cannot continue to depend on the selfish interests of a handful of big businessmen or on the cold calculations of profits drawn by a few tycoons in their air-conditioned offices. ... The problems of the Republic can be solved only if we devote ourselves to fight for it with the same energy, honesty, and patriotism our liberators displayed when they founded it.[3]

---

[3] Fidel Castro, *History Will Absolve Me*, trans. Carmen González Díaz de Villegas (Havana: Editorial José Martí, 1998), 66–7.

Outlining five revolutionary laws that the 26th of July Movement would have instated to create a socialist, redistributive, constitutional Republic, the speech articulated Castro's revolutionary beliefs and aspirations and was later published as the manifesto of the Cuban revolution.

In response, the court handed Castro a fifteen-year prison sentence, a more merciful judgment than many of the revolutionaries received. He joined his brother Raúl and several of the movement's organizers in prison on the Isle of Pines; here, he developed the increasingly Marxist views that informed the revolution that carried Cuba for the next half-century.

In 1956 Castro was released under a general amnesty granted by the Batista government, and he traveled to Mexico, where he reorganized the 26th of July Movement with the aid of Argentine Ernesto "Che" Guevara, an ardent socialist. On December 2 of that same year, they launched the next phase of the Cuban revolution: a force of just over eighty Cuban dissidents landed the yacht *Granma* near Playa Las Coloradas on the eastern coast, where they met with resistance from the Batista military. Only twelve of the original force survived the first day, and they fled to the Sierra Maestra. Over the next three years, though small in number, they instigated a bloody guerrilla war, spreading socialist ideology through the Cuban countryside, winning support from rural peasants, and coordinating with the Communist Party in Santiago and Havana. On January 2, 1959, Fidel Castro's 26th of July Movement seized Santiago de Cuba. Two days later Guevara took Havana, and Batista fled to the Dominican Republic. In a speech to the people of Santiago, Castro advocated civil liberties for all people, including freedom of speech, freedom of the press, open discussion and dissent, and workers' rights.

He declared, "Here in Cuba it is the people, and the people alone, who must decide who is to govern them."[4] It is important to note the emphasis on popular government in Castro's rhetoric at the time. In the same speech, he indicated that he had no intention of taking power in Cuba. Yet, it was not a popular election, but a mandate of leaders of the 26th of July Movement that instated Cuba's first revolutionary president, Manuel Urrutia. When Castro became prime minister and the head of the Council of State, it quickly became evident that Castro would be in charge of the new government.

When we examine Cuban and U.S. relations in the post–Cold War era, it is important to first understand the foundations upon which the contemporary conditions and conflicts in Cuba were built. In the early stages of the Cuban revolution, the United States had been ambivalent about the changes taking place, offering no definitive statements on its position regarding the

[4] Fidel Castro, "Speech Delivered to the People of Santiago, Cuba," January 3, 1959.

Castro regime, while quietly boosting its intelligence programs in the country. In 1960, however, Castro's leadership took a drastic left turn, beginning with a land reform program, in which the government seized property from the middle and upper classes for redistribution. By the end of 1961, the state controlled 80 percent of industry, 30 percent of agricultural land, and 90 percent of exports. Declaring its socialist sympathies, Castro's government nationalized land and capital held by foreign companies, most notably American banks, railroads, port facilities, sugar plants, and oil refineries. Castro's moves attracted Washington's attention in part because they threatened American economic and political dominance in the region. Declaring a "fight for a liberated Latin America," Castro pushed back against what many Cubans had long considered U.S. imperialism.[5] The Cuban government followed this up with a successful widespread literacy campaign and socialization of the health-care sector.

At this time in the early 1960s, Havana established its first ties with Moscow. In February 1960, Anastas Mikoyan, Krushchev's aide, made a deal with Castro to buy 1 million tons of Cuban sugar per year for five years, to be repaid in hard currency, oil, and agricultural machinery, to be accompanied by an interest-free loan of U.S.$100 million for industrial equipment.[6] Later that year, Castro issued the First Declaration of Havana, in which he announced Cuba's alliance with the Soviet Union:

> The People of Cuba strongly condemn the imperialism of North America for its gross and criminal domination, lasting for more than a century, of all the peoples of Latin America. ... That domination, built upon superior military power, upon unfair treaties, and upon the shameful collaboration of traitorous governments, has for more than a hundred years made of Our America ... a backyard of the financial and political empire of the United States.[7]

This speech marked the beginning of Castro's anti-U.S. attitude, which has since become a nearly institutionalized facet of U.S.-Cuban relations. Such rhetoric, in part, enabled Castro to shore up his own ascendancy, as it instilled among the Cuban people a sense of national pride and allowed them to project their indignation for Cuba's social and economic ills onto an external power.

In response to Castro's actions, the Eisenhower administration declared a partial economic embargo against Cuba in October 1960 on all exports

---

[5] Richard Gott, *Cuba: A New History* (New Haven: Yale University Press, 2004), 183.
[6] Ibid., 182.
[7] Fidel Castro, "The First Declaration of Havana," speech delivered to the people of Havana, Cuba, September 2, 1960.

except food and medical products. With Cuba accepted into the Soviet fold, Eisenhower's advisers believed that Cuba posed a serious threat to the security of the entire region. Although almost no policymakers in Washington could have imagined it, the economic embargo policy would persist for more than forty years.

In addition to the economic embargo, successive U.S. administrations pursued clandestine efforts to overthrow the Castro regime, including the Bay of Pigs operation in 1961. Dispatched under final orders that came from President John F. Kennedy, a group of CIA-funded Cuban exiles invaded Cuba to stage a coup against Castro. They hoped to establish a democratic, antisocialist (read: pro-U.S.) government after eliminating the communist opposition. However, the mission's organizers had underestimated both the military capabilities of the new Cuban government and the popularity that Castro enjoyed among the poor rural populations. Castro met the dissidents with a substantial military force and quickly routed them.

The Bay of Pigs operation is largely regarded as a monumental failure in U.S. policy in Latin America. Not only did it expose the United States' willingness to sacrifice its ethical foreign policy foundation for the sake of containing communism, but it also shored up Castro's ascendancy in Cuba. By quelling the U.S.-sponsored insurrection, Castro emerged as a symbol of heroism, the defender of the "oppressed" Latin American people. Yet, despite suffering serious international condemnation for their involvement in the disastrous intervention, the CIA and Department of Defense continued to explore the possibility of an overthrow, arming and training guerilla forces in the Caribbean under programs like President Kennedy's Operation Mongoose.

By the late 1970s, the United States no longer engaged in direct destabilization efforts in Cuba. The Bay of Pigs model had been abandoned, and subsequent administrations took a "hands-off" approach, employing the embargo as the primary coercive "stick" against the Castro regime. Aimed more at "containing" communism within Cuba than at eliminating it, the embargo became an almost immutable aspect of U.S. policy, with little variance even after the Cold War.

SOVIET WITHDRAWAL AND A NEW CUBAN ECONOMY

During the Cold War, Cuba was a determining factor in the United States' containment policy in the hemisphere. Following the Bay of Pigs, policymakers in Washington believed that it would be more efficient – and internationally acceptable – not to force a transition in Havana, but rather to disallow the communist regime from exporting the *revolución* to its neighbors, especially in

Central America. In other words, Cuba had to be "quarantined" to keep the plague of communism from spreading throughout the region. While pressuring Cuba through economic means, consecutive presidential administrations took more assertive actions in other countries, such as Venezuela and Nicaragua, ostensibly to keep new communist revolutions from taking root. U.S. diplomat George F. Kennan first articulated a policy of containment in 1947 as an effort to apply "counter-force at a series of constantly shifting geographical and political points" to "promote tendencies which must eventually find their outlet in either the break-up or the gradual mellowing of Soviet power."[8]

The collapse of Soviet communism and the country's withdrawal from Cuba in 1991 dealt an unexpected blow to Cuba. Many observers predicted the end of the Castro regime and the collapse of Cuba's economy, which had been based on sugar production to satisfy the Soviet trading bloc's needs. Once Cubans realized that the socialist system could not support itself, they would call for reforms, preferably democratic ones. Some analysts predicted a dramatic change within a matter of months, and President Bush agreed: "I've got a pretty pessimistic prospect there for Fidel Castro down there in Cuba, very pessimistic for him, because it is so hard to be the only one that still thinks communism is a good idea."[9] As would become evident in the next several years, these estimations were not altogether incorrect. Beginning in 1991, Cuba entered a period of devastating economic crisis, which put a tremendous strain on the socialist regime.

Cuba's economic troubles came to light in the 1980s, when the Cuban government realized that the cash-crop system that allowed the nation to fill a niche market in the Soviet economic complex was a highly unstable and dangerous arrangement. The nation's sugar revenues had decreased substantially since 1984, due to abysmal world sugar prices, natural disasters in Cuba, and increased protectionism in international markets. As a result, Cuba grew increasingly more dependent on Soviet subsidies. Castro attempted to reform this system and diversify the economy with an initiative called the Rectification of Errors and Negative Tendencies. Begun in 1986, the program decreased subsidies and tariffs, increased and diversified food production to reduce the dependency on imports, and rejected outright the liberal, open-market reforms that the Soviet Union was advocating in Eastern Europe. Cuba also started an

---

[8] U.S. Department of State, "Kennan and Containment, 1947," Timeline of U.S. Diplomatic History, 1945–52, http://www.state.gov/r/pa/ho/time/cwr/17601.htm (accessed August 6, 2007).

[9] President George W. Bush, Presidential News Conference, December 26, 1991.

austerity initiative aimed at decreasing consumption to free up public funds for Cuba's expansive social programs.

Historians will continue to debate whether these reforms had a positive impact on Cuba's economy in the long run. Policies that attempted to recentralize and diversify the country's economic production may have done just enough to keep the Cuban economy from totally failing after the Soviets abandoned the island. On the other hand, the regime's refusal to liberalize the Cuban economy more comprehensively may have intensified the crises that Cuba experienced throughout the 1990s.

Between 1991 and 1993, the Cuban economy declined rapidly under the intense strains caused by the loss of its primary trading partner. In 1989, 63 percent of Cuba's sugar, 95 percent of its citrus, and 73 percent of its nickel went to the Soviet Union. In return, the Soviet Union provided 63 percent of the island nation's food imports and 80 percent of its agricultural and industrial machinery. By 1992 trade between the two countries had fallen by 70 percent. Cuba also experienced an energy crisis, as oil imports from the Soviet Union decreased from 13 million tons in 1989 to 5.3 million tons in 1993.[10] Ultimately, after the Soviet Union revoked its sugar subsidies, the Cuban economy plummeted; the GDP fell a record 14.9 percent in 1993.[11]

GEORGE H. W. BUSH AND EVOLVING CUBAN POLICY

As Cuba entered this "special period" of economic emergency, the U.S. government under George H. W. Bush became concerned increasingly with the deteriorating humanitarian conditions on the island. At this time in 1992, the primary piece of legislation driving U.S. policy toward Cuba had remained unchanged for thirty years. The Trade Expansion Act of 1962, which had extended President Eisenhower's 1960 economic embargo indefinitely, prohibited the U.S. government from pursuing diplomatic relations and from supporting multilateral loans and aid until it was "determined that Cuba is no longer dominated or controlled by the foreign government or foreign organization controlling the world Communist movement."[12] But now, the fear of communist expansion in the region had dissipated. Moreover, preoccupied with its own economic and social crises, Cuba was no longer interested in exporting its socialist revolution around the world; Cuba's policy focus

---

[10] Gott, *Cuba: A New History*, 287.
[11] Ana Julia Jatar-Hausman, *The Cuban Way: Capitalism, Communism and Confrontation* (West Hartford, CT: Kumarian Press, 1999), 46–8.
[12] *Trade Expansion Act of 1962*, HR 11970, 87th Cong., 2nd sess., October 11, 1962.

was becoming increasingly "domesticated." As a result, new issues such as human rights and democratic reform became key concerns for the Bush administration.

Such domestic concerns were at the crux of the Cuban Democracy Act (CDA), sponsored by Representative Robert Torricelli (D-NJ) and ratified in by Congress in 1992. The legislation stated, "The government of Fidel Castro has demonstrated consistent disregard for internationally accepted standards of human rights and for democratic values. It restricts the Cuban people's exercise of freedom of speech, press, assembly, and other rights."[13] Indicating that the United States now had "an unprecedented opportunity to promote a peaceful transition to democracy in Cuba,"[14] the act reflected a dramatic reframing of the motivations driving U.S. policy. Washington no longer aimed to contain communism but to instill in Cubans the democratic ideals of free political discourse, labor rights, and free and fair elections, as well as American-style free market reforms.

Although the rhetoric of the new legislation represented an important shift from Cold War thinking, the operational policies included in the act actually differed very little from the 1962 Trade Expansion Act. The CDA upheld the president's power to enforce the decades-long economic embargo and maintained restrictions on aid to Cuba until a democratic transformation occurred. The CDA augmented the president's power to enforce the now-conventional embargo policy, enabling him to sanction other nations engaging in trade with and giving assistance to Cuba.

In addition, the CDA included a brief statement of consent allowing the government to provide assistance to nongovernmental organizations promoting "nonviolent democratic change in Cuba." The legislation also reauthorized Radio Martí and TV Martí, American news services that broadcast from Miami, Florida, across the Caribbean basin. Similar to Radio Free America, the programs delivered more than five hours of newscasts, several hours of political analysis and commentary daily, and statements about U.S. policy, including the U.S. president's weekly address to the nation. Although the Office of Cuba Broadcasting, which directed the programs, maintained that it conformed to international broadcasting guidelines and simply filled in the "information gaps caused by over four decades of Cuban government censorship," Radio and TV Martí gave rise to serious conflict between Washington and Havana. Castro, claiming that the United States was

---

[13] *Cuban Democracy Act of 1992*, HR 5323, 102nd Cong., 2nd sess., September 4, 1992, Section 6001, 1.
[14] Ibid.

violating international law, launched a major effort to jam the broadcasts a few days after the programs were launched. Yet they still reached all but the most populated cities in Cuba.

During this time, many critics in the Anti-imperialist school argued that Congress was merely inventing new reasons to exercise its hegemonic will over Cuba. In this view, Castro's human rights violations were the new "communism," another justification for the U.S. government's imposition of American-style political systems on its back-door neighbor.[15] Hard-liners in this camp accused the U.S. Congress of pandering to American corporate interests who were looking to cash in on new investment opportunities as Castro liberalized foreign trade.

Critics in the Establishment school, however, countered that the Bush administration was acting in the best interest of democracy and freedom in Cuba. If Washington – Bush included – was truly interested in promoting democracy in Cuba, then the damaging effects that sanctions would have on relations with other countries, which these advocates insisted would be only temporary, were necessary and worthy costs. Many believed that, in this case, the goals of the CDA matched up with the U.S. government's true intentions.

IMMIGRATION AND DEMOCRACY: DOMESTIC DISPUTES?

As Bill Clinton entered the presidency, a series of political and economic changes impacted Cuba, creating a wave of domestic crises that, somewhat unexpectedly, spilled over into the United States. Responding to what was quickly becoming a financial disaster, Castro placed discretionary control of the Cuban economy in the hands of Finance Minister Carlos Lage, who decentralized the state's control of foreign trade and invited foreign corporate and industrial investment with the promise of 49 percent ownership in joint-venture projects. Lage also coordinated with European investors to boost the tourism industry. Then, in August and September 1993, Castro issued several decrees that reintroduced the U.S. dollar into the unstable peso economy, opened more than 100 service-sector businesses for private ownership, and created agricultural cooperatives to replace large state-owned farms and plantations.

In a surprising move, the Cuban leader also improved the conditions for political participation in Cuba. In 1992 he encouraged the National Assembly to amend the 1976 constitution; it excised the document's overt

---

[15] Kimberly A. Elliott, "Economic Sanctions," in *Intervention into the 1990s: U.S. Foreign Policy in the Third World*, ed. Peter J. Schraeder (Boulder, CO: Lynne Rienner, 1992), 100.

Marxist-Leninist and anti-Christian language and made provisions for the direct election of representatives to the National Assembly. However, the Cuban Communist Party still remained the only legal political organization; candidates for legislative office had to be hand-selected and approved by "el máximo líder."

To further promote "civic participation," Castro disseminated his sweeping economic reforms for ratification by public referendum. These efforts, though they did not meet the United States' demands for democratic processes, restored public confidence in Castro's government.

Simultaneously, Castro pursued a number of policies that reminded the Cuban people that they still lived under a repressive socialist regime. The administration rationed food, gas, and oil and periodically cut power to decrease consumption. It also redistributed thousands of laborers to rural areas to increase agricultural production and cut public spending in every sector except health care and education. Furthermore, Castro cracked down on public dissent, authorizing the military and Communist Party para-militaries to arrest and assassinate people who spoke out against the regime. He denied most of the Cuban population exit visas to the United States and other, more liberalized countries in the region.

The persistent economic decline of the so-called special period of economic rationing and restructuring, when coupled with the dramatic political changes taking place in Cuba, heightened public discontent. Tensions reached a boiling point on July 13, 1994, when a group of seventy-two dissidents commandeered a tugboat from the port in Havana and headed for the Florida coast. Castro ordered a fleet of Coast Guard vessels to pursue the fleeing expatriates. They attacked the boat and sunk it, killing forty-one people on board.

The so-called 13 de Marzo tragedy caused a vehement public reaction in both Cuba and the United States. In August 1994 several hundred Cubans organized the first major political demonstrations against the Castro regime since the 1960s. For about a week, several hundred protestors rioted on the Malecón, a scenic avenue along Havana's historic harbor. They demanded economic liberalization, sweeping political changes, and permission to leave the island. In response, Castro relented and opened the borders to anyone who wanted to leave. Needless to say, many did (Figure 12.1).

At this point, we can only speculate as to why Castro conceded on the emigration issue: he may have responded to the upsurge of popular discontent or he may have hoped to place a strain on the United States and its immigration policies in retaliation against the CDA. Moreover, he may have wanted to relieve some of Cuba's economic pressure; by allowing

FIGURE 12.1. Cubans build a raft in Cojimar, near Havana, Cuba, during the massive exodus to the United States in August 1994. (Photo: Marcelo Salinas.)

people to escape Cuba, he reduced the number of citizens receiving socialized services – and thus government spending – as well as the number of unemployed and underemployed. Perhaps a more accurate assessment, though, is that Castro had to make some crucial decisions to keep himself in power. As was the case during the Cold War era, the Cuban president rarely acted as a "textbook" socialist. Rather, he pursued his own brand of what many observers have called "Fidelismo," a dynamic and flexible political model that ensured, above all, that Fidel Castro remained on top. His apparent "leniency" on economic concerns and expatriation policy during this "special period," while perhaps indicative of profound changes in the Cuban political consciousness, most probably shows that Castro was willing to make small sacrifices in the short run to ensure his ascendancy over the long term.

WET FOOT–DRY FOOT

After Since the Cold War period, the United States held a relatively idiosyncratic immigration policy toward Cuba. Unlike just about every other country in the world where normal immigration and asylum rules applied, due to the long-standing hostility between Washington and Havana, the United States had granted automatic asylum to anyone who left Cuba for the United States, with or without a valid exit visa. From 1990 to 1993, just over 8,000 Cubans came to the United States through this program. During the early 1990s, though, the policy faced heightened criticism, as members of Congress pointed to the discrepancies between immigration policy for Cuba and Haiti. As thousands of Haitian "boat people" fled the violently oppressive Cédras regime, the U.S. Coast Guard rounded them up and detained them in Guantánamo Bay (located, somewhat ironically, in Cuba) to await immigration status verification. Congressman Charles Rangel (D-NY), among others, accused both the Bush and Clinton administrations of racial discrimination, because most of the Haitians were Afro-Caribbean, while most Cuban refugees were lighter-skinned mestizos. As Representative Harry A. Johnston (D-FL) commented, "It sends a terrible message to have two different policies for two different islands."[16]

After the Malecón riots in 1994, as nearly 30,000 Cuban "refugees" flooded the United States, President Clinton realized the full extent of the dilemma that the preferential immigration policies had created. On one hand, he knew that allowing that many people into the United States would be neither popular nor economically viable in the Gulf Coast states. Clinton was personally aware of the problems that such a tide of immigration could create. During the Mariel Boatlift in 1980, in which 125,000 Cubans entered the United States after Castro had authorized a similar mass expatriation, a group of Cuban refugees rioted in Arkansas, where Clinton served as governor. The ensuing violence contributed significantly to his failure to be reelected later that year.

On the other hand, though, Clinton found himself under serious pressure from both Democrats and Republicans in Congress to continue to accept Cuban immigrants. Clinton knew that if he tightened the refugee policy, he could face accusations of being unsympathetic to the suffering of Cuban nationals, a criticism that would certainly undermine the credibility of U.S. democracy-promotion initiatives on the island.

Finally, on August 18, Clinton abandoned the historical policy, stating simply, "The people leaving Cuba will not be permitted to come to the United States." He bolstered the Coast Guard flotilla in the Gulf of Mexico, ordering them to detain unauthorized persons leaving Cuba for the United States and to

---

[16] Carol J. Doherty, "Influx of Cubans Forces Clinton to Halt Automatic Asylum," *CQ Weekly*, August 20, 1994.

hold them in U.S. military bases in Guantánamo Bay and Panama. By the end of September, more than 21,000 Cubans had been detained.

On September 1 Clinton and Castro agreed to hold negotiations over immigration policy. Castro sent President of the National Assembly Ricardo Alarcón, and Clinton sent Deputy Assistant Secretary of State Michael Skol. After nearly two weeks of deadlocks, the emissaries agreed that the United States would accept 20,000 Cuban refugees per year, but would not accede, as Alarcón insisted, to any changes in the embargo policy. The revision became known as the "wet foot–dry foot" policy, because it permitted Cubans who made it to shore to apply for residence, while it enforced the practice of detainment for those intercepted on the water.

These negotiations represented a significant step in U.S.-Cuban relations. Not since 1984 had the United States so drastically revised its operational policies toward Cuba. Alarcón's concessions in the deal (he had wanted the United States to accept an additional 130,000 refugees) reflected the severity of Cuba's crisis. The fact that the nation's still-crumbling economy and destabilized political system could not support its own population seemed to indicate that Cuba was even closer to dramatic change than Washington had originally supposed. Furthermore, many Cuban Americans considered the deal a great victory, although they had previously accused Clinton of "ignoring" the plight of suffering Cubans. If the island nation was actually in as depressed a state as it appeared, they judged, then keeping disaffected Cubans "trapped" inside Cuba might hasten the demise of the Castro regime.

The new immigration policy also demonstrated an important characteristic of U.S. policy toward Cuba in the post–Cold War era: many decision makers in Washington still thought of U.S.-Cuban relations as a "zero-sum game." Along these lines, although communism was now at the bottom of Clinton's list for policy considerations, his administration, as well as many members of Congress, viewed Skol's diplomatic success as a loss for the Castro regime and, necessarily, a win for the United States. If we contrast this way of thinking with, for instance, the motivations behind the United States' initial collaboration with Argentina during its economic crisis, U.S. intentions may seem somewhat anachronistic. U.S.-Cuban relations still stand as a glaring exception to the patterns of regional convergence we have seen in other cases. Although the United States often operated according to relatively "progressive" principles during the post–Cold War period, Cuba policy is a strong reminder that at times the United States continues to fall back on Cold War methods and the Big Stick in dealing with its Latin American neighbors.

BIG STICK REDUX: HELMS-BURTON

Seeing that the refugee crisis had pushed Castro's administration closer to the edge of losing control of Cuba, Congress looked to give the struggling dictator a final shove. In 1995 Senator Jesse Helms (R-NC) and Representative Dan Burton (R-IN) sponsored coordinating bills to stiffen the economic sanctions against Cuba. Finally submitted in 1996 as the Cuban Liberty and Solidarity Act, the legislation codified all existing sanctions against Cuba, placing power over Cuba policy in the hands of Congress instead of the President. It also authorized U.S. companies to file suits against Cuban nationals and international corporations who had purchased land expropriated during the nationalization of the 1960s. Finally, it reaffirmed the president's authority to deny aid to other countries trading with Cuba, as stipulated under the Cuban Democracy Act of 1992.

The new legislation included a somewhat contentious provision for humanitarian and democracy-focused aid in the event that Cuba instated a "democratically elected government ... that results from an expression of the self-determination of the Cuban people."[17] Such a government would not only have to comply with the requirements of free, fair, and internationally observed elections but would also have to make considerable progress in promoting full civil liberties, free public discourse, and basic human rights. More controversially, the new government would have to undertake measures to return U.S. property expropriated during the 1960s nationalization to its original owners. Furthermore, the bill stipulated that neither Fidel Castro nor his brother Raúl could be affiliated in any way with the new administration.

The Cuban Liberty and Solidarity Act codified U.S. expectations of Cuba's governmental system, defining democratic political structures in explicitly American terms. Notably, it was the first piece of legislation since the 1960s aimed at promoting political reorganization. Because of its overtly oppositional intent in undermining the Castro regime, many critics in the United States and abroad opposed it. At this stage, even President Clinton threatened to veto the bill because it contained provisions for sanctioning U.S. trading partners doing business with Cuba.

While the bill was being considered, however, Clinton received intense pressure from various fronts. Particularly influential was the Cuban expatriate community in the United States, whose most vocal policy advocacy

---

[17] *Cuban Liberty and Solidarity (LIBERTAD) Act of 1996*, HR 927, 104th Cong., 2nd sess., January 3, 1996.

group was the Miami-based Cuban-American National Foundation (CANF). Throughout the 1980s and into the 1990s, this group called for continuing or increasing pressure on the Castro regime, advocating what one scholar labeled the "squeeze school."[18] It argued that any easing of the embargo against Cuba would signify an acceptance of Castro's oppressive rule. Throughout the Cold War, the CANF occupied a highly important niche in the policy-making machine. Led by Jorge Mas Canosa, the CANF created organizations to study how Cuba's economic and political climate might change after Castro left office and contributed funds to several presidential and congressional campaigns, including U.S.$300,000 to Clinton's campaign in 1992.[19] A study by the Center for Public Integrity in 1997 found that, after receiving U.S.$120,000 from CANF, Robert Torricelli (D-NJ) made a complete turnaround in his position on Cuba policy and, as a result, proposed the 1992 Cuban Democracy Act.[20] Interestingly, several members of the CANF and its associated arms, which include the Cuban-American Foundation and Free Cuba Political Action Committee, were also accused of funding a series of bombings in Havana in 1997, threatening to harm advocates for a conciliatory Cuba policy, and attempting at least two assassinations against Castro during the 1990s.[21]

On the other hand, though, some Establishment critics have demonstrated that throughout the 1990s CANF was not as influential as it seemed. In fact, as longtime Cuba watcher David Reiff points out, CANF actually had little say in Clinton's decision to formulate a new Cuban immigration policy.[22] Additionally, the group met with resistance from a large body of Cuban Americans on specific policy aims; for example, 65 percent were in favor of a provision in the Helms-Burton legislation permitting medical supplies to be sent to Cuba. Many Cuban Americans were "bitterly critical" of Mas Canosa's control of the organization, and a number of smaller Cuban exile organizations opposed to CANF's hard-line stance, such as the Cuban Committee for Democracy and the Cuban Commission on Human Rights, began to curry political favor.[23] Their call for a policy of open

---

[18] Gillian Gunn, *Cuba in Transition: Options for U.S. Policy* (New York: Twentieth Century Fund, 1993), 55.

[19] Ann Louise Bardach, "Our Man in Miami," *New Republic*, October 3, 1994.

[20] Patrick J. Kiger, "Squeeze Play: The United States, Cuba and the Helms-Burton Act," Investigative Report (Washington, DC: Center for Public Integrity, 1997).

[21] Maxine Molyneux, "The Politics of the Cuban Diaspora in the United States," in *The United States and Latin America: The New Agenda*, ed. Victor Bulmer-Thomas and James Dunkerley (Cambridge, MA: Harvard University Press, 1999), 295.

[22] David Reiff, "From Exiles to Immigrants," *Foreign Affairs* 74, no. 4. (July–August 1995): 86.

[23] See ibid., 76–89.

communication with the Castro government in order to promote peaceful democratic transformation found open ears in Congress.

Other less "orthodox" domestic interest groups exerted considerable influence over the passage of the Helms-Burton Act. Farmers in the Midwest and in Florida, with the backing of several farm-state Republicans and Democrats in Congress, initiated a dialogue about relaxing the sanctions on agricultural products. To support their arguments for liberalizing trade policy, these politicians pointed to statistics that indicated a US$1 billion loss per year in agricultural trade. Additionally, many U.S. corporate interests claimed that the Helms-Burton legislation was outdated in demanding remunerations for American-owned commercial property that was confiscated in the 1960s. Oil companies Texaco and Shell, as well as several sugar companies, had long subsumed those losses and were now hoping to reestablish ties with Cuban businesses. These interests quickly became important to the Helms-Burton debate as Castro continued to open Cuba to international investment.

The pressure that the Clinton administration met regarding its Cuba policy was not only external. Many of Clinton's advisers engaged in repeated heated debates throughout the latter half of the 1990s. In 1995 Dennis Hays and Nancy Mason, director and deputy director, respectively, of the State Department's Cuba Bureau resigned in the face of conflict over the immigration crisis. In response, Clinton created a new administration position, special advisor on Cuban affairs, and appointed Richard Nuccio to the post. This represented a decisive turning point in Clinton's Cuba policy as Nuccio advocated a new agenda, which he called Track II and which complemented the embargo with bridge-building democracy promotion and economic development. As he explained in an interview with the *Washington Times* shortly after his nomination, the United States needed to respond "in carefully calibrated ways to positive developments" in Cuba.[24] Despite these changes, one administration official criticized Clinton's Cuba policy for "being made by the political staff, not the foreign-policy specialists."[25]

All this is to say that even within the Clinton administration there was considerable dispute about policy toward Cuba, reflecting the fact that "administration" often does not mean a single actor. Moreover, traditional

---

[24] Richard Nuccio, quoted in Soraya M. Marino, "U.S.-Cuban Relations during the Clinton Administration," *Latin American Perspectives* 29, no. 4 (July 2002): 54.
[25] Philip Brenner and Peter Kornbluh, "Clinton's Cuba Calculus," *NACLA Report on the Americas* 29 (September–October, 1995): 35.

U.S. attitudes toward Cuba were shifting in Washington, despite the U.S. government's continued hostility toward Castro in operation.

Early in 1996 a dramatic event ultimately pushed Clinton to endorse the Cuban Liberty and Solidarity Act. After Clinton instituted the "wet foot–dry foot" policy, a group of Cuban American exiles who called themselves "Brothers to the Rescue" started an illicit refugee smuggling operation. With a small fleet of personal aircraft and boats, the Brothers flew over the Gulf of Mexico and picked up Cubans attempting to cross the waterway to the United States secretly. Both Clinton and Castro had issued cease and desist orders, but the group continued operating. Then, on February 24, 1996, as two of the Brothers' planes flew over Cuban waters north of Havana, Castro ordered several MiG-29 fighter jets to shoot them down. The backlash from this attack on U.S. citizens – albeit criminal citizens – dissolved any of Clinton's previous objections to the Helms-Burton Act. He signed the bill on February 28 and followed it with the Declaration of a National Emergency, which suspended all travel to Cuba (with an exception for academic purposes). He and George W. Bush would continue to renew the declaration for the next decade.

Immediately after the passage of Helms-Burton, a debate erupted over the efficacy of long-term sanctions to promote democratic reform abroad. On the one hand, some critics of the new legislation believed that the renewed embargo would exact its most troubling revenge on the Cuban people and not on the Castro regime. Other critics supposed that the United States was suffering the greater loss, given that Cuba, whose economy had begun to turn around in 1996, was satisfying its domestic demand with other international trading partnerships. Economists estimated that free trade with Cuba could yield between U.S.$2.1 billion to U.S.$5 billion annually for the United States alone. In 1997 John S. Kavulich, president of the U.S.-Cuba Trade and Economic Council, stated before the House Ways and Means Committee:

Generally, if a country institutes a unilateral trade sanction, the government and citizens of the targeted country will design and implement short term, medium term, and long term commercial and economic strategies designed to minimize [its] impact. ... Over time, a unilateral trade sanction becomes an expected "cost of doing business" [for the government in the sanctioned country].[26]

In this line of reasoning, the unilateral embargo had long outlasted its useful life. Further critics of the Cuban Liberty and Solidarity Act capitalized on

---

[26] John S. Kavulich, President of the U.S.-Cuba Trade and Economic Council, Inc., "The Use and Effect of Unilateral Trade Sanctions." Testimony before the House Ways and Means Committee, 105th Cong., 1st sess., October 23, 1997.

this argument and asserted that the embargo was ineffective, unable to exert enough pressure on the Castro regime to effect any sort of substantive change. In fact, they claimed, the embargo was one of the key reasons that Castro was able to make it through the "special period" during most of the 1990s. The Castro administration had made great use of its propaganda machine to "externalize" the enemy, taking the focus off his own regime's failings and placing blame on the United States.

On the other hand, some of the more conservative analysts in the Establishment school maintained their view that the embargo was in fact protecting American interests. Though Cuba had encouraged foreign investment during the 1990s, it still ranked as one of the worst climates for commercial development in the world. They also pointed to Castro's persistent intractability on human rights. The Cuban military continued to arrest and kill political dissenters; after the *balsero* crisis of 1994, the Castro regime returned to punishing people who attempted to leave illegally. Furthermore, Havana showed no sign of moving toward a representative governmental system that met the demands of the Helms-Burton Act. As Representative Ileana Ros-Lehtinen (R-FL), a Cuban American and one of the most ardent supporters of a tough Cuba policy, insisted, "Attaching an economic cost to bad behavior acts as a disincentive. ... Sanctions express commitment to norms of international conduct, human rights, and non-aggression. Sanctions reinforce such norms by holding the aggressors accountable. Sanctions go beyond rhetoric and promises, and convert policy into action."[27] According to this camp, any relaxation of the embargo would represent an unmerited endorsement of Castro's refusal to work toward democratic progress, a goal that many in Washington – Democrat or Republican, Anti-imperialist or Establishment – could agree on.

Such contentious debates continued throughout Clinton's presidency. Pope John Paul's visit to Cuba in 1998, in which he criticized both the climate of repression in Cuba and the "oppressive economic measures – unjust and ethically unacceptable – imposed from outside the country," only added fuel to the fire. Similarly, the Elián González dilemma in 2000, which embroiled the American public in fierce dispute, forced the Clinton administration to reconsider both its immigration policy and the Helms-Burton Act. The Coast Guard picked up the eleven-year-old Cuban boy after the boat carrying his mother and several other escapees sank off the coast of Florida. His mother died in the accident, his father still lived in Cuba, and several of his relatives

---

[27] Representative Ileana Ros-Lehtinen, "The Use and Effect of Unilateral Trade Sanctions," Testimony before the House Ways and Means Committee, 105th Cong., 1st sess., October 23, 1997.

FIGURE 12.2. Protesters march in front of the Office of Interests of the United States in Havana, December 9, 2000, as U.S. government officials met with the father of Cuban Elián González to resolve the family's virulent international custody dispute. (Photo: Reuters/Raphael Perez.)

had settled in Miami. The family fought heatedly over who should have custody, leaving the U.S. government at a loss over whether the boy qualified for refugee status and could thus be permitted to stay in Miami. The boy's fate was held up for several months due to slow court proceedings; eventually, the U.S. Supreme Court ruled that the boy should return to Cuba with his father. The issue caused a deep rift in the Cuban American exile community and pitted hard-line lobby groups such as CANF against the U.S. government. Because the Gonzales case created such an uproar in the United States (few will forget the dramatic photographs of U.S. troops armed with automatic rifles bursting in to take the boy from his family home in Miami), it likely influenced Clinton's decision to endorse a congressional bill permitting food and medical products to be exported to Cuba as he left office (Figure 12.2).

GEORGE W. BUSH'S NEW INITIATIVE

As president, George W. Bush seemed to fall in line closely with his post–Cold War predecessors regarding Cuba policy. Despite growing bipartisan pressure in Congress to relax the embargo, in July 2001 Bush demonstrated his firm support of the Cuban Democracy and Cuban Liberty and Solidarity Acts by appointing Otto Reich, a staunch anti-Castroite, as the assistant secretary of state for Western Hemisphere Affairs. Almost a year later, Bush fully articulated his stance on Cuba under the New Initiative for Cuba, which would provide assistance to pro-democracy, nongovernmental organizations in Cuba, boost the operations of news (Anti-imperialist critics would say propaganda) broadcasts to the island, and fund scholarships for Cuban students to learn how to build democratic civil and social institutions. Bush outlined his administration's policy in a speech delivered to Cuban-Americans in Miami on the 100th anniversary of Cuban Independence, May 20, 2002:

The goal of the United States, the goal of our policy towards Cuba is not a permanent embargo on Cuba's economy; our goal is freedom for Cuba's people. Full normalization of relations with Cuba, diplomatic recognition, open trade, and a robust aid program will only – only – be possible when Cuba has a new Government that is fully democratic, when the rule of law is respected, and when the human rights of all Cubans are protected.[28]

With characteristic rhetorical flair, Bush declared, "Mr. Castro, once – just once – show that you're unafraid of a real election."[29] Bush's speech indicated that his intentions for Cuba policy were very similar to those that had developed during the previous Bush and Clinton administrations. However, the Initiative for a New Cuba represented a significant redirection of operational policy. While the initiative continued to uphold the economic embargo, it shifted away from what many in Washington perceived as a "stagnant" policy of embargo to more "proactive" measures for democratization such as funding anti-Castro dissidents.

The Bush administration crafted this new policy partially in response to changing dynamics in Cuba. As Castro entered his seventy-fifth year, Cuba's central planning committees turned dramatically away from the liberalizing policies of the 1990s, in an apparent attempt to preserve the socialist state in the event of Castro's departure from power. Earlier in 2002 Castro had passed a constitutional amendment through the National Assembly that declared the socialist system "irrevocable." His administration followed this by recentralizing Cuba's financial planning structures and banking system. Amazingly, Cuba seemed to be heading back to the 1980s, abandoning the market-style "structural adjustment" reforms that had led to economic recovery in 1996. The Bush administration hoped that the Initiative for a

---

[28] President George W. Bush, "Remarks on the 100th Anniversary of Cuban Independence in Miami, Florida," Office of the Press Secretary, May 20, 2007.
[29] Ibid.

New Cuba would "hook" the Cuban people at a time when political and economic change was already taking place on the island.

Over the next two years, though, Castro's government clamped down even further on Cuba's economy, reversing much of the liberalization that had come about during the "special period." In July 2003 Castro removed the U.S. dollar from the Cuban economy and replaced it with a new "convertible peso" system. He forced almost half of the nation's small number of private entrepreneurs back into public employment by revoking their licenses. The regime also restricted foreign investment by renationalizing property held by international companies operating in Cuba.

Castro also clamped down on civil society and human rights, most visibly by arresting political dissidents. In 2002 a group of activists working collectively as the Varela Project submitted a petition with more than 11,000 signatures requesting a public referendum to implement gradual and peaceful democratic procedures and free market reforms. Under the Cuban constitution, the Cuban people have the right to propose new legislation with a petition from 10,000 citizens. Yet Castro flatly rejected the proposal. In March 2003 the Cuban military arrested seventy-five political dissenters, journalists, opposition leaders, and activists and, on April 11, 2003, ordered the execution of three men who commandeered a ferry to escape to the United States. Moreover, Castro showed no sign of changing his position on economic and political reform.

Responding to these developments, in 2003 the Bush administration created the Commission for Assistance to a Free Cuba. Much like Track II under Clinton, the commission's aim was to coordinate with and finance pro-democracy activists and nongovernmental organizations to identify efficient ways to promote liberal reform. Yet Bush's initiative met with serious bipartisan resistance in Congress when a Government Accountability Office report on U.S. Democracy Assistance to Cuba revealed that the commission had failed to finish reviewing several aid recipients before distributing funds and had failed to supervise how the funds were spent.[30]

The administration also encountered substantial pressure from members of Congress who wanted to relax the economic embargo. During the fiscal year 2003 and 2004 appropriations deliberations in Congress, representatives Jim Davis (D-FL) and Jeff Flake (R-AZ) attempted to attach amendments ending the embargo and travel restrictions to the House Treasury-Transportation

---

[30] See United States Government Accountability Office, "Foreign Assistance: U.S. Democracy Assistance for Cuba Needs Better Management and Oversight," *GAO Report to Congressional Requesters*, 109th Cong., 2nd sess., GAO-07-147, Washington, DC, November 2006.

Bill; Senator Byron Dorgan (D-ND) included similar language in the Senate version. However, the provisions were eventually removed, as Bush threatened to veto the entire bill if it contained any language regarding Cuba.

Additionally, the Bush administration clashed with the American farm lobby and U.S. businesses on the embargo. These interests, seeking to secure their place in Cuba's expanding international trade markets, argued that the potential for U.S.-Cuban trade exceeded U.S.$3 billion. Nevertheless, Bush remained firm, restricting exports of food and medicine by implementing a "cash up-front" regulation on all commerce with Cuba.

Complicating the Bush administration's domestic concerns regarding Cuba were Castro's renewed attempts to reassert Cuba's status as a prominent foreign policy player. In a shift away from the isolationist policies of the "special period," Castro had begun to court Venezuela's President Hugo Chávez and China's President Hu Jintao in 1999. Through a series of exclusive trade agreements, Castro agreed to export agricultural products and "subsidized" medical care in return for cheap Venezuelan oil. The two leftist leaders recognized their countries' "mutual interest" and integrated their economies by reducing duties and tariffs and entering into joint ventures.

In 2001 Castro began to pursue relations with China, and the leaders of both nations signed a series of agreements formalizing their cooperation in technological development, education, and trade. In 2006 Cuba's biotechnology sales to China expanded by 90 percent. China also received nearly 50 percent of Cuba's nickel, whose price leapt 160 percent between 2005 and 2006. Sino-Cuban trade, which totaled U.S.$1.8 billion in 2006, contributed significantly to Cuba's economic growth in this period. In 2006 the Ministry of the Economy and Planning in Havana reported an astounding 12.5 percent GDP growth in 2006, but American and European estimates placed it at a more conservative level, between 7 percent and 9.3 percent.

Cuba's ties to the anti-American "Bolivarian" government in Caracas and the communist regime in Beijing placed a tremendous strain on U.S. policy, above all because these two governments had the ability to support Havana through trade and financial subsidies. The Bush administration's open relations with both countries, in addition to American dependence on Venezuelan oil, significantly diminished the credibility of the administration's stringent policy toward Cuba. How, critics asked, could the United States justify its harsh treatment of the Castro regime, while recognizing other, perhaps equally repressive regimes as legitimate? Furthermore, Cuba's robust economic growth during the Bush administration seemed to negate any impact that the embargo could have had on Cuba's economy. As one observer pointed out, the long-standing policy of economic isolation had become largely "symbolic."

TIME FOR A CHANGE?

Despite Bush's democracy promotion initiatives, the most prominent component of U.S. policy toward Cuba – the economic embargo – remained virtually unchanged at the end of the first decade of the twenty-first century. As Fidel Castro began to release his almost half-century grip on Cuban society, beginning with his illness and temporary transfer of power to Raúl Castro in 2007 and followed by his decision in February 2008 not to accept another five-year term as president, the social and political climate in Cuba remained stagnant, as did the United States' operational policies toward the island nation. This raises a number of challenging questions about the role of the United States in the Western Hemisphere. For one, why has the United States maintained such a singular focus on removing Castro, even in the postideological period? Is Washington genuinely concerned with the state of human rights, the rule of law, and free market economics in Cuba? Or has the attitude of mutual hostility between Havana and Washington become so institutionalized that nothing short of an end to not just Castro but also the ideology of "castroism" will remedy it? Given Bush's aggressive rhetorical response to Raúl Castro's presidency, it is difficult to say with any certainty.

Moreover, if we look back at the debates in Washington surrounding Cuba policy, we see that there was a serious lack of consensus on what, exactly, the United States should be doing, despite the continuity of policy in operation. Supporters and critics of the embargo did not adhere rigidly to party lines, and key policy decisions often came about because immediate domestic concerns pushed decision makers to support them. The relative uniformity of Cuba policy is not, in fact, the result of agreement in Washington. Rather, the actions that Washington ultimately undertakes are often the product of a tremendous diversity of interests.

13

The Haitian Dilemma

with Katie Hunter and Marshall Worsham

Almost a decade into the twenty-first century, Haiti's seemingly intractable economic and political turmoil makes it the most tragic country in the Western Hemisphere, as well as the object of some of the most perplexing U.S. policies since the Cold War. Successive presidential administrations in the United States have struggled to find effective policies that would help create a more stable political, economic, and social climate in Haiti so that Washington could "forget" again about this small island nation. Yet, given Haiti's countless internal issues, U.S. and Haitian interests have not converged to create a functional, mutually beneficial relationship. Indeed, to many American observers, Haiti's leadership has been exceptionally uncooperative. As Madeleine Albright, U.S. representative to the United Nations, expressed in a statement before the UN Security Council in August 1994, "We have provided every opportunity for the de facto leaders in Haiti to meet their obligations. But patience is an exhaustible commodity."[1]

In the post–Cold War era, George H. W. Bush, Bill Clinton, and George W. Bush all attempted to influence political developments in Haiti, especially as those events threatened to send thousands of Haitian refugees toward American shores. The three administrations' policies appeared to be driven by Woodrow Wilson's famously paternalistic quip that he wanted his Latin American neighbors to "elect good men." In an echo of Woodrow Wilson's "gunboat diplomacy" during the U.S. occupation of Haiti in 1915, in 1994, and again ten years later, the United States sent its military forces

---

[1] Madeleine K. Albright, "Shared Resolve in Restoring Democracy in Haiti," statement before the UN Security Council, August 15, 1994.

into Haiti in an attempt to restore order and promote democracy in a country that had known stability only as a dictatorship.

Some would view American interventions in Haiti as "postmodern" in the sense that they were motivated not by traditional Cold War security issues but rather by domestic and humanitarian concerns. With the end of the Cold War and the communist threat, these successive U.S. presidential administrations had the flexibility to enact policies aimed at prioritizing democratic and economic progress for Haiti, in what some would characterize as a "do-good" foreign policy. Similar to the United States' efforts in Somalia in 1992 and 1993, Haiti policy contained a strong humanitarian component on both the rhetorical and intentional levels.

Still, U.S. policy in Haiti has been haunted by the shadow of the Cold War. For example, critics accused the George W. Bush administration of using covert actions to undermine the authority of Haiti's President Aristide, which led to his ouster in 2004. For these critics, there was nothing "postmodern" about the Bush administration's policies in Haiti. Rather, its policies simply added a new twist to the Big Stick.

Yet, even if Washington wanted to "do good," that did not mean that it succeeded. In fact, Haiti is a case study of tragic failure in well-intentioned foreign policy. Despite overwhelming American military power and massive economic aid, the United States was unable to "fix Haiti" through nation building. Moreover, the disappointments in Haiti seem to indicate that, though the United States wields a great deal of power in relation to its neighbors, its influence may be quite tenuous. In this case, Washington's massive and sustained effort to build democracy in Haiti has failed miserably.

Post–Cold War U.S. policy toward Haiti has been riddled with controversy, particularly with regard to immigration and Washington's relationship with the divisive Haitian leader Jean Bertrand Aristide. In the 1990s Haiti's ongoing refugee crisis elicited a litigious American public response, which in turn influenced the aggressive policy decisions made by the Bush and Clinton administrations. Some historians believe that Washington paid attention to Haiti in the post–Cold War era only because of how much influence it had on domestic politics. In fact, in the height of the refugee conflict, the actual conditions of the Haitian people were often subordinated to a domestic political game, in which liberal and conservative politicians and activists used Haiti's grim reality to score political points against each other. Scholar Robert Pastor's "whirlpool" metaphor again applies, where in the post–Cold War era the United States largely ignores its Latin American neighbors until a crisis erupts to "suck Washington in."

Haiti presents a fascinating case because it defies the typical pattern of political criticism. Contemporary observers and historians, particularly those on the left or in the Anti-imperialist camp, tend to censure American military interventions in the hemisphere, arguing that such operations are intended to make these countries safe for U.S. business and usually end up impeding democracy. Yet, during the interventions in Haiti in 1994 and 2004, many on the left believed that even *more* military involvement, not less, might have been the solution.

ANOTHER "SOB"

Haiti made its first appearance in the American political consciousness in 1915, when a turbulent domestic conflict led to the gruesome beheading of President Jean Vilbrun Guillaume Sam. When a similar situation developed across the border in the Dominican Republic, President Woodrow Wilson decided to take action, ordering American forces to occupy Haiti. U.S. forces remained for nineteen years, during which time they influenced elections, drafted a new constitution, and assumed nearly total control of the Haitian government. It was democratization by force, Wilson's own style of "gunboat diplomacy."

After U.S. forces departed, Haiti continued to be plagued by political instability, particularly as a result of the deep social and economic divisions that existed between Haiti's small group of wealthy mulatto elites and its poor, black majority. American know-how on elections and economic improvement was unable to uproot these entrenched structures within Haiti's political and economic institutions. In fact, in the years following the American occupation, the country saw further stratification of these groups, as a series of blatantly fraudulent elections gave rise to a dynasty of authoritarian presidents from the privileged class.

In 1957 François Duvalier emerged from the turmoil as the Haitian president. A rural black doctor, he won a sizable though contested majority in that year's elections. "Papa Doc" Duvalier, however, soon stood as the epitome of terror and tyranny in Haiti. His private militia, the Tonton Macoutes, brutally terrorized all political opponents and added one of the most virulent chapters to the nation's already violent history.

By 1965 Washington had started to regard Papa Doc's militant "presidency" as a relatively stable force in the hemisphere, which otherwise seemed constantly in danger of the "invasion" of communist ideologies. Referring to Duvalier's counterpart in the Dominican Republic, Rafael Trujillo, Secretary of State Cordell Hull said, "He may be a son of a bitch, but he's our son of a bitch."[2] Like Trujillo, Duvalier was one of Washington's Cold War "SOBs," those right-wing Latin American leaders who were reliably and predictably anticommunist. Duvalier leveraged his favored position to extract economic aid from the United States, threatening to run to Cuba – and, by association, the Soviet Union – if Washington failed to comply with his requests. Duvalier remained in control until his death in 1971, at which time his despotic rule passed to his son Jean-Claude. "Baby Doc" Duvalier upheld his father's tradition of tyranny, and the United States continued to provide aid, further ignoring the reality of Haiti's deteriorating domestic conditions.

Ultimately, though, a popular and violent reaction against Duvalier's attempt to make himself "President for Life" in February 1986 forced the Reagan administration to take heed. As Baby Doc Duvalier fled the island nation, it became obvious, as it had with Trujillo, that the United States' unapologetic support of the Duvalier regime had undermined its goals for democracy in the region. The Duvaliers' policy of systematic repression, long endured by Haiti's poor, had created a climate of instability that threatened to invite communism into its open arms.

Now intent on "saving" Haiti at this critical moment, Reagan sent a delegation led by Lieutenant General Henry Namphy to assist the interim National Council of Government (CNG) in strengthening democratic institutions and drafting a constitution. Easy peace seemed forthcoming, but neither Reagan nor the CNG had fully anticipated the impact of Duvalierism's legacy on Haiti's society and politics. As one observer explained,

The government in Haiti under the Duvaliers regime became a patrimonial system that functioned on a patronage and spoils basis. The government recruited *Tonton Macoutes* (paramilitary thugs) to maintain political control and resorted to extortion to meet financial needs. Those who were not part of the Duvaliers clique were left to fend for themselves. Under Jean Claude Duvalier, corruption was honed to perfection, and the greed of the elites was more evident.[3]

Duvalierism, while fattening friends and impoverishing the rest of the population, created an immense gap between the wealthy and poor, the consequences of which became evident in 1987 when democratic elections were interrupted by a massacre of dozens of voters. Ex-Duvalierist military officials led the attacks against political opponents, urged on by prominent Haitians who had thrived under Duvalier. The situation initiated a four-year

---

[2] Robert D. Crassweller, *Trujillo: The Life and Times of a Caribbean Dictator* (New York: Macmillan, 1966), 213.

[3] Jean Pierre Jean-Marie, *U.S. Policy toward Haiti, 1991–1994* (Ann Arbor, MI: ProQuest Information and Learnings, 2005), 27.

period of instability and violence, in which a pattern of democratic elections and violent countercoups ushered in five different governments.

HAITI'S HISTORIC ELECTION

After nearly two centuries of domestic turmoil and violently repressive rule – for which, no matter its intentions, the United States was partly responsible – Haiti saw a glimmer of democratic hope in the immediate post–Cold War era. Unlike the rigged elections and unconstitutional Duvalier referenda of years past, the elections of December 16, 1990, actually provided the Haitian people a chance to choose a new leader. By the end of the week, an approximate 68 percent majority of voters had picked Roman Catholic priest Jean Bertrand Aristide to be their next president, in what an international team of observers deemed an "open, fair and peaceful election."[4]

The 1990 election, financed by millions of dollars in aid, the majority of it supplied by the United States, marked a major change in U.S. policy toward Haiti. After years of supporting the tyrannical Duvaliers and the brief succession of military dictatorships that had ruled in their wake, the Bush administration came out in strong support of Haiti's endeavor at democratic progress. No longer preoccupied with the threat of communism, the United States appeared to "put its money where its mouth was," reinforcing its rhetorical policy of democracy promotion in the region by funding the country's first real democratic election. Yet critics questioned the use of U.S. funds, particularly the Bush administration's financing of candidate Marc Bazin. Many critics wondered how the United States could claim to support hemispheric democracy while using its sizable economic influence to secure an electoral outcome in line with its own interests.

Others, however, wondered if the Bush administration would accept Aristide's presidency at all. Many conservatives in Washington had been concerned about a victory for Aristide, whom they feared would incite further unrest with his fervent promises to purge Haiti's government of Duvalierists and redistribute the wealth of the country's elite to its 6 million impoverished black citizens.

As the polls cleared, the Bush administration faced the challenge of aligning its rhetorical, intentional, and operational policy aims. Bush administration officials often remained vague or tight-lipped about the fiery

---

[4] Robert Glass, "Duvalier Legacy Hangs over Haiti's New Democracy," Associated Press, December 19, 1990.

FIGURE 13.1. President of Haiti Jean-Bertrand Aristide gestures as he addresses the nation during a speech at the National Palace in Port-au-Prince, Haiti, 1995. (Photo: Marcelo Salinas.)

Aristide. For instance, when asked about the priest, Ambassador Alvin Adams Jr. claimed "our interest is in the process, not the outcome" of the elections.[5] Rhetorically, the administration supported the ideal of democracy, independent of specific candidates. Operationally, however, it had placed a high value in candidate Marc Bazin and his Movement for the Installation of Democracy. Ultimately, though, the administration stuck by its rhetorical position when the election results were announced, openly endorsing Aristide as the clear winner (Figure 13.1).

It soon became apparent that, whatever else he might be, Aristide was far from a saint. Reports surfaced that he was inciting his supporters to "necklace" their political opponents by placing flaming automobile tires over their heads, a shocking practice that originated during the South African apartheid. Thus, while Aristide had fought courageously for the progress of democracy in Haiti, he himself was becoming yet another Haitian leader with "authoritarian tendencies," a reality that added to the complexity of U.S. policies.

Bernard Aronson, Bush's assistant secretary of state for inter-American affairs, promised that the United States would "extend political and financial

[5] Pamela Constable, "For the US, No Choice but Optimism after Haiti Vote," *Boston Globe*, December 23, 1990.

support" to Aristide's government upon his inauguration in early February.[6] Things looked ominous well before then, however, when a former Duvalier official named Roger Lafontant tried to seize the presidential palace from the interim government. Proclaiming, "I'll never deny that I'm a Duvalierist," Lafontant soon faced a mob of Aristide's supporters, who flooded the streets and demanded the help of the Haitian army.[7] Haitian soldiers responded to the call by arresting Lafontant.

This promising sign seemed to indicate two positive changes in Haiti: first, that the army's once questionable loyalty to Aristide was now sound; and, second, that Duvalierism's control in Haiti had finally come to an end. Washington quickly denounced the coup attempt, and Aristide's inauguration went forth as scheduled. U.S. concerns about Aristide gradually dissipated after his first few months in office, during which time the priest toned down his anticapitalist, anti-Western rhetoric in favor of a more conciliatory approach toward foreign nations (and foreign aid).

One sign of Aristide's new attitude was the warm working relationship he pursued with U.S. ambassador Alvin Adams Jr., who said of the Haitian president, "He has gotten off to a very credible start. The process is well begun."[8] Aristide expressed similar optimism for Haiti at a UN conference in late September: "Democracy has won out for good," he said. "The roots are growing stronger and stronger."[9]

THE CEDRAS COUP: WHAT TO DO?

Adams and Aristide couldn't have been more wrong in their predictions. While his popularity among certain U.S. officials might have been soaring, Aristide could not escape the intense opposition of the Haitian elite and military. To them, his quasi-socialist agenda of industrial nationalization, land reform, and redistribution of wealth was downright hostile. On September 30 mutinies that had started at an army base and police station the previous night erupted into an all-out rampage in downtown Port-au-Prince. Rebellious soldiers seized the presidential palace, captured Aristide, and held him at army

---

[6] Howard French, "New Leader of Haitians Offers U.S. a Wary Hand," *New York Times*, December 23, 1990.

[7] Michael Norton, "Lafontant Was Prominent in Duvalier Dictatorship," Associated Press, January 7, 1991.

[8] Howard French, "After Six Months of Changes, Haiti Is Surprised by Its Leader's Moderation," special to the *New York Times*, August 4, 1991, sec. 1, pt. 1, 16.

[9] Michael Norton, "Aristide Believed Democracy Had Taken Root in Haiti," Associated Press, October 1, 1991.

headquarters until Venezuelan, French, and U.S. officials could negotiate to save his life. Ambassador Adams escorted Aristide to the airport, where the deposed president boarded the plane that would take him into exile.

President Bush quickly condemned the coup. Calling for "an immediate halt to violence," he demanded a "restoration" of Aristide and the "democracy" that the United States had helped establish with its contributions to the election.[10] State Department officials announced the suspension of all U.S. military and economic aid allotted to Haiti unless the new military junta, led by Aristide's former military commander in chief General Raoul Cedras, agreed to step down.

The crisis in Haiti led to hemispheric convergence in that both the United States and Latin American governments agreed that Haiti's crisis needed to be addressed. In June 1991 the OAS had passed the landmark Santiago Resolution, which codified the member nations' commitment to supporting democracy in the hemisphere. Calling for regional unity in "defense of hemispheric democracy," the Santiago Resolution mandated an emergency OAS meeting to decide on a coordinated multilateral response in the event of a coup in the region. On October 8, 1991, the OAS Permanent Council convened and, after a series of failed negotiations with the Cedras regime, instated an embargo against Haiti and a freeze on its assets. To many observers, this was a critical effort at hemispheric solidarity. Had it succeeded, it may have provided substantive proof that the region had entered an era of unity in its interests and goals.

Yet, despite good intentions, President Bush met with harsh criticism that the embargo only harmed already impoverished Haitians. As the economic situation worsened and the military gave no sign of stepping down, some began asking about the possibility of using U.S. military force to restore democracy. While a few administration officials mentioned the potential for such action to the press, it never appeared to receive serious consideration. The Bush administration seemed convinced that the embargo would succeed.

THE REFUGEE QUESTION

In the months after Aristide's ouster, driven by the economic and political chaos in their country, thousands of Haitians set out on rickety rafts in order to seek refuge in the United States. The Bush administration responded to this growing crisis by maintaining the Reagan administration's policy of rescuing

---

[10] George Gedda, "U.S. Suspends Aid to Haiti, Demands Return of Elected Government," Associated Press, October 1, 1991.

Haitians on the high seas and then taking them to the U.S. naval base on Cuba's Guantánamo Bay in order to have their refugee status determined. Following Bush's May 24 Kennebunkport Order, U.S. Coast Guard vessels began intercepting hundreds of refugees. President Bush even sent 500 Marines to Cuba in anticipation of the need for screenings.

In the months immediately following, it became clear that the Coast Guard and the facilities at Guantánamo were not equipped to handle thousands of asylum seekers. Bush already faced the wrath of many human rights groups and members of Congress like Representative Charles Rangel (D-NY), who called the policy "racist and discriminatory."[11] These critics argued that the administration was keeping Haitians out because they were black and poor, an especially unfair policy in light of the United States' automatic acceptance of political refugees from nearby Cuba. Rangel's remarks were indicative of a bitter debate on Haiti policy that continues to this day. Stated simply, liberal critics, many of whom would fall into the Anti-imperialist school, have accused successive administrations of either not doing enough to help Haiti's embattled leader of the poor (i.e., Aristide) or even actively working to conspire against Aristide and his base of supporters.

Bush continued to defend himself against such criticism, which only increased after he began sending some of the intercepted Haitians back to their homeland from Guantánamo Bay. Claiming that the policy was intended to keep Haitians from making the extremely dangerous sea voyage, President Bush received judicial backing in January 1992 when the Supreme Court overruled a court injunction from November that held refugee repatriation to be unlawful. As refugees kept coming, Bush again changed his policy. In May he announced that any intercepted Haitians would immediately be sent back to Haiti (Figure 13.2).

By this time, more than 37,000 Haitians had tried the leave their country. The United States sent back nearly two-thirds of them under the policy, provoking further outrage among more liberal factions of Congress and the public. Claiming that U.S. policy was both heartless and racist, protesters, including former tennis star Arthur Ashe, staged a rally outside the White House in September, urging the president at least to grant temporary asylum to the refugees.

Bush knew that allowing thousands of Haitian refugees to flood America's shores would not be a popular or economically viable solution to Haiti's democracy dilemma, no matter how bad the humanitarian crisis had become. He also hoped that sending back the refugees would cause hardships for the

[11] Charles Rangel, in a televised interview with *CNN Crossfire*, transcript #583, May 29, 1992.

FIGURE 13.2. Haitian migrants rescued in the Windward Pass, a stretch of ocean northwest of Haiti where thousands of boat people began the 600-mile (970-kilometer) journey to Florida, sit on the deck of the U.S. Coast Guard's 210-foot Medium Endurance Cutter *Valiant*. (Photo: Reuters/Ho New.)

Cedras junta, which he believed might buckle under the pressure of a deprived and desperate population. In the face of both the embargo and refugee policy, however, Cedras still had not budged. Yet, Bush would not have to face Haiti's woes much longer because of his electoral defeat that November.

BILL CLINTON: OVERCOMING THE SOMALIA SYNDROME

Sworn in almost sixteen months after Aristide's ouster, President Clinton entered the Oval Office to growing concern over the Haitian crisis. The junta showed little sign of backing down, and the number of those fleeing Haiti were rising again. While he endorsed the embargo, Clinton repeatedly denounced the Bush administration's "cruel policy" of refugee repatriation. He pledged to change it once he took office.

But President Clinton broke his promise mere days after his inauguration. He had been informed in early January of a raft construction project that would allow more than 100,000 Haitians to cross the Gulf. Faced with the potential influx of thousands of Haitians, Clinton announced on January 14, 1993, that Bush's repatriation policy would remain in effect until further notice. He explained, "I think this is a policy for the moment. I still believe that people who leave their country, come into ours, are entitled to some refugee hearing before being summarily turned back."[12] Clinton indicated a hope that repatriation would be temporary and that a quick return to political stability in Haiti would relieve the immigration problem. But the refugees kept coming, and the Coast Guard continued to intercept and turn back tens of thousands of Haitians.

Criticized for his politically expedient decision, Clinton lost the trust of many of his former supporters on Haiti policy, including several members of the Congressional Black Caucus. Clinton learned early that, at least politically speaking, there were no easy solutions to the Haitian dilemma.

In order to shore up support and to quell opponents' criticism of his lack of foreign policy command, Clinton pledged to commit U.S. resources to restoring Haiti's democracy and its deposed president. At a news conference early in the year, the president stated that "we want to step up dramatically the pace of negotiations to restore President Aristide" and that the "United States is committed strongly to a much more aggressive effort to ... over the long run, work with the people of Haiti to restore conditions of economic prosperity."[13]

Unsurprisingly, Aristide balked at any terms that would allow military leaders to govern alongside him upon his return to Haiti. Ever since his ouster, the former president had been adamant about his restoration as Haiti's sole leader. Backed by activism centers like TransAfrica, a human rights and justice organization that promotes political and social equality for Africans and people of African ethnicity, as well as by several members of the Congressional Black Caucus, Aristide demanded that Clinton set and adhere to a date for his return.

Despite the rhetoric on the campaign trail that suggested he would pursue a radical new policy toward Haiti, President Bill Clinton continued the Bush administration's bifurcated approach toward the junta in hopes that this "resignation to change" would soon lead to the return of democracy. In early June, Clinton announced stiffer sanctions against Haiti, including a freeze on all U.S. assets of those who had done business with the junta and a successful push for a worldwide, UN-imposed embargo against the country.

[12] Holly Idelson, "Supreme Court: Administration Holds to Policy of Haitian Repatriation," *CQ Weekly*, February 27, 1993, 462.
[13] President William Clinton and Haitian President Jean-Bertrand Aristide, "U.S. Support for Democracy in Haiti: News Conferences," March 16, 1993, U.S. State Department Dispatch, March 22, 1993, 12.

Wielding these punitive policies as "sticks," the administration balanced them with the "carrot" of diplomatic immunity for Haiti's illegitimate leaders if they decided to step down peacefully. Finally, in response, General Cedras announced he was ready to negotiate for his junta's removal and Aristide's return.

The Governor's Island Accords

On July 4, 1993, President Clinton triumphantly announced that Aristide and members of the junta had reached an agreement called the Governor's Island Accords. During a separate meeting, the deposed president and the junta members negotiated the agreement, which called for Cedras's resignation, amnesty for all participants in the illegitimate government, and an end to the UN's multilateral embargo. Aristide was to nominate a candidate for the post of prime minister, which would be filled before his return. Most notably, it set a date – October 30, 1994 – for the president's homecoming.

While outside supporters called the agreement a foreign policy success, critics cautioned against premature victory celebrations. They claimed the Haitian military might shake up Aristide's supporters before the return date or disallow his return. Indeed, reports of increased harassment leading up to the date forewarned what was to come. In one incident, members of the reemerging Tonton Macoutes reportedly dragged a prominent Aristide backer from a church service and assassinated him outside on the street.

But Aristide, determined to return, upheld his part of the agreement and nominated a candidate for prime minister in late July. The UN lifted the embargo soon after. Clinton had pledged U.S.$47.5 million in U.S. aid to Haiti as well as several hundred peacekeeping troops.[14] With signs pointing in every direction, the American president could only wring his hands in anticipation. Only time would tell if the junta would uphold its end of the bargain.

The *Harlan County* Affair

President Clinton would not be wringing his hands much longer. In fact, like millions of other Americans, he would be shaking his head in disbelief on October 3, when word came that eighteen American soldiers in Somalia had been killed in a rebel ambush. Americans stared in horror at their television screens at scenes of Somalis dragging a U.S. soldier's naked body through the streets. For the Clinton administration, Haiti was far from mind.

---

[14] Secretary of State Warren Christopher, "Shaping a New World: U.S. and Brazilian Leadership in a Democratic, Prosperous Hemisphere," U.S. Department of State Dispatch, March 4, 1996.

About a week later, however, Haiti reappeared on the radar screen. To prepare for the transition to democracy and to demonstrate to the junta that the United States was serious, Clinton ordered the U.S.S. *Harlan County* to Haitian shores. Aboard the ship were 200 lightly armed American soldiers, sent to precede the UN force that would later come to train the country's army.

On October 11 the ship approached Port-au-Prince, only to find a Cuban tanker in the berth where it was supposed to dock. On shore, a violent mob of anti-Aristide, neo-Duvalierist protestors paraded around the port. Brandishing sticks, pistols, and machetes, the mob chanted anti-American slogans at the ship. The soldiers aboard the *Harlan County* waited all day for orders, while listening to Haitians' cries of "Somalia! Somalia!" in the distance. The following day, the White House ordered a retreat as it was reluctant to let the conflict escalate. To put it mildly, the decision to withdraw, reached by Clinton and the members of his National Security Council, was not well received by the international community. UN and OAS officials publicly denounced the retreat, while members of Congress lambasted Clinton for doing "serious damage" to U.S. foreign policy credibility.

The retreat had played in the junta's favor; with Cedras reinvigorated, the situation in Haiti worsened steadily. Just days later, amid other incidents of violence, Aristide's newly appointed minister of justice was gunned down in the streets of Port-au-Prince. Fearful of similar reprisals, the UN and OAS evacuated all human rights observers on the island. And, in defiance of the Clinton administration, Aristide, and the international community, the junta let the October 30 deadline come and go. More than ever, the Cedras regime seemed resolved to tighten its grip on Haiti.

Considering the Options

Much of the criticism directed at U.S. involvement in Haiti was reduced to the *Harlan County* affair, which many called a "foreign policy disaster." Critics claimed that the Clinton administration, by turning U.S. policy into "empty threats," could no longer be counted on to uphold the United States' commitment to hemispheric democracy. Many also cited the *Harlan County* debacle as proof of the fruitlessness of attempts to compromise with an illegitimate authoritarian regime. Yet, administration officials maintained that, while it was a mistake, overall the "disaster" had little impact on the progress of democracy in Haiti.[15]

---

[15] Richard Feinberg (Special Assistant for Inter-American Affairs to President Clinton, 1993–6), in a telephone interview with the author, March 16, 2007.

Nevertheless, these criticisms came as a setback to the Clinton administration, given the apparent progress that had been made following the
Santiago Resolution. In addition, Congress was beginning to question the
effectiveness of the multilateral initiatives in Haiti. In a February 9, 1994,
statement to the House Subcommittee on Western Affairs, Representative
John L. Mica (R-FL) pointed to statistics indicating that UN sanctions were
"doubling infant mortality" and that "little of the aid being sent to Haiti to
help the poor is getting through."[16] Though the embargo was designed to
punish the economic elite and Cedras's supporters, many argued that it was
in fact taking a much greater toll on the poor.[17]

Clinton also faced constant protest over the continued policy of Haitian
refugee repatriation. The refugees crossed the Caribbean in droves, propelled
by what several human rights groups cited as some of the worst violence on
record in the country. One of the military's methods of repression, reportedly
used against suspected Aristide sympathizers, was "chopping off their faces
with a machete."[18]

President Clinton had to recalibrate his approach to Haiti's crisis in light
of the junta's strengthened grip on Haiti and rampant criticism at home.
Clinton finally changed the refugee policy to allow hearings for those caught
on the high seas after Randall Robinson, the director of TransAfrica, went
on a twenty-seven-day hunger strike in protest – a publicity move that
dancer Katherine Dunham had previously used on the Bush administration.
Clinton also acknowledged his government's failings in Haiti, publicly
stating that "we ought to change our policy; it hasn't worked."[19] Despite
his earlier pledges to Haiti, Clinton's actions thus far had effected little
more change than those of his predecessor.

The Clinton Intervention

Clearly fed up, President Clinton decided it was time to risk testing Cedras's
dramatic threat: "I am the pin in Haiti's hand grenade – if pulled an explosion
will occur." In July the U.S. military began training exercises off the coast of
the Bahamas. Observers claimed that the practice operations resembled what

[16] Gideon Rose, "Haiti," in *Economic Sanctions and American Diplomacy*, ed. Richard
   N. Haass (New York: Council on Foreign Relations, 1998), 66.
[17] "Haiti: Official Says Poor Are Getting Aid," *CQ Weekly*, February 12, 1993, 342.
[18] Tom Post, Spencer Reiss, Peter Katel, Karen Breslau and John Berry, "Getting Ready,"
   Newsweek (July 25, 1994): 16–18.
[19] Elaine Sciolino, "Failure on Haiti: How U.S. Hopes Faded," special report to the *New York
   Times*, April 29, 1994, sec. A, 1.

might happen in the case of an invasion of a "small Caribbean island." The prospect of military action seemed further confirmed with the UN ratification of Resolution 940, which called on member nations to form a U.S.-led multinational force and "use all means necessary to restore Aristide."[20] All the signs pointed toward an imminent American invasion.

In an address to the nation on September 14, 1994, Clinton told the junta leader, "Your time is up."[21] Claiming that the invasion, later known as Operation Restore Democracy, would be "limited and specific," he informed the American public that 20,000 combat troops would be sent in order to oust the junta and halt the violence.[22] These troops, he claimed, would be replaced by a UN peacekeeping force, which would help establish a stable government in Haiti to pave the way for Aristide's return.

In a last-ditch effort to convince the junta to leave peacefully, Clinton sent a team led by former president Jimmy Carter, Democratic senator Sam Nunn, and former chairman of the Joint Chiefs of Staff Colin Powell to Haiti to deal with Cedras one final time. They had forty-eight hours to negotiate with the junta leader over terms of his departure.

The team gave Cedras two options: he could either leave without a fight or lead his troops against what Powell listed to him across the negotiating table – "two carriers, two and a half infantry divisions, 20,000 troops, helicopter gunships, tanks, artillery."[23] Knowing that his ragtag army would stand little chance against such force, Cedras agreed at the last moment to hand the presidency back to Aristide and to leave the country by October 15. Cedras actually kept his word and resigned on October 10. A triumphant Aristide returned home five days later.

Ironically, it was the generally dovish, Democratic president who came close to ordering an armed military intervention into Haiti. While Clinton gradually became less of a stranger to military interventions during his tenure, the atrocities in Somalia and the ensuing *Harlan County* affair further complicated the Haiti crisis for the president and sidetracked any further moves at direct intervention on the island. The Clinton administration recovered from these "Vietnam and Somalia syndromes" only when it became clear that all other approaches, including the embargoes and asset freezes, had failed.

---

[20] Jean-Marie, *U.S. Policy toward Haiti, 1991–1994*, 159.
[21] Evan Thomas, John Barry, Douglas Waller, Eleanor Clift, Bob Cohn, Karen Breslau and Peter Katel, "Here We Go Again," *Newsweek* (September 26, 1994): 22–24.
[22] "Excerpts of Clinton's Speech on Haiti," Agence France-Presse (September 16, 1994).
[23] Colin Powell with Joseph E. Persico, *My American Journey* (New York: Random House, 1996), 600.

Yet, even this decision did not go uncontested. Clinton's critics on Haiti were not just liberal Democrats; in fact, certain Republicans in Congress, including Senate Minority Leader Bob Dole (R-KS) and Senator Jesse Helms (R-NC), voiced their opposition to sending troops to Haiti. Exhausted by the situation in Somalia and wary to grant Clinton the power to deploy troops elsewhere, both senators sponsored unsuccessful budget amendments to prohibit military action in Haiti unless authorized in advance by Congress.

Now the Hard Part: Nation Building

President Clinton worked to uphold the stated goals of the mission, vowing to withdraw all U.S. combat troops that had landed with the multinational force by the end of February 1996.[24] But in order to ensure that Haiti was stable enough for its troops to leave, the U.S. government had to address the crucial task of training Haiti's police forces, still rife with corrupted elements of the Cedras regime.

The Clinton administration funded programs to hire new Haitian recruits and trained many of them on U.S. soil, sending them back to Haiti in hopes that they would stabilize the domestic situation enough for UN peacekeepers to take over. By September 1995, just 2,660 of the original 20,000 U.S. combat troops remained, and by March of the next year, that number had dropped to around 400. That same month, UN mission troops, with mainly humanitarian operations, took over from the multinational force.

Wary of a "slippery slope" situation that could lead to a protracted military occupation, the Clinton administration ordered the Pentagon to remove its "boots on the ground" in Haiti quickly after the invasion. Yet, the United States still maintained a very significant force of engineers, peacekeeping troops, and citizens assisting with humanitarian efforts.

Despite the relative peace following the invasion, neither Haiti's political nor security front looked any better. In the parliamentary elections of June 1995, Aristide's Lavalas Party received an overwhelming majority of the vote. Robert Pastor, a former Carter administration official and an electoral observer from the Carter Center, called the elections "the most technically disastrous" of any he had ever witnessed.[25] In many areas, eligible citizens were kept from voting, and many ballots were burned. Aside from Lavalas, all party coalitions boycotted the results, and U.S. officials urged the

---

[24] Robert I. Rotberg, "Clinton Was Right," *Foreign Policy* 102 (Spring 1996): 135–41.
[25] Michael Norton, "Losing Party Hails Carter Center Report Condemning Haiti Election Count," Associated Press, July 21, 1995.

government to schedule another election round. As Clinton officials quickly realized, intervening in Haiti was easy when compared to the task of building a stable democracy and economy.

December 1995's presidential elections were tainted, although not by blatant corruption and electoral fraud. Many Haitians called them a sham because they considered the winner, René Préval, to be Aristide's hand-picked successor. An agronomist by trade and Aristide's premier before the coup, Préval was criticized for being controlled by the newly returned president, whose term limit was already nearing expiration. Préval won with an astonishing 88 percent of the vote out of a field of fourteen candidates. However, a later report indicated that only 15 percent of voters showed up at the polls.[26] This served to undermine Clinton's claim that Haiti had just held "impressive" democratic elections.

For its part, the Clinton administration continued to keep a watchful eye on Haiti, sending envoys such as the newly appointed secretary of state Madeline Albright to facilitate compromise between Préval and opposition legislators at crucial moments. Within the administration, a senior official under Clinton reflected, "There was no question in anybody's mind that the Clinton administration was absolutely committed to restoring democracy in Haiti."[27]

But in Washington, opinion remained divided, especially in Congress, as to how the United States should continue to support the country. After learning of the reports of fraud and ballot tainting from Haiti's 1995 parliamentary elections, several Republican legislators – many of whom had never trusted Aristide – demanded that Clinton withhold aid to the nation.[28] The Republican majority in Congress also battled the president over aid to Haiti, successfully cutting funds for the police training program later that year after it received word that squad members had carried out politically motivated assassinations.

The United States spent more than U.S.$550 million to address these issues in Haiti in the last half of the 1990s. But money, goods, and humanitarian workers alone simply were not enough to address the multitude and severity of Haiti's crises. Without a working parliament, the country could not even pass a budget resolution to coordinate aid-funded expenditures. Préval's slowness to implement certain structural reforms caused many multinational lenders and investors to back out on financial commitments to the country.

---

[26] "Clinton Lauds Free Haitian Polls," Agence France-Presse, December 26, 1995.
[27] Feinberg, interview, March 16, 2007.
[28] "Haiti, U.S. Republicans Renew Campaign against Aristide," *IPS*, June 29, 1995.

Still reeling from the effects of the embargoes, Haiti's economy remained in shambles, further dashing many Haitians' hopes for the better future Aristide had once promised them so eloquently. Perhaps worst of all, Haiti's citizens seemed to have lost faith in the democratic process. Fraudulent and postponed elections, coupled with the lack of a trustworthy judiciary and police force, only made the already dire economic and social situation worse.[29]

The Clinton administration's worst fears were confirmed. Many critics argued that administration officials, in their haste to extract American troops, had failed to facilitate a stable enough environment for fair, nonviolent political processes to take place. Some claimed that it was impossible to expect democracy to take root so quickly in a nation where it had never existed in the first place. Following the withdrawal, Haiti quickly destabilized, as its police forces became increasingly corrupt, organized crime syndicates with drug connections emerged, and human rights violations, including extrajudicial killings, increased.[30] In addition, opponents of Préval attacked government officials, and violence escalated among rival political parties.

Despite how little or how much it had contributed to Haiti's supposed "restabilization and democratization" process, the Clinton administration retained hope that conditions would improve in the small island nation. Yet, in January 1999, President Préval dissolved the Haitian parliament after a political deadlock over the appointment of Préval's education minister, Jacques-Edouard Alexis, as prime minister. In response, President Clinton and international actors suspended nearly U.S.$500 million in aid. By 2000 Préval was feeling substantial multilateral pressure to hold legislative elections.[31]

In stark contrast to the failure of the international economic sanctions lodged against the Cedras regime in 1994, this renewed multilateral diplomatic effort seemed to make real progress. Finally, after Clinton offered Préval the "carrot" of several million dollars in funding for Haiti's 2000 elections, the Haitian leader budged.[32] However, in May, Aristide's party again cleaned house, sweeping almost all of the open seats in parliament. As the December

[29] Jean-Germain Gros, "Haiti's Flagging Transition," *Journal of Democracy* 8, no. 4 (October 1997): 94–109.
[30] U.S. Bureau of Democracy, Human Rights, and Labor, "Country Reports on Human Rights Practices 2000" (Washington, DC: GPO, February 23, 2001).
[31] "Haiti: Human Rights Developments," *HRW World Report, 2000* (New York: Human Rights Watch, 2001), http://www.hrw.org/wr2k1/americas/haiti.html (accessed June 24, 2006).
[32] Maureen Taft-Morales, "Haiti: Developments and U.S. Policy since 1991 and Current Congressional Concerns," *Congressional Research Service* (Washington, DC: Library of Congress, January 19, 2005), 5.

deadline for presidential elections neared, with Préval unable to run again because of restrictions on consecutive presidential terms, it soon became clear who would succeed Préval.

The unshakable ex-president Aristide, who had helped fuel Haiti's now-inflamed domestic situation while exiled and persecuted, came to the forefront again. Announcing his candidacy months before the election, Aristide won handily with a reported 91.5 percent of the vote. Estimated turnout was well below a quarter of the voting population.[33] Most Haitians likely knew the results far in advance.

GEORGE W. BUSH'S POLICIES IN HAITI

Haiti was not the only country that underwent a change of leadership in 2000. Just weeks before Aristide's election, George W. Bush, himself the winner of a highly contested election, stood poised to take office as the next president of the United States. During the first few years of the Bush presidency, however, Haiti received little attention.

The Bush administration was more than happy to have other nations and international organizations do the heavy lifting on diplomatic and democracy-building efforts with regard to the Haiti situation. Indeed, both before and during the United States' engagement in wars in the Middle East, Bush took a peripheral approach to Haiti, largely relying on the OAS to help Haiti rectify its deepening governmental crises.

The Bush administration did not completely ignore Haiti's political predicaments during the president's first term in office. On the contrary, it upheld the freeze on aid to Haiti in response to the Haitian government's failure to remedy the flawed parliamentary elections of 2000, ostensibly to send a message to the Haitian authorities that its disruption of democracy would not be tolerated.

By 2003 President Bush had also put U.S.$2.5 million behind the OAS's efforts to promote compromise between Aristide, Haiti's fledgling parliament, and the warring political factions.[34] For Bush, this was perhaps the ideal position for the United States, as it allowed his administration to back up his rhetorical support for the OAS and its initiatives in Haiti without having to make more than a monetary commitment.

---

[33] Ibid.

[34] Marc Grossman, Under Secretary of State for Political Affairs, "U.S. Policy toward Haiti," Testimony before the Senate Foreign Relations Committee, 108th Cong., 2nd sess., July 15, 2003.

One likely reason for the relative standoffishness toward Haiti was the reluctance of the Bush administration to throw U.S. weight in Aristide's corner. Many of the administration's top officials had worked for Republican members of Congress during the 1990s and were not big supporters of Aristide. More specifically, it was an open secret that many individuals in the Bush administration, including State Department official Otto Reich, fiercely distrusted the Haitian president and were ready to be rid of him.

Aristide faced more criticism later that year when he ordered the arrest of dozens of people implicated in a raid on Haitian police stations and then held them in custody without a warrant.[35] He faced yet another coup attempt in December 2001 when several armed men stormed the National Palace in Port-au-Prince. Incensed by the attack and by claims that it had been a "set-up" in order for Aristide to crush dissent, his supporters responded by torching the opposition parties' headquarters.

Conservatives in Washington also claimed that Aristide had begun to incite the violence directly when, in one of his fiery speeches, he announced a "zero tolerance crime policy," under which it was "not necessary to bring criminals to court."[36] His Haitian supporters, critics declared, had taken this as a rallying call for vigilante justice. Critics also began to draw comparisons between Duvalier's brutal Tonton Macoutes and the newly emergent *chimères*, the thugs that Aristide and his supporters reportedly hired from the slums to do their bidding.[37] Such evidence further darkened Aristide's already shady record on human rights.

The Bush administration's top officials believed that Aristide would continue to worsen Haiti's crises and prevent the efficient use of humanitarian aid. Many liberal politicians and observers, however, criticized the Bush administration and leaders of other nations that were withholding aid for further burdening Haiti's impoverished and violence-stricken population. The Bush administration's refusal to sanction the IMF's release of U.S. $200 million in funds, as well as its significant cuts in humanitarian relief to Haiti since Clinton's tenure, they said, had exacerbated the political and social turmoil as much as Aristide's rhetoric. Liberal critic James Dobbins, who served as Clinton's special representative to Haiti from 1994 to 1996, explained, "This administration continued to provide counsel and moral

[35] "Haiti: Human Rights Developments," *HRW World Report, 2000.*
[36] "Haiti: Human Rights Developments," *HRW World Report, 2002* (New York: Human Rights Watch, 2003), http://www.hrw.org/wr2k2/americas7.html (accessed June 20, 2006).
[37] Mark Falcoff, "Where Does Haiti Go from Here?" Latin American Outlook, *American Enterprise Institute for Public Policy Research*, April 2004, 2.

support to the opposition but ... provided no assistance to the Haitian government. The result was a somewhat unbalanced relationship in which they seem to have an intimate relationship only with the opposition."[38] Many critics of the Bush administration's foreign policy, particularly from the Anti-imperialist school, also pointed to the president's repatriation of the refugees and his sanctioning of the arrest of hundreds of Haitians who arrived on Florida's shores in 2001 as further proof of the administration's hard-line stance on Haiti's government and its abandonment of the nation's impoverished citizens.

2004: Another Aristide Exile, Another Military Intervention

In January 2004, when Haiti's bicentennial celebration was scheduled in Port-au-Prince, a series of violent riots and protests rocked the capital. Police officers and armed gang members reportedly hired by Aristide attacked demonstrators, prompting the U.S. government to condemn the government and push hard for new elections. Increasingly, Haiti began to turn against Aristide. Several thousand citizens staged a march in the Haitian capital and demanded his resignation. The opposition and violence worsened as armed rebels began seizing control of Haiti's cities just weeks later.

In addition to backing multilateral mediation efforts, the Bush administration continued pushing for compromise in Haiti. Both Assistant Secretary of State Roger Noriega and Secretary of State Colin Powell tried talking to Aristide, assuring him that a solution would not have to entail his early departure from office. But Aristide's opponents would bargain for nothing less. Violence increased to the point where, in late February, several U.S. Marines were deployed to protect the U.S. Embassy. Powell, Noriega, and officials from other nations kept pushing compromise, urging Aristide to negotiate directly with the armed rebels who had begun closing in on Port-au-Prince. But with Aristide vehemently refusing to back down, the rebels said there was no chance of a deal.

When the rebels reached the capital, hell broke loose in Haiti. U.S. officials began to adopt a new approach, at least publicly, when they questioned Aristide's "fitness to govern" and asked him to "re-examine" his position on remaining in office.[39] Whether in response to American insistence, the chaos

---

[38] Quoted in Janine Zacharia, "Washington v. Aristide: Oppo Research," *New Republic*, March 3, 2004, 13.

[39] "U.S. Questions Aristide's 'Fitness' to Govern Haiti," Agence France-Presse, February 29, 2004.

outside the National Palace walls, or both, Aristide fled his country on February 29, 2004. Once again, the divisive president found himself in exile, this time in the Central African Republic. And, once again, Haiti found itself at a crossroads.

The same day Aristide left Haiti, the UN Security Council adopted a resolution authorizing the deployment of a "multinational interim force" for three months, mainly to create a "secure and stable environment" in the country.[40] The Bush administration changed its policy from earlier that year when it had refused Aristide's requests to send peacekeeping troops and spearheaded the contingent forces of more than 3,000 soldiers. They went with the immediate intention of securing Haiti for its transition to an interim government headed by Supreme Court Justice Boniface Alexandre.

Three months would prove too short a time to stabilize the country, especially given the continued violence and largely incomplete disarmament process. Though American ambassador James Foley had announced in March 2004 that the United States "would not walk away from Haiti before the job was completed," the United States' deep involvement in Iraq would make that a difficult task.[41] Sending just over half of the first UN forces, the Bush administration could seemingly do little to restore order in Haiti, especially because the Pentagon claimed they would not act like "cops on the beat."[42]

Indeed, it is still debatable whether the administration's operational policies actually matched its rhetorical and intentional position: U.S. forces were committed to the mission for only three months and were withdrawn promptly. Furthermore, the United States contributed only U.S.$116 million for the first fourteen months of the operation, a figure representing only one-eighth of the total mission budget.[43]

Another key factor in this episode was the fact that the Pentagon had no desire to send its forces into Haiti. Clinton's arguably unsuccessful occupation of Haiti was still fresh in the minds of many officials in Washington. According to a statement by Senator Christopher Dodd (D-CT), the mission a decade earlier cost the United States more than U.S.$2 billion. Even before the withdrawal in 2001, Haiti neared the same destabilized condition it had

---

[40] "Replacement of U.S.-Led Force in Haiti with UN Peacekeeping Mission," *American Journal of International Law* 98, no. 3 (July 2004): 587.

[41] "Will America Finish the Job, This Time?" *The Economist*, March 6, 2004.

[42] Ibid.

[43] U.S. House, United States Government Accountability Office, *Peacekeeping: Cost Comparison of Actual UN and Hypothetical U.S. Operations in Haiti*, 109th Cong., 2nd sess., February 2006 (Washington, DC: GPO, 2006), 4.

been in before the intervention. In the eyes of many policymakers, it would have been difficult for the president and his administration to justify sending more permanent forces – especially to a country where the United States had few political or economic interests.

However much or little the administration's standoffishness contributed to Haiti's renewed turmoil, violence still ruled the streets. Haiti's police force of several thousand proved far too few to quell the violence; in fact, squad members themselves were the ones responsible for many of the crimes. In addition, the UN-led disarmament process was extremely slow, mainly due to the fact that the UN failed to offer incentives for rebels to hand over their weapons. Also, President Bush faced increased criticism for cutting aid and failing to do more to build up the country's economy, which is what many claimed that Haiti really needed to begin the process of democratization and stabilization. As Charles Rangel (D-NY) expressed, "We are just as much a part of this coup d'etat as the rebels, as the looters, or anyone else."[44]

In addition, the Bush administration had to contend with the wrath of Aristide, all the way from Africa. Alleging that U.S. Marines had kidnapped him and forced him into exile that February night, he blamed the Bush administration for Haiti's continued crises. The question of Aristide's kidnapping or rescue continues to be disputed. Critics saw the Bush administration's murky "neoconservative" agenda at work in Aristide's removal. While all the facts are not clear, it was alleged that the Bush administration had worked through democracy promotion organizations such as the International Republican Institute (IRI) in an effort to bolster groups opposed to Aristide. U.S. ambassador Brian Dean Curran said in January 2006 that Stanley Lucas, the IRI director in Haiti, had instructed Aristide's opposition to refuse to cooperate with the Lavalas Party in an effort to "cripple" the government, an accusation that Lucas denied.[45] Nevertheless, for many Anti-imperialist critics, these sorts of efforts were proof positive that the Bush administration was interested in supporting only a certain form of democracy, one that fit the administration's own ideologies or interests. In any case, according to Curran, the accusations made the United States' responsibilities in Haiti "infinitely more difficult."[46]

---

[44] Quoted in Erich Marquardt, "Haiti's Experiment with Democracy Subverted Once Again," *Power and Internet News Report*, March 4, 2004, http://www.pinr.com/report.php?ac=view_report&report_id+148&language_id=1 (accessed June 2006).

[45] Walt Bogdanich and Jenny Nordberg, "Democracy Undone: Mixed Signals Helped Tilt Haiti toward Chaos," *New York Times*, January 29, 2006.

[46] Ibid.

Because the situation in Haiti hardly had improved, the UN reauthorized the peacekeeping force for six months, bolstering its numbers to 8,000 troops, including a contingent from China. This new force took over in June 2004, arriving just after severe floods in the southern part of the country caused considerable death and destruction. The U.S. government had left fewer than a dozen of its own soldiers and had contributed none to the new UN mission, which still fell two-thirds short of promised troops by that September.

As violence and protests continued in certain areas of Haiti, observers went as far as to call it "guerrilla warfare" between the former president's supporters and his opposition. To top it off, Haitian police officers reportedly were terrorizing the slums of Port-au-Prince, with some officers executing those believed to be supporters of the former president.

The interim government and Prime Minister Latortue were criticized for allowing and even condoning such actions. Even in Aristide's absence, his remaining legacy and the remaining instability in the country made democracy seem like a perpetually lofty goal. Nevertheless, elections were scheduled for 2005; the UN Security Council even extended its troops' mandate until 2006 in order to see to it that the elections took place. Hope, however small, still existed for Haiti.

Democracy Promotion?

As the months following Aristide's departure wore on, many asked exactly what the Bush administration had done to contribute to Haiti's strides toward democracy. For a presidential administration so intent on promoting democracy worldwide, some critics claimed, it had done too little. The extent of the United States' commitment to Haiti since Bush's inauguration, aside from its small troop contribution to the first UN contingent, had focused primarily on economic and social development. The administration continued to endorse the Caribbean Basin Trade Partnership Act of 2000 and the subsequent Trade Act of 2002, both programs that eliminated duties and quotas on apparel and textile industry materials for Haiti. Statistics indicated that Haiti had taken advantage of the trade preferences by expanding its manufacturing sector; the nation's apparel exports to the United States had increased from U.S.$176.5 million to U.S.$218.2 million in 2004, and the figure continued to grow.[47]

---

[47] Office of the United States Trade Representative, *Sixth Report to Congress on the Operation of the Caribbean Basin Economic Recovery Act*, 109th Cong., 1st sess., (Washington, DC: GPO, December 31, 2005), 3–13.

Additionally, Bush promoted reforms within the Inter-American Institute for Cooperation on Agriculture (IICA). After the WTO Doha round negotiations in November 2001, the Bush administration pushed IICA to open discussions on agricultural trade liberalization in the Americas, giving preference to struggling countries like Haiti. Between fiscal year 2004 and 2006, Congress set aside $870 million for security, stability, economic growth, and humanitarian aid initiatives in Haiti.[48]

Without U.S. troops in Haiti, however, many questioned what good these programs would do given the country's continual instability. But in light of U.S. military involvement elsewhere, especially in Iraq, the Bush administration argued that troops were stretched too thin to "stabilize" another nation. But the president could hardly afford to abandon Haiti completely. While he had openly mocked Clinton's attempts at "nation building" in Haiti and other countries during the 2000 election campaign against Vice President Al Gore, George W. Bush now faced a situation in the Middle East much grander than any faced by his predecessor. Given Bush's fervent vows not to back out of Iraq and to promote democracy on a global scale, it would be hard to justify ignoring a struggle for democracy taking place in his country's own "backyard."

A NEW FUTURE FOR HAITI?

While the United States might have found it easy to promote democracy and fair elections through rhetoric, the lead-up to the scheduled December 2005 elections was anything but painless. In fact, renewed acts of violence and a rash of kidnappings made the situation look worse than ever. Pro-Aristide militants had reportedly killed several UN soldiers, and Haiti's under-equipped and understaffed police force had hardly proved any match for their machine guns. Compounding the problems was the sluggish pace of voter registration. A number of logistical problems postponed the elections four times. Hope that the democratic process would take hold in Haiti was quickly fading.

But finally, on February 7, 2006, Haitian voters went to the polls. And they elected none other than René Préval – the only president ever to have completed a full term – to be their next president. As was all too common in Haiti, the elections were accompanied by controversy. Haitian electoral officials, in order to avoid a runoff and to ensure that Préval won more than

---

[48] U.S. Bureau of Western Affairs, "US Assistance to Haiti," Fact Sheet, May 25, 2006, http://www.state.gov/p/wha/rls/fs/2006/66935.htm (accessed July 2006).

a 50 percent vote majority, removed 85,000 blank ballots from the count.[49] Predictably, this provoked an outcry among several of the other candidates. This time, however, the new president stepped in, asking his supporters to remain calm and to leave violence out of their celebrations. And this time, mostly, they did.

The Bush administration proclaimed the elections a success and wholeheartedly endorsed Préval. Undoubtedly relieved at Préval's willingness to establish a coalition government and to distance himself from Aristide, the United States, as put by Secretary of State Condoleezza Rice, "wants this government to succeed."[50] For Washington policymakers, political and economic stability in Haiti could not have come a moment sooner.

The months following Préval's inauguration became a period of rare political stability. Préval made gains in promoting the political incorporation of different parties by opening parliamentary positions to opposition members. He also qualified Haiti for debt relief under the IMF's Heavily Indebted Poor Countries initiative. Additionally, the IMF, World Bank, Inter-American Development Bank, and the European Union pledged several million dollars in development loans and grants. The U.S. Agency for International Development signed an agreement with Préval on September 15, 2006, pledging U.S.$492 million over three years, U.S.$128 million of which was confirmed in the its budget for fiscal year 2007.

To be sure, Haiti had a much greater impact on U.S. post–Cold War policy than its size or global standing might indicate. Indeed, it is somewhat surprising that this island nation's turbulent past and equally tumultuous present figured so heavily in the policies of the three U.S. presidential administrations since the collapse of Soviet communism. The crises in Haiti elicited a blowback in Washington on par with the drug war in the Andes and the Cuban embargo, and while it may seem counterintuitive, Haiti played a prominent role in bringing democracy promotion to the forefront of U.S. policy in the Americas.

Despite the island's lack of geopolitical importance and economic strength, Haiti highlights several important trends in U.S.–Latin American relations in the post–Cold War era. Notably, it reflected a growing interconnectedness among the different countries in the region. Several Establishment observers pointed to the invocation of the Santiago Resolution during the Clinton

---

[49] Carol J. Williams, "Haitian Election Celebration Clogs Capital; The Decision to Declare Rene Preval the Winner without a Runoff Sets Off Revelry in the Streets, but Draws Criticism from Two of His Opponents," *Los Angeles Times*, February 17, 2006.

[50] Ibid.

administration as evidence of a new hemispheric solidarity. Whether or not this is accurate, the multilateral coordination in dealing with Haiti did demonstrate that, increasingly, a crisis in one country affects the others in the region. In addition, Haiti reflects the rising importance of intermestic issues in U.S. policy and adds a complex but very useful example for determining whether the United States has moved "beyond the Big Stick." Still, it remains to be seen whether Haiti will maintain its elevated standing in the American political consciousness, or if Washington again will forget about this tiny, star-crossed Caribbean nation.

14

The United States and Mexico

with Katie Hunter

BETWEEN A TOAST AND A TUNNEL

On September 6, 2001, at the beginning of his first state dinner, President George W. Bush raised his glass to make a toast. Bush spoke warmly of the evening's guest of honor, a fellow head of state who also had taken office just months before. Rather than a "traditional" ally such as Canada or Britain, Mexico's President Vicente Fox sat on the receiving end of the new American president's commendations: "The United States has no more important relationship in the world than our relationship with Mexico. Each of our countries is proud of our independence, our freedom, and our democracy. We are united by values and carried forward by common hopes."[1] At first, it might seem strange that Bush had named Mexico as the nation with whom the United States' shared its most significant ties. But, over the past quarter century, the United States' relationship with Mexico has become one of increasing importance and interdependence. As President Bush's toast indicated, in an era when concerns about democracy, drugs, economic liberalization, and terrorism supersede those of communism, Mexico matters greatly to the United States.

Despite Mexico's increasing importance to Washington, U.S. policies toward its southern neighbor do not mimic its policies toward other close partners such as Britain or Canada. On the contrary, Mexico's gradual ascension in status to one of the United States' most important policy allies has been shaped by a variety of factors in the post–Cold War context,

---

[1] President George W. Bush, "Remarks by President Bush and President Fox in an Exchange of Toasts," The State Dining Room, The White House, Office of the Press Secretary, September 6, 2001.

including tremendous bilateral trade, a massive shared border, illicit drugs, legal and illegal immigration, and cultural "cross-fertilization."

Today, each nation's mutual influence extends beyond the border region. For example, ubiquitous Tex-Mex restaurants across the United States and Mexican laborers at construction sites as far north as Maine illustrate Mexico's tremendous influence on U.S. society. Similarly, the plethora of American-owned *maquiladora* factories, American tourists and expatriate retirees, and billboards advertising Coca-Cola in cities like Tijuana and Cancún are testaments of America's influence on Mexico. Furthermore, on the same day that presidents Bush and Fox dined in Washington, more than half a million crossings took place at ports of entry along the U.S. border with Mexico – a number that does not include the estimated thousands of *illegal* crossings. In addition, each day, thousands of commercial trucks that cross the border, sometimes carrying goods made tariff-free by NAFTA, in other cases carrying drugs, illegal immigrants, or weapons.

Just two days after Bush and Fox's soiree, Mexican authorities arrested six leaders of a high-profile Mexican drug cartel. One of the arrested leaders was wanted in the United States on charges that he had helped build a tunnel 1,416 feet long and 65 feet deep beneath the border to smuggle drugs into the United States.

BORDERS AND THE INTERMESTIC AGENDA

The U.S.-Mexico border brings into focus myriad issues that directly affect the United States' national security, prosperity, and domestic stability. Once largely regional concerns, border security and illegal immigration now weigh heavily on the minds of Americans across the country. No longer confined to border cities like San Diego and Tucson, public anxiety over Mexican emigration has cropped up from Spokane, Washington, to Savannah, Georgia, especially because migrant workers and their families are now more likely than ever to reside in these parts of the country.

The increased national concern over border security, which encompasses economic, national security, and drug trafficking issues, introduces a level of complexity to the U.S.-Mexico relationship that did not exist before and during the Cold War. At times, such complex issues transcend political partisanship, as evidenced by the fierce opposition President George W. Bush faced from many Republican members of Congress over his initial proposal in 2001 to grant a pathway toward legal status for some of the 3 million to 4 million Mexicans living illegally in the United States. Many criticized the president for rejecting his conservative roots in championing what they considered a type of liberal "amnesty." Interestingly, President Clinton experienced a similar type of criticism, as members of his own party and constituency protested vehemently against his push for NAFTA and more aggressive border patrol policies.

The intermestic nature of the U.S.-Mexican relationship and the public response to it prompts the United States to watch Mexico with rapt attention. Take, for example, Proposition 187, a contentious proposal championed by California Governor Pete Wilson in 1994 that would have prohibited the state's undocumented migrants from attending public schools and receiving emergency state-funded health care. While the plan provoked outrage among American citizens and politicians who considered it draconian, its passage revealed intense domestic concern about illegal immigration, the overwhelming majority of which came from Mexico.

The proposition's passage by a majority vote of around 60 percent came on the heels of Congress's approval of NAFTA, which also raised domestic alarm based on the widespread belief that NAFTA would send American jobs southward to Mexico. Similar fears, such as Mexicans taking jobs away from American citizens and forcing the country to adopt bilingual education, have since permeated national discourse, as have fears about insufficient border security in the wake of the September 11 terrorist attacks. The persistence of such "hot button" issues during the past two decades, particularly around U.S. election times, illustrates the domestic significance of U.S. policy toward Mexico.

Yet domestic issues and their increasing importance to U.S. policy provide just part of the story surrounding Mexico's significance to the United States. During the Cold War, given Mexico's relative stability and its facade of a functional democratic system, the United States was content to leave Mexico alone, despite the fact that its "democracy" consisted of a single party ruling the country in a semiauthoritarian fashion for several decades. In the 1980s, however, Mexico began a gradual but dramatic process of actual democratization. In 2000 Vicente Fox was the first Mexican president in more than seventy-one years to come from a party other than the Institutional Revolutionary Party (PRI). Mexico's democratic "maturation" encouraged Washington to engage its southern neighbor more closely and more seriously throughout most of the post–Cold War era.

In another sign of Mexico's "maturation," Mexico's leaders (not to mention public opinion) have come to oppose periodically the United States on many of its critical domestic, bilateral, and even international policies. Just days before his official visit in 2001, Fox challenged Bush to expand the American policy of merely granting "residency status" to illegal Mexicans in the United States to a general amnesty for these same illegal Mexicans. Two years later, as a temporary member of the UN Security Council, Mexico would vote against the U.S. invasion of Iraq, illustrating how in the post–Cold War era, Mexico has been able to act primarily in its own interests, even as those interests conflict with those of the United States.

Mexico has never ranked consistently at the top of the U.S. policy priority list. President Bush, who perhaps had the closest ties of any American president to a Mexican head of state, was criticized for neglecting relations with Fox in the wake of the terrorist attacks of September 11, 2001. Many claimed that Bush, in diverting his attention to the Middle East and tightening America's borders, dropped the ball on a promising partnership.

The period soon after September 11, 2001, though it was characterized by certain divergences in U.S. and Mexican interests, did not cause irrevocable harm to the nations' relationship. When Mexico's ambassador to the UN claimed that "the U.S. isn't interested in a partnership of equals with Mexico, but with a tight relationship of convenience and subordination" and that the United States sees Mexico "as a backyard," President Fox immediately removed him from his post.[2] Thus, while at times difficult to balance national interests and a burgeoning partnership, the deepening of the U.S.-Mexico relationship illustrates how the United States has reprioritized its Latin America policies in the post–Cold War era.

HISTORICAL BACKGROUND: NOT-SO-GOOD NEIGHBORS

George W. Bush was not the first U.S. president to acknowledge the importance of strong relations with Mexico; officials in President Jimmy Carter's administration coined the term "special relationship" to describe the United States' ties with Mexico. The U.S.-Mexico "special relationship," however, never resembled Winston Churchill's original notion of a diplomatic "two-way street" between London and Washington where both nations cooperated in a mutually respectful and constructive manner. U.S.-Mexican relations improved dramatically only in recent decades.

Early U.S.-Mexican relations smacked of the confrontational and interventionist Big Stick approach. Land issues motivated a majority of the United States' involvement with Mexico, with the United States usually gaining land at Mexico's expense. Several of these disputes turned bloody and Mexico lost much of its treasured territory to the United States through

---

[2] John Authers, "Mexico's ambassador to the UN Sacked after Speech Critical of US," *Financial Times* (London), November 19, 2003, 4.

treaties and sales, leaving some Mexicans with deep-seated reservations about any dealings with the "Colossus to the North."

President Woodrow Wilson's dealings with Mexico in the early twentieth century reveal a great deal about the attitudes that historically characterized U.S.-Mexican relations. Responding to public concerns about Mexico's civil war and its potential effects on the United States, in 1916 Wilson sent 10,000 U.S. troops into Mexico to hunt down Francisco "Pancho" Villa after the rebel leader raided a New Mexico town that same year. This occurred after the downfall of Mexico's President Huerta, whom Wilson helped to topple through the sale of weapons to Huerta's opponent Venustiano Carranzo.[3] Wilson disagreed with the "undemocratic" manner in which Huerta had seized power, eventually shelving his administration's "nonrecognition" policy toward the Huerta administration when the new Mexican leader refused to step down. Ironically, under President Taft, the U.S. government had supported Huerta in *his* overthrow of President Francisco Madero.

These instances are indicative of the often confrontational and interventionist approach that the United States employed during the first few decades of the twentieth century. Wilson reinforced this view in a 1913 speech about Mexico's civil war, in which he claimed "those conditions touch us very nearly. Not merely because they lie at our very doors. ... Mexico has a great and enviable future before her, if only she would choose and attain the paths of honest constitutional government."[4] Such rhetoric illustrated the asymmetrical, litigious, and undeniably paternalistic relationship between the United States and Mexico at the time.

Despite their political disagreements, throughout the twentieth century the United States and Mexico found many incentives (primarily economic) to work together. Most of the impetus for cooperation arose from sheer necessity and expediency, given the nations' proximity to one another. Mexico depended on the United States as an export market and a source of foreign investment capital. In addition, the United States' demand for labor, which increased during World War II, resulted in a more formalized program for bringing Mexicans to the United States for work. Created in 1946, the Bracero Program was a first major step toward institutionalizing what had already become a popular occurrence – Mexican migration to the more prosperous, and labor hungry, North.

---

[3] Ibid.
[4] "Address of the President of the United States on Mexican Affairs," *American Journal of International Law* 7, no. 4 (October 1913): 284.

Nevertheless, the two nations rarely let bilateral economic cooperation stand in the way of their own respective national interests. The Cold War era, in particular, constituted a period of "bargained negligence," during which the United States combated communism and pursued trade liberalization while Mexico pursued protectionist economic policies and economic growth.[5] Despite ongoing trade relations and labor migration during the Cold War, exemplified by the steady growth of *maquiladora* factories along the border, a relative coolness persisted between Washington and Mexico City during that time.

In contrast, the years leading up to the 1989 Soviet collapse saw a marked increase in bilateral cooperation. National events and concerns in each country, including the United States' war on drugs, Mexican emigration to the United States, and Mexico's economic crisis in the early 1980s precipitated much of this necessary collaboration. Many critics have characterized such events as instances of the United States' "crisis response" approach to Latin America.

GEORGE H. W. BUSH AND MEXICO: A PROMISING PARTNERSHIP?

During a trip to Mexico in 1990, House Majority leader Richard Gephardt (D-MO) stated what, to many, might have seemed obvious. Claiming that the United States too often had "taken the relationship for granted" with the "huge country on our border," Gephardt asserted that "if we can successfully deal with their problems, if their economy can prosper, we'll really save ourselves a lot of problems."[6]

Two other politicians with goals similar to Gephardt's had already hit the ground running. Elected just months apart in 1988, President George H. W. Bush and Mexico's President Carlos Salinas de Gortari both committed to cultivating better bilateral relations. Salinas confirmed his goodwill toward the United States at a state dinner held in his honor by President Bush, stating that "the time has come to derive mutual benefits from the advantages of the border that joins us" (Figure 14.1).[7]

[5] Jorge I. Domínguez and Rafael Fernández de Castro, *The United States and Mexico: Between Partnership and Conflict* (New York: Routledge, 2001), 18.

[6] Jon Sawyer, "Gephardt Views Mexico as Land of Opportunity," *St. Louis Post-Dispatch*, January 21, 1990.

[7] "As Delivered Remarks and Toast by Mexican President Carlos Salinas de Gortari during the State Dinner Given in His Honor and in the Honor of Mrs. Salinas de Gortari by the President and Mrs. Bush, The White House," *Federal News Service*, October 3, 1989.

FIGURE 14.1. U.S. president George H. W. Bush offers a toast to his host, Mexican president Carlos Salinas during a luncheon in Monterrey on November 27, 1990. During his two-day visit, the American and Mexican leaders discussed trade and immigration. (Photo: Reuters/Gary Cameron.)

Neither president, however, could ignore the contentious issues surrounding their burgeoning friendship. Salinas's victory had been marred by cries of widespread electoral fraud after reported computer failures – attributed by many to tampering by the PRI – delayed vote tallies for several days. Several of the leftist opposition parties refused to recognize Salinas as the legitimate president. Bush, however, did not let that stand in the way of his desire to acknowledge and engage Salinas.

Behind his administration's accommodating position was Bush's optimistic belief in Salinas's potential to be a strong partner in the push for what Bush believed would be their countries' mutual economic gain. Educated at Harvard like his predecessor President Miguel de la Madrid, Salinas had promised to continue de la Madrid's process of privatization and opening the country to more foreign trade and investment. These initiatives were radical departures from the conventional, inward-looking PRI policies that Mexico had adopted in the decades leading up to the 1982 debt crisis. Salinas's stated commitment to negotiate with Washington on the potential lowering of Mexico's trade barriers also gave the Bush administration incentive to embrace his presidency.

In addition, Salinas represented the ruling party that for more than six decades had maintained a stable (if far from fully democratic) regional presence. Although Salinas's election had certainly been circumspect, President Bush chose to engage Salinas rather than criticize his election and interfere in Mexico's internal politics. Given the relative consistency with which the United States had recognized Mexico's presidents in other dubious elections, Bush had no historic precedent for breaking ties, even as others in Washington began scrutinizing Mexico's "democracy" more closely.

Other concerns, including Mexico's enormous debt and a perceived failure to cooperate fully with the U.S. government in the drug war, plagued the relationship. Despite Bush's high hopes, Mexico was proving to be a challenging partner. When the president appointed national security hawk John Negroponte as ambassador to Mexico, some viewed it as Bush's readiness to take seriously the issue of border security. Yet the selection had an unsettling effect in Mexico and the broader region, given Negroponte's association with the Reagan administration's controversial Central America policies during his tenure as ambassador to Honduras. Mexican opposition parties and journalists decried Negroponte's appointment, with one front-page newspaper article calling it "an unfriendly and threatening gesture."[8]

Bush did show his respect for Mexico and the new bilateral partnership by praising Salinas publicly for several early political moves, including the arrest of several well-known drug traffickers involved in bribing local and state governments. Still, U.S. officials knew that effectively fighting the drug trafficking problem in Mexico would take much more effort. In addition to producing nearly 30 percent of the marijuana and 40 percent of the heroin that came into the United States, Mexico still served as the primary shipping point for nearly a third of Colombian cocaine.[9] At the same time, the Mexican government had come under fire for the slow investigation of the widely publicized 1985 murder of U.S. Drug Enforcement Agency (DEA) agent Enrique "Kiki" Camarena Salazar, whose killers included some former Mexican police officers. For many Washington officials, this event reinforced the belief that Mexico was an unwilling or incapable ally in the war on drugs.

Many members of Congress manifested this opinion in their attempt to overturn Bush's "certification" of Mexico for its cooperation in the drug war. In both 1988 and 1989, Foreign Relations Committee chair Senator Jesse Helms (R-NC), an outspoken critic of the PRI, introduced a bill to override the certification and related financial aid for Mexico. In 1988 the

---

[8] Jane Bussey, "Mexico Unhappy with New Envoy," *Guardian* (London), February 6, 1989.
[9] Richard Johns, "Mexico Cracks Down on Drug Traffickers," *Financial Times* (London), March 2, 1989, 3.

bill passed in the Senate by a vote of 63 to 27, an outcome that could have enacted sanctions against Mexico in accordance with a 1986 certification law. Though it did not pass in the House later that year, the bill's reappearance indicated that the U.S. Congress would consider seriously the terms of the U.S.-Mexico relationship.

From the Yukon to the Yucatan: The Push for Regional Free Trade

In addition to addressing Mexico's debt and economic stagnation stemming from the 1982 default of the peso and ensuing financial crisis, Bush and Salinas were also well on their way toward creating what would become a revolutionary trilateral North American trade bloc. While the concept of a regional free trade agreement had been on the books since the early 1980s, it was not until well into Bush's presidency that the final package – NAFTA – began to take shape.

The North American trade bloc proved a controversial idea from its inception, igniting criticism on both sides of the border. Although he would later initiate free trade talks, President Salinas resisted initially, citing the Uruguay Round of the General Agreement on Tariffs and Trade (GATT), begun in 1986, as sufficient. He also expressed concern over the different economic levels between the United States and Mexico, questioning whether a "common market would provide an advantage to either country."[10] However, Salinas soon reconsidered based on frustrating GATT negotiations and the lack of investment and trade opportunities presented by Europe.[11]

Salinas's decision to pursue trade integration represented a decisive break from Mexico's past economic policy pursuits. Whereas Salinas's predecessors had striven for economic isolation, the new president sought integration with the United States, Canada, and other world economic powers in order to secure the elusive development Mexico had missed persistently during the twentieth century. In 1989 Salinas spoke in favor of a strong bilateral trade agreement with the United States as a "fundamental" part of the "consolidation of the program of economic reform" created in the wake of Mexico's debt crisis.[12]

[10] Larry Rohter, "North American Trade Bloc? Mexico Rejects Such an Idea," *New York Times* November 24, 1988, sec. D, 1.
[11] Clyde Farnsworth, "Mexican–U.S. Pact Reached on Trade and Investments," *New York Times*, October 3, 1989, sec. A, 1.
[12] John Driscoll and Philip Bennett, "Salinas on Trade Ties and the Drug Fight," *Boston Globe*, October 1, 1989, 20.

By 1989 the United States was already Mexico's largest export market, and Mexico itself was the third most popular location for U.S. exports. The United States already shared a similar pact with Canada, and the virtual collapse of the Uruguay GATT round in December 1990 encouraged the Bush administration to push even harder for a free trade agreement. Yet, despite the president's intensified requests, Congress remained divided; Democrats, in particular, blackballed the accords, even though negotiators intentionally left out the contentious issue of labor migration. Many in Congress also retained their skepticism toward Salinas and the PRI, claiming that the party's singular rule called into question its ability to function as a democratic party that would uphold fair labor and environmental practices.

Once the U.S. Congress felt assured it would have the final say on any agreement that the United States, Mexico, and Canada might reach, it renewed fast-track authority and let plans proceed in May 1991. With congressional approval, formal talks began in June to resolve such issues as the countries' conflicting national policies on health and safety standards for consumer goods. These negotiations dragged on for months, but finally, on December 17, 1992, mere weeks before the end of his term, Bush signed the completed NAFTA – a whopping document more than 2,000 pages long.

While the accord's text centered largely on technical minutiae, NAFTA encompassed far more than market economics. Namely, the Bush administration hoped that the agreement's market impact and the ties it facilitated between the two nations would help Mexico progress toward democratization.

However, NAFTA's passage of the executive branch did not mean it had universal acceptance. While the Bush administration and the more Establishment supporters of the agreement believed it would serve both countries' interests, just as many observers disagreed. Some argued that the United States was "warming up" to Mexico only because Mexico was warming up to trade. Several members of Congress reiterated that the pro-NAFTA camp seemed to be searching unscrupulously for new markets for U.S. businesses to exploit, citing as evidence the fact that many of the accord's safeguards, such as environmental and labor protections, were tied up in complicated side agreements.

Moreover, for NAFTA and for Mexico's democratization to be successful, the two countries would have to make serious headway on the more contentious issues between them. NAFTA, in bringing the United States and Mexico closer, would thrust issues such as illegal immigration and drug trafficking into the spotlight.

Drugs, Immigration, and a Dose of Democracy?

While pushing for the free trade of goods with Mexico, President Bush made it clear that certain things should not cross the United States' southern border: illegal migrants and illicit drugs. These issues were prominent in the wake of the Reagan administration's heightened border security and drug interdiction efforts and the comprehensive immigration law passed in 1986. Early in his presidency, Bush backed an Immigration and Naturalization Service (INS) proposal to dig a "border ditch" in southern California, which would serve the dual purpose of averting drug smuggling and illegal migration from Mexico. The plan incited considerable anger on the Mexican side, prompting Bush to drop the idea.

Many in Washington were also still angry over what they considered Mexico's slow investigation of the death of DEA agent Enrique Camarena. The tension surrounding the Camarena affair reached an entirely new level, however, when U.S. agents arrested Mexican doctor Humberto Álvarez Machaín for his involvement in Camarena's death and then shipped him to the United States to stand trial. Salinas vehemently opposed what his government referred to as a "kidnapping," stating that he "would not permit anybody, not drug traffickers nor their pursuers, to violate Mexican rights."[13] He also threatened to desist aiding U.S. antidrug efforts if Machaín was not returned.

The manner in which Machaín's capture and trials had been conducted was proof positive for many observers that the United States had not shed the arrogance – or Big Stick – with which it had conducted Mexico policy in the past. The U.S. government certainly would not allow Mexican officers to arrest an American citizen in his own country and ship him southward to stand trial. Anti-imperialist critics pointed to the budding friendship's double standard – the two independent nations would work together for mutual gains, but Mexico's sovereignty could be violated if it served U.S. interests. Judge Stephen Reinhardt on the U.S. Court of Appeals recognized the negative implications of the United States' actions in his statement for the case of another Mexican citizen standing trial in the United States for Camarena's murder: "If we are to see the emergence of a 'new world order' in which the use of force is to be subject to the rule of law, we must begin by holding our own government to its fundamental legal commitments."[14]

In a clear display of national autonomy, Salinas decided in July 1992 to refuse antinarcotics aid from the United States. As Ignacio Morales

---

[13] Michael Isikoff, "U.S. Won't Return Mexican Doctor," *Washington Post* April 21, 1990, sec. A, 18.
[14] "U.S. Court Orders Mexican's Release," Associated Press, October 20, 1991.

Lechuga, the senior official in charge of Mexican drug-control programs explained, "if you are a guest in a house, you can't act like the host."[15] He also maintained that the move did not mean that Mexico was "lowering its guard in the struggle against narcotics"; the nation would continue to accept the presence of U.S. DEA agents within its borders.[16] Nevertheless, the Salinas administration's position caught many in Washington off guard. Given the enormous power imbalances and potential diplomatic consequences of a cold shoulder from Washington, at this time few Latin American states were willing – or able – to take such a bold stand against the United States. That Mexico was able to do so in 1992 indicated not only what the nation's "special relationship" with the United States signified but also how the end of the Cold War had paved the way for these sorts of unexpected and unprecedented outcomes.

PRESIDENT CLINTON AND MEXICO: HANDLE WITH CARE

The incoming Clinton administration faced many challenges with respect to ties to Mexico: Clinton's support for NAFTA and his party affiliation boded well for the push of the trade agreement through a Democratic majority Congress; yet Clinton, as well as many NAFTA skeptics in Congress, maintained that the free trade agreement would need to incorporate protective measures for laborers, American businesses, and the environment if it were to be approved. In addition to cultivating goodwill with Salinas in order to get NAFTA off the ground, Clinton also would have to take a strong stance on the bilateral issues of drugs and immigration. Clinton would also need to negotiate deftly on other volatile issues such as illegal immigration, especially after the withdrawal of Zoë Baird from her presidential appointment as attorney general after it was discovered that she had hired two illegal Peruvian immigrants as housekeepers. In light of the early criticism he received in Washington over his lack of foreign policy directive, Clinton could not afford to bungle NAFTA – or fail to sustain good relations with Mexico.

Aside from the looming trade issues, Clinton proved conciliatory toward Mexico and Salinas over Machaín's arrest, claiming that "when another nation is willing to obey the law ... the United States should not be involved in kidnapping."[17] Salinas also attempted to appease Clinton

---

[15] Tim Golden, "Mexico Says It Won't Accept Drug Aid from the United States," *New York Times*, July 26, 1992, sec. 1, 14.
[16] Ibid.
[17] Nancy Benac, "Clinton Meets Mexican president, Plans Quiet Weekend in Arkansas," Associated Press, January 9, 1993.

by readily agreeing to press for the side agreements on lingering trade issues, labor, and the environment to ensure NAFTA's passage. Yet, while both presidents appeared optimistic about the future of the accord, NAFTA would be just one of many bumps (albeit a big one) on a bilateral roller coaster ride that included a severe financial crisis and a Marxist guerrilla insurrection.

Domestic concerns in the United States over Mexico-related issues intensified during the mid-1990s and were manifested in measures like Proposition 187 and anti-free-trade protests. Clinton also faced an overwhelming array of foreign crises during his tenure, not in the least of which were Mexico's economic catastrophe and problems with drug-related corruption. If President Bush had seen the birth of the "special relationship," it was Clinton who would contend with its growing pains.

Netting NAFTA

Placing NAFTA's passage first on his "to do" list, President Clinton knew that it would take some hard bargaining to reach side agreements acceptable to Mexico, Canada, and especially the U.S. Congress. Congressional Democrats and Republicans alike were concerned about Mexico's notoriously poor labor conditions. Furthermore, many worried about a spike in pollution levels and the potential impact of cheap, imported Mexican goods. Senators Larry Craig (R-ID) and John Breaux (D-LA), motivated by pressure from sugar interests in their home states, sent Clinton a thirty-three-signature letter opposing NAFTA for the toll that cheap Mexican sugar would exact on American beet and cane farmers.

Despite criticism, Clinton believed that NAFTA had potential to alleviate rather than create problems between the United States and Mexico. For one, if Mexico were able to support its own population, fewer Mexicans would have reason to cross the border illegally in search of jobs. So even in the face of fervent opposition from some of his most dedicated political constituents, foremost among them the AFL-CIO and other labor unions, Clinton pushed the NAFTA proceedings forward in 1993. After several months of haggling, on September 14, 1993, all three nations signed the side accords, which Congress ratified two months later on November 20, 1993.

NAFTA achieved the remarkable feat of bringing 360 million people together in a legislated free trade zone that spanned from "the Yukon to the Yucatan." Compromise resulted in success; yet compromise also had resulted in what many critics considered to be "toothless" agreements that lacked real capability of enforcing labor and environmental regulations.[18] The agreements were worded vaguely, with the labor provision citing its purpose as "enforcing basic workers' rights" and "increasing employment and improving working conditions and living standards in each country" without stating any concerns or issues in particular.[19] Once again, the United States had sidestepped more contentious issues, particularly between itself and Mexico, in order to make bigger gains and keep up good relations.

While it remained to be seen if NAFTA would prove as economically successful as was expected originally, it did bring the United States even closer to Mexico, its historically "distant neighbor," in what some considered a major step toward a more equitable and conscientious partnership. Other events, however, soon threatened the relief and goodwill surrounding NAFTA's ratification.

Countering the Crises

On January 1, 1994, the day that NAFTA went into effect, residents in Chiapas, Mexico, heard gunshots ringing in the New Year, as the Zapatista National Liberation Front (EZLN) seized several government offices and transit routes in the provincial capital of San Cristóbal de las Casas and surrounding towns. Amid anti-NAFTA cries and calls for "land and revolution," six people were killed, a number that increased drastically in the coming weeks as the insurgency wore on. From a public relations standpoint, NAFTA was not off to a good start.

Over the course of this same year, further destabilization and panic in Mexico occurred in the wake of the assassination of Salinas's "handpicked" presidential successor Luis Donaldo Colosio. The Clinton administration extended a U.S.$6 million dollar line of credit (as discussed in Chapter 6) in hopes of propping up the peso and subsequently assuaging the fears of U.S. investors. For his part, Salinas scrambled to choose another "successor," naming Colosio's former campaign manager and fellow American-educated economist Ernesto Zedillo as the new PRI candidate. Although Salinas considered several factors when making his choice of whom to support, his selection nevertheless indicated an eagerness to placate both Washington and Wall Street. Furthermore, Salinas showed a willingness to stabilize his

---

[18] Maxwell A. Cameron and Brian W. Tomlin, *The Making of NAFTA: How the Deal Was Done* (Ithaca, NY: Cornell University Press, 2000), 187.

[19] Gary Clyde Hufbauer and Jeffrey Schott, *NAFTA Revisited: Achievements and Challenges* (Washington, DC: Institute for International Economics, 2005), 18.

country and appease local critics, who still considered the nation a de facto autocracy, by allowing foreign electoral observers and appointing a special prosecutor for electoral fraud.

Although the U.S. Congress announced full confidence in Mexico's electoral process, Washington nevertheless took preemptive measures to help ensure that elections were legitimate. The U.S. Agency for International Development spent more than half a million dollars on a team of observers for the vote on August 21, 1994.[20] Despite outcries over alleged electoral fraud from opposition party candidates, Zedillo was declared the winner in what the U.S. and other observation teams deemed a generally free and fair election.

Yet Mexico's situation became increasingly tenuous in late 1994 in light of the peso's stunning devaluation. The Clinton administration's coordination of another aid package, which this time included IMF funds, prompted concerns in Congress about an unwise use of U.S. dollars. Clinton, however, insisted that the package was "not a bailout" and maintained that the move was, above all, made in the interests of one country – the United States. In his State of the Union address, the president claimed that he extended the aid (via the Exchange Stabilization Fund program), "not for the Mexican people, but for the sake of the millions of Americans whose lives are tied to Mexico's well-being. If we want to secure American jobs, preserve American exports, safeguard America's borders, then we must pass the stabilization program and help to put Mexico back on track."[21]

Clinton was particularly concerned with how weakened economies in Latin America could complicate his pet project – a free trade area of the *entire* Americas, or FTAA. The president also knew he would have a hard time justifying the value of an FTAA to Congress if NAFTA continued to produce less than expected results and Mexico's economy continued to falter. Indeed, as a top economic adviser to President Clinton explained, "Since we have become increasingly interconnected with emerging markets, both through financial flows and trade, we estimate that it's at least possible that over the next two years if this contagion factor were big enough, it might cost a percentage point off of our GDP growth in the next two years."[22] Such a stark forecast did not bode well for the future of hemispheric free trade. Thus

---

[20] David Clark Scott, "Anxious, Hopeful Mexico Set for Historic Vote," *Christian Science Monitor*, August 17, 1994, 10.

[21] President William Clinton' "State of the Union Address," Office of the Press Secretary, January 28, 1995.

[22] Laura Tyson, Chair of Council of Economic Advisors, Press Briefing, White House Briefing Room, Washington, DC, January 20, 1995.

Clinton, to indicate how Mexico fit "strategically" in the scope of U.S. interests, provided a "fact sheet" to the House and Senate detailing potential effects of the peso crisis, including an "over 30% rise in illegal immigration" of Mexicans coming northward for work. The Clinton administration knew how crucial intermestic issues had become in the eyes of Americans – and how these issues would shape Washington's policies toward Mexico.

It seemed that putting Mexico "back on track" was not simply a duty undertaken in the interests of helping out a neighbor and increasingly close "amigo." Many critics, in fact, called it another instance of Washington acting primarily in its own interest, with Mexico looking on as a powerless bystander to its own internal affairs. Yet, in this case, the United States' interests clearly converged with those of Mexico, which certainly wanted to heal its crippled economy. Moreover, given the impact that a potential economic collapse in Mexico could have on other Latin American econo-mies, on hemispheric trade, and on security in the region, arguably Clinton was also looking at the interests of the entire hemisphere when he proposed the aid package.

Thou Shalt Not Trespass: Testing the Boundaries of the "Special Relationship"

For both Mexico and the Clinton administration, 1994 and 1995 were difficult years. Faced with foreign policy crises in Haiti and the Balkans, Clinton had more than his fair share of diplomacy to conduct and security interests to consider. With respect to Mexico, he faced not only a trading partner with an imploding economy and shaky political climate but also a nation drawing increasing ire for being what many Americans viewed as a source of their domestic troubles.

In early 1994 a number of states with a high number of illegal residents, including Florida, Texas, and Arizona, brought lawsuits against the federal government demanding compensation for the strain on their social services. Most telling, the birth and passage of Proposition 187 in California in 1994 prohibited illegal immigrants from attending public schools and from receiving emergency medical treatment and forced citizens to report any such person who openly sought these services.

The move represented a major break from what might have once been viewed as a singularly "Washington Beltway" policy toward Mexico. California sent the federal government a glaring message with its vote: either act more aggressively to confront illegal immigration, or we will take matters into our own hands. Largely ignored during the preceding Bush administration, border security surfaced so forcefully that Clinton (and his chances at reelection) could not afford to disregard it.

Director of Immigration and Naturalization Services (INS) Doris Meissner claimed that "Washington has heard that message," which Attorney General Janet Reno followed up on with the announcement of a new border security initiative named Operation Gatekeeper.[23] The plan, "specifically tailored for California," pledged to put 200 more INS agents in the San Diego border region in the following 100 days and 700 new agents in the Southwest border area in the 1995 fiscal year.[24] Reno also promised financial aid to California in order to defray the costs of incarcerating illegal immigrants charged with crimes.

The attorney general also reminded critics of other border operations carried out under Clinton's tenure to counter the accusation that the president was "soft" on border security. In 1993 the administration had authorized Operation Blockade, which took the unprecedented step of placing agents on the border to catch illegal crossers there instead of waiting until after they had entered the United States. This was followed in February 1994 by the Clinton administration's request from Congress for a $368 billion border patrol budget increase, which covered the cost of 1,000 agents and various high-tech security measures.

Yet critics countered that Clinton had taken up the security issue only in response to congressional initiatives in early 1993. In addition, many criticized Clinton for failing to address what they considered the root of the troubles in states like California – namely, immigrants *already* living illegally within the United States. The federal lawsuits and Proposition 187 propelled the issue onto Congress's list of priorities, where it steadily rose in importance after the "peso crisis" (and Clinton's "fact sheet") hit congressional floors. By 1995, sensing that the new Republican majority in the House and Senate were prepared to take him to task on the issue, especially after his initially successful border operations were criticized for shifting traffic to more remote points of entry, a long-reluctant Clinton began addressing immigration directly.

In early 1995 Clinton included $1 billion in the budget for immigration reform, which included strengthening border patrol, compensating states for strains on their social services, and hiring more officials to enforce sanctions against employers who knowingly hired illegal immigrants. He also secured the passage of the Illegal Immigration Reform and Immigrant

---

[23] David Adams, "INS Chief Sounds Alarm over Immigration Crisis," *St. Petersburg Times*, March 29, 1995, sec. B, 1.

[24] "Reno Initiative Claims to Control Immigration," *New York Times*, September 18, 1994, sec. 1, 40.

Responsibility Act of 1996, which authorized $12 million for new border security measures, increased penalties for alien smuggling, and pushed for the development of programs to target illegal migrants at their place of employment in the United States.

Aside from its surge in popularity and its intermestic nature, the illegal immigration issue had the distinction of remaining a largely unilateral measure in an era when the U.S.-Mexico "bilateral partnership" had developed such increasing significance. Similarly, the drug front would prove to be another realm where the United States' self-interests ultimately would take precedence over cooperative, transparent efforts.

Clinton and Zedillo Tackle Drugs

Along with immigration, Washington could not escape another looming problem: the war on drugs. Given its enormous debt to the United States following the peso crisis, Mexico had little room for real resistance against U.S. antidrug efforts, especially given its agreement to a wider exchange of drug intelligence information as one condition of the 1995 financial loan package. Still, President Zedillo proved more willing than any other leader in Mexico's history to partner in the drug war. In 1995 Zedillo announced that Mexico's military would have a greater role in antidrug efforts; he and Clinton then negotiated an agreement in which the United States would supply Mexico's military with equipment and training.

Zedillo and Clinton also established a "high level contact group" composed of officials from both countries in March 1996 to collaborate on antidrug efforts, establishing several working groups to address problems like "illicit arms trafficking, chemical precursor control, and demand reduction."[25] Zedillo's own successes on the drug front included the arrest and extradition of several traffickers in high-profile cartels operating near the Gulf of Mexico and in Tijuana.

The Mexican president's actions, however, could not fully counter the power of the cartels or the corruption within his nation's government and security sector. The drop in the amount of drug seizures from 1996 to 1998 was an ominous sign, though perhaps not as disturbing as the high number of military and civilian officials arrested in Mexico on drug-related charges. Particularly damning was the 1997 arrest of Mexican drug czar General Jesús Gutiérrez Rebollo on charges of involvement with a major Mexican

---

[25] Jesus Silva-Herzog, Mexican Ambassador to the United States, "Mexico's Efforts to Combat Drug Trafficking," letter to the editor, *Washington Post*, September 24, 1996, sec. A, 16.

drug trafficker, which came just three days before Clinton's choice of whether to certify Mexico in the drug war. But, like his predecessors, Clinton refused to sacrifice generally good relations to chastise Mexico.

Many in Congress, however, were fed up with what they viewed as excessive executive branch generosity. The House voted to give Mexico ninety days to bolster its antidrug efforts, a demand that linked admitting more U.S. narcotics agents into the country to certification. The Senate crafted a more lenient measure, though it still mandated that Clinton report to Congress in six months on Mexico's progress in specific drug-related areas. In 1998 Mexico again faced the prospect of decertification; yet Congress again voted to maintain Mexico's good standing.

For better or for worse, the certification process upheld the notion of "cooperation" as a thin veil for Washington's undeniably self-interested efforts in the war on drugs. Perhaps more indicative of these self-interests, however, were the U.S. government's antidrug operations in Mexico that existed far outside the realm of bilateral and domestic efforts. The most prominent was Operation Casablanca, a three-year undercover operation in Mexico led by the U.S. Customs Service. The operation culminated in 1998 in Nevada with the arrest of more than 100 employees of leading Mexican banks on charges of laundering illegal drug money. Knowing nothing of the operation, the Mexican government was outraged, with Zedillo citing a wrongful incursion of Mexico's "national sovereignty." Nevertheless, Zedillo further stepped up antidrug efforts, announcing a U.S.$500 million program in February 1999 to help reduce money laundering and to interdict more drug shipments.

Clinton-Zedillo Winds Down

In light of the power asymmetry in the relationship, Mexico could provide little more than rhetorical condemnation of certain U.S. actions. While Zedillo expressed his outrage at Proposition 187, which he called the result of "great ignorance about the phenomenon of migration to the United States," he could do little about it given that the issue rested entirely in the United States.[26]

The Zedillo administration also continued its commitment to democratization, granting Mexico's Federal Electoral Institute increased power and virtual independence from presidential control. In 1997 Clinton

[26] William E. Clayton Jr., "Zedillo Rebuts Wilson with Human Rights Concern," *Houston Chronicle*, November 24, 1994, sec. A, 34.

acknowledged the process when he met officially with the leaders of the principal Mexican opposition parties, the PAN and the PRD. But it was at the end of Clinton's tenure, in July 2000, when Mexico would make its greatest stride yet toward democracy. The election of Vicente Fox, candidate for the conservative PAN party, marked a watershed event in Mexican history and for future bilateral relations.

Thus, by the end of his own presidency, Clinton could be credited with having addressed some of the critical bilateral issues that Bush left untouched. Arguably, though, the U.S. Congress, Clinton's reelection campaign, and citizens from states like California put the pressure on the president to respond to illegal immigration, border security, and drug trafficking. The loan package and Operation Casablanca, while largely the Clinton administration's initiatives, seemed to be driven as much by "crisis response" as by policy prescience. However, Clinton had increased border security drastically: by the end of his term, there were nearly 9,212 border patrol agents, twice the total there had been in 1993.[27] And while the efficacy of these stepped-up efforts was questionable, Clinton had managed to carry them out while still maintaining good relations with Zedillo, to whom he extended a lifesaving loan in a time of fiscal crisis. Mexico had indeed made a slow but steady economic recovery in the late 1990s.

These developments also contributed increasingly to a two-faced U.S.-Mexico relationship. One side showed a friendly partner, eager to engage Mexico economically and to work with it to confront mutual problems like drug trafficking. The other side, found throughout U.S.-Mexico history, retained distrustful tones, engaged in covert operations, and fortified its "fences" in the interests of national security. The two sides had come into conflict as closer economic ties generated by NAFTA led to questions and concerns over labor and migrant flows. It would remain to be seen whether the United States and Fox could reconcile them.

COWBOY DIPLOMACY: GEORGE W. BUSH AND VICENTE FOX

In a twist of irony, Mexico's momentous election in 2000 preceded what would shortly become the United States' own hotly disputed election process. Even in the midst of the U.S. electoral crisis in Florida, however, Fox's

---

[27] Wayne A. Cornelius, "Death at the Border: Efficacy and Unintended Consequences of U.S. Immigration Control Policy," *Population and Development Review* 27, no. 4 (December 2001): 661.

election was promising for U.S.-Mexican relations based on the optimism in his grand policy initiatives. Once-critical members of Congress rained down approval for Mexico's president, whose conservatism and business background made him particularly popular among Republicans. Representative Jim Kolbe (R-AZ) referred to him as "a visionary" who "says things you'd never hear a politician say, much less a Mexican politician."[28]

If we ignore Kolbe's arguably paternalistic attitude, we see that such "things" included Fox's push to make NAFTA into a "common market" allowing both goods and workers to move freely across borders, as well as his determination to convince the still-undeclared American president to support the idea.[29] Fox's desire for stronger ties to the United States, embodied in an agreement he called "NAFTA plus," also indicated just how far the partnership had progressed from the days when a free trade accord had seemed unlikely and even undesirable.

Fox's eager commitment to fight drug trafficking and money laundering made him appealing to Washington, as did the fact that he represented what was perhaps a clean break from the long-entrenched and heavily corrupted PRI.

When Texas governor George W. Bush was declared winner of the U.S. presidential elections, hope for Mexico and the United States seemed to burn its brightest yet. Bush clearly felt at home with Fox, a fellow conservative and businessman in charge of the nation that had literally always been on his doorstep. Fox expressed his affinity for Bush as well, presenting him with a pair of cowboy boots during his first foreign policy trip to Fox's ranch in San Cristóbal, Mexico, in February 2001. Thanking Fox for the gift, Bush said he looked "forward to deepening our friendship. ... But I look forward even more to forging a deeper partnership between our great nations."[30]

The two presidents agreed at that meeting to create a "Partnership for Prosperity" that would promote increased U.S. investment in Mexico. They also agreed to restructure the U.S.-Mexico Binational Commission (BNC), created in the 1980s, to enable a more efficient response to drug trafficking, energy, and the ever-pressing issue of migration. Both presidents had also earlier championed the idea of creating more legal channels to bring

---

[28] Peter W. Cohn, "Congress Casts Hopeful Eye on Mexico's Transition," *CQ Weekly*, November 18, 2000.

[29] Traci Carl, "Fox Looks for Change North of the Border," Associated Press, November 30, 2000.

[30] President George W. Bush, "Remarks by the President to State Department Employees," Press Release, State Department, Washington, D.C., February 15, 2001.

Mexican labor to the United States, though Bush stopped short of endorsing Fox's plan for completely "open borders." Refraining from making any concrete plans on the immigration front, Bush and Fox agreed to establish high-level talks on the issue in the coming months.

But Bush soon needed tangible policies to show that he and Fox were about more than chat and cowboy boots. Several Republican senators from states with large immigrant populations were already pushing a guest-worker program, a type of plan that Bush himself had rhetorically championed, which would include providing legal status for Mexicans residing illegally in the United States. The estimated number of these immigrants stood at 4.5 million in 2001, an increase since the early 1990s that had been fueled in part by Mexico's economic crisis and the pull of higher wages in "El Norte."[31]

Neither administration wanted to squander goodwill or waste time. U.S. secretary of state Colin Powell and Mexican foreign minister Jorge Castañeda met in April for initial talks on immigration, and Bush and Fox saw each other again in late April 2001 at the Summit of the Americas, where Bush pledged to obtain the fast-track authority that Clinton had failed to renew in order to secure a hemispheric free trade accord. The results of NAFTA, while generating only modest GDP growth for both nations, had still shown significant trade increases and little of the dreaded "sucking sound" of U.S. jobs going southward that many critics had predicted. Given this fact, Bush, as well as Fox, felt it was time to push for expanded trade throughout the hemisphere.

These efforts led to the June announcement of a joint border security program, which included measures that each country had refused to take in prior years. For its part, the U.S. government agreed to address the "balloon effect" to more-isolated border crossing points that its border patrol policies had caused in recent years, and Mexico broke precedent by conceding to stop migrants before they crossed in hazardous regions.

Such promising steps also came with setbacks, as the temporary-worker bill championed earlier in the year collapsed in Congress that July 2001. But the obstacle proved only minor to Bush and Fox, who continued to discuss immigration policy and the legal residency proposal throughout the following months. Relations remained as encouraging as ever at Bush's first state dinner that September, where the president issued his all-important toast. Mexico

---

[31] Frank D. Bean, Jennifer Van Hook, and Karen Woodrow-Lafield, "Estimates of Numbers of Unauthorized Migrants Residing in the United States: The Total, Mexican, and Non-Mexican Central American Unauthorized Populations in Mid-2001," special report, *The Pew Hispanic Center*, January 24, 2002, 2.

was no longer just a neighboring country in which the United States had important interests. It was an *amigo*.

Redefining Relations: September 11th

Yet not even a week later, the U.S.-Mexico relations began to sour. The terrorist attacks of September 11, 2001, shook the United States to its core and prompted outpourings of sympathy and solidarity from leaders and nations around the world. As the Bush administration began its global war on terror, Mexico's immediate declaration that it would not supply troops for any U.S. military efforts rubbed some in Washington the wrong way. Mexico's government also began expressing concerns about the future of bilateral relations, particularly as they concerned border security and illegal immigration. Once touchy subjects, they had turned suddenly into downright critical concerns, as national security and fighting terrorism became the United States' utmost priorities. Bush called Fox to reassure him that he had not forgotten his commitments to improving immigration policy in the wake of the attacks; yet his words rang hollow as the administration increased its border security efforts. These included the Enhanced Border Security and Visa Entry Reform Act of 2002, which strengthened regulations for legal entry, and the Homeland Security Act, passed in November 2002, which established an entirely new Department of Homeland Security to oversee and revitalize the Immigration and Naturalization Service, long criticized for its slow processing of immigrant residency applications and failure to keep track of foreign visitors within U.S. borders.

With these measures and Bush's push in February 2002 for an $856 billion increase in INS funding for "border protection and other counter-terrorism programs," any progress toward temporary-worker programs or increased immigration flows had been sidetracked indefinitely.[32] Now, national security was the name of the game.

Dedicating the once multifaceted INS fully to the task of enforcing border security, Washington attempted to send of the message of "don't you dare" to potential border crossers. Bush did reach out to Fox, as well as to Canadian prime minister Jean Chrétien, on border security matters: in March 2002 the leaders discussed a "Smart Border Initiative," which would streamline customs and expedite interhemispheric travel for citizens of the three nations.

---

[32] "Agency by Agency: The President's Opening Bid," CQ *Weekly Online*, February 9, 2002, http://library.cqpress.com/cqweekly/weeklyreport107–000000376731 (accessed July 11, 2007).

However, Bush's reiteration that "the United States has no more important relationship ... than the one we have with Mexico" appeared increasingly incongruent with the unfolding post-9/11 bilateral relationship.[33] At
that moment, Mexico's "importance" to the United States was more about
strategic security matters than about previous plans to create more immigration channels and pathways to legal citizenship. Chairman of the Congressional Immigration Reform Caucus, Representative Tom Tancredo's
(R-CO) comments in defense of a beefed-up border security program were
telling of this new mentality: "The defense of our nation begins at this
nation's borders. And if we can't control our borders, the question of whether
we are going to be successful in this war is subject to debate."[34]

This kind of congressional sentiment did not resonate well with Fox,
who had expressed frustrations earlier that year with stalled talks on
immigration, stating "there can be no privileged U.S.-Mexico relationship
without actual progress on substantive issues."[35] Fox canceled his trip to
Washington in August 2002 to protest the execution of a Mexican man in
Texas. Observers perceived a chilly distance between the presidents when
they met later that year, especially with Fox's increasing sense of having
been left out in the cold on previously joint-policy initiatives. With Bush's
mind increasingly on national security and Iraq, common ground and enthusiasm on tackling these issues – the essence of amigo diplomacy – seemed to
have disappeared.

The rift widened drastically when in March 2003 Mexico, acting as a
rotating member of the UN Security Council, failed to support a resolution
authorizing U.S. forces to enter Iraq. Popular opinion in Mexico stood largely
opposed to the war, given that most Mexicans believed that it was driven by
the United States' thirst for oil, contributing substantially to Fox's refusal to
put his country in the United States' "coalition of the willing."

Border (and Immigration) Blues

Despite the cool bilateral relationship, hope for a new immigration accord
grew as many legislators in Congress realized the necessity of a bold,

---

[33] U.S. Office of the Press Secretary, Press Conference by President Bush and President Fox,
   Palacio de Gobierno, Monterrey, Mexico, March 22, 2002, www.whitehouse.gov.
[34] Jorge Amaya, "Opening America's Borders: Mexico Is Not Our Enemy," *Denver Post*
   September 30, 2001, sec. F, 1.
[35] Kevin Sullivan and Mary Jordan, "Fox Laments 'Stalled' Relations between U.S., Mexico;
   Leader Says His Credibility Is Being Undermined by Bush's Failure to Speed Immigration
   Reform," *Washington Post*, May 10, 2002, sec. A, 28.

decisive (and cohesive) policy. The drastic increase in deaths of migrants attempting to cross the border in particular convinced Republican senator John McCain (AZ) of the need to create the legal migration channels once proposed by Bush and Fox. He cosponsored a bill for a guest-worker program that would allow migrants to come to the United States and eventually apply for permanent residency. The bill also included a pathway that illegal residents could take to become legalized, a provision that appeared (in varying forms) in a few other bills that session as well.

Fierce opposition, however, came from members such as fervent anti-immigration advocate Representative Tancredo, who considered such provisions as "amnesty" for people who had broken the law. But the bill gained support among other members and eventually formed the basis for President Bush's plan on immigration, which he presented in his 2004 State of the Union address. The president stressed that a temporary worker program for illegal immigrants would protect the country by allowing border patrol "to focus on true threats to our national security."[36] Bush also attempted to differentiate his plan from an "amnesty" to counter critics in Tancredo's camp, stressing that the program would grant citizenship only to those who "respect the law, while bringing millions of hardworking men and women out from the shadows of American life."[37]

As the immigration bills gained traction in Congress, public debate began to focus more seriously on the matter. Immigrant advocacy groups rallied support for a citizenship track, arguing that punitive measures would only harm people who had contributed culturally and economically to U.S. society. Critics countered that illegal residents' strain on social services and their breach of U.S. law constituted grounds for punishment or even deportation. Such arguments resembled those which had surrounded past legislative proposals, including the 1986 immigration act and the Illegal Immigration Reform and Immigrant Responsibility Act passed ten years later. Interestingly, though, the potential threat posed by illegal residents to national security now factored more prominently in public dialogue; yet the fundamentals of the debate about a heavily intermestic issue remained the same.

The same old issues, however, began to precipitate more local and "novel" responses. In early 2005, a group of Arizona citizens began patrolling the state's southern border as part of the Minuteman Project, an initiative of

---

[36] President George W. Bush, "State of the Union Address," United States Capitol, Washington D.C., Office of the Press Secretary, January 20, 2004.
[37] Ibid.

retired accountant and former Vietnam veteran Jim Gilchrist, who claimed he was "going down there to assist law enforcement."[38] Like Proposition 187, the Minutemen's arrival illustrated that key issues related to Mexico policy were highly intermestic. Instead of the strain on social services, the Minutemen cited damage to their property as well as the general threat to national security as justification for their fight against illegal immigration.

While the Minutemen incited widespread controversy for their vigilante approach to catching border crossers, no one could deny that illegal crossings had become a substantive issue when Arizona governor Janet Napolitano (D) and New Mexico governor Bill Richardson (D) each declared a "state of emergency" in August 2005 in order to obtain more federal and state funds for law enforcement efforts at the border. Calling it an act of desperation, Richardson voiced domestic frustrations when he said that such funding would be needed "until Congress and the feds deal with this issue."[39]

A New Partnership?

The arrival of the Minutemen and Congress's continual failure to pass an immigration bill irritated the Mexican government. Yet during that same year, promising signs of regional cooperation also emerged. In March 2005, Bush met with both Fox and Prime Minister Steven Harper of Canada in Baylor, Texas, where the three agreed to create the Security and Prosperity Partnership (SPP). The SPP would establish working groups that would advise each government of target goals of cooperation and integration in the realms of border security and trade, which had become an important regional issue with the rise of competition from China and India (Figure 14.2).

Yet while the SPP might have been the strongest collaborative move for the three regional governments since the creation of NAFTA, it still failed to address illegal immigration to the degree that Fox and Bush had promised nearly four years prior. The House's passage of the Real ID Act earlier that year, which sought to prohibit states from issuing driver's licenses to illegal immigrants and removed state restrictions on border fence construction, further strained relations. The latter provision proved divisive in Congress, particularly when Rep. Duncan Hunter (R-CA) proposed a U.S.$2 billion plan for the construction of a fence along the entire

---

[38] "Modern Minutemen Plan Border Patrols; Group Denies It Seeks Vigilante Justice," *Grand Rapids Press* (Michigan), February 21, 2005, sec. A, 4.
[39] Ralph Blumenthal, with Ginger Thompson, "Citing Border Violence, 2 States Declare a Crisis," *New York Times*, August 17, 2005, sec. A, 14.

FIGURE 14.2. President George W. Bush, Mexico's President Vicente Fox, and Canada's Prime Minister Stephen Harper stand in front of the Chichen-Itza Archaeological Ruins in March 2006. (Photo: Courtesy of the White House Photo Office/Kimberlee Hewitt.)

2,000-mile border. Even the Bush administration, which considered strategic border fences an integral part of the government's comprehensive immigration plan, refused to support the proposal, due to its cost and potential unpopularity.

Despite its continued efforts to construct a plan that would enhance national security without being too punitive or too lenient toward illegal immigrants, the Bush administration continued to confront conflicting domestic demands on these issues from Congress, interest groups, and the American public. Bush also had to contend with more than a decade's worth of largely inefficient border control measures and immigration policies, including the virtually unenforced provision of the 1986 immigration reform act that mandated fines for employers who hired illegal immigrants. Yet even now the notion of employer sanctions encountered domestic opposition, particularly from among strong probusiness Republicans who made a direct link between America's prosperity and the cheap and available labor provided by undocumented individuals.

At the same time, critics (whose ranks also included a sizable congressional Republican contingent) contended that the estimated 11 million illegal immigrants were putting a heavier strain than ever on America's public schools, health care services, and social programs. These concerns, when combined with arguments about the "fairness" and "effectiveness" of immigration and border security policy, created an issue that, generally unconstrained by party lines, was extraordinarily complex and received attention on a national level.

Congress tried again to solve the immigration issue, changing pace by pushing for plans that focused more on immigrant labor than on the prior year's more border-oriented policy. Senate Judiciary Committee Chair Arlen Specter (R-PA) devised a bill that included a generous guest-worker program and created a "pathway" for illegal immigrants to achieve legal residency status.[40] The Senate finally approved a bill in May 2006 that included a process for residency that differed depending on how long a person had lived illegally in the United States; yet victory would prove elusive, given that the House too had drafted its own bill that emphasized border security and felony penalties for illegal immigrants. By the year's end, the 109th Congress still had no uniform, comprehensive solution to illegal immigration and border security to offer up to an impatient president.

While President Bush pushed congressional attempts to secure residency pathways and worker programs at a meeting with senators in April 2005, he nevertheless furthered his "balancing act" on immigration by asking for increased spending on border security in the following year's budget. He also made trips to several border states in an attempt to placate legislators who criticized his residency pathway proposal as an "amnesty" to illegal migrants. Yet Bush did not forget to emphasize his other less punitive plans for immigration policy reform when he once again met with President Fox. At an SPP summit in March 2006, Bush attempted to assure Fox of his steadfast dedication to immigration reform, stressing that "by 'comprehensive,' I mean not only a bill that has border security in it, but a bill that has a worker permit program in it."[41]

---

[40] Elizabeth Crowley, "Hot Immigration Issue Splits Member's Views," *CQ Weekly*, March 6, 2006, 609.

[41] Ginger Thompson and David Sanger, "Bush Reassures Mexico Leader of His Backing for Immigrants," *New York Times*, March 31, 2006, sec. A, 6.

Both presidents, however, publicly recognized that the issue now rested in the U.S. Congress's hands. Unfortunately for Fox, this fact kept him from seeing the passage of a comprehensive immigration policy – a goal set at the very beginning of his presidency – before his term expired that year.

AMLO, Calderón, and the Future of Bilateral Relations

The unrealized immigration deal dealt one more blow to Mexico's outgoing president, who had been roundly criticized during his term for failing to deliver on promises to reduce domestic unemployment and poverty. A good deal of the condemnation came particularly from leftist Mexican presidential candidate and former Mexico City mayor Andrés Manuel López Obrador, widely known as "AMLO." A proponent of industry nationalization and socialist-style programs whose specialty was energizing crowds with fervent anticapitalist speeches, AMLO caused worry for many in Washington over the future of U.S.-Mexico relations (and for a continuation of the "leftward" trend that seemed to be developing throughout Latin America at the time). Yet his hesitancy to criticize the Bush administration and the United States suggested that AMLO, despite his populist leanings, recognized the importance of bilateral ties with Washington.

The Bush administration and the United States, however, were undeniably more relieved when conservative PAN candidate Felipe Calderón, who had served as secretary of energy under Fox, was reported to have won the vote that July. Yet AMLO and his supporters fervently disputed Calderón's thin margin of victory and organized mass demonstrations against what they called a dubious election. Mexico, despite all the strides it had made toward democratization and electoral reform in recent years, was still haunted by the memories of elections past. Yet, while there had been a few cited "irregularities" in vote tabulation, electoral observers reported no systematic fraud. Many Mexicans soon grew weary of AMLO's pledges to set up a parallel government, and the fallout over the election gradually quieted after a Mexican high-court ruling declared Calderón the undisputed winner.

Perhaps unsurprisingly, President Bush had recognized Calderón's victory long before the September court decision and prepared to welcome the new president to the White House that November. Calderón, disinclined to exude the same shiny optimism for relations that his predecessor Fox had in 2001, instead emphasized his opposition to the new border fence initiative while in Washington. He indicated his strong desire for economic growth and reform, saying "it is a better solution to build one mile of roads in

Michoacán than to build 10 miles of walls in Texas."[42] Calderón also made it known that the immigration issue would not overshadow his commitments to fighting crime and drug trafficking, which had been displaced in bilateral talks by the issue of terrorism. In the first few months of his term, Calderón extradited several Mexican traffickers, including the alleged leader of the notorious Gulf Cartel, to the United States. The new president also involved Mexico's military directly in the war on drugs and crime, even ordering soldiers to pull up marijuana and opium plants.

Despite praise from Washington for his efforts, Calderón could hardly hope to shift the Bush administration's focus off of the war on terror. Bush's diminished leverage with a now Democrat majority Congress and the continued turmoil in Iraq made progress on bilateral promises to tackle issues like drugs, crime, immigration, and trade unlikely. Yet Calderón, despite his rhetorical recognition that "priorities changed" after September 11, would not let Bush forget the Mexican president's priorities, reasserting at a March summit that "it is now time ... to direct our relationship toward a path of mutual prosperity."[43]

PAST EXAMINATIONS, FUTURE EXPECTATIONS

Ironically, in 2007 Calderón now reminded the United States of the importance of the countries' bilateral relations. At the meeting in the provincial city of Mérida, he reiterated Bush's words: "there is no relationship the world over that is more relevant to the United States than the one with Mexico."[44] After centuries of cold and even periodically hostile relations, these words recalled, despite recent rifts, how far the "special relationship" had come. Instead of avoiding "El Norte" and attempting to go it alone, Mexico's leader was now pressing the United States to renew the commitments it had made – as far back as the George H. W. Bush presidency – to reform immigration and fight cross-border drugs and crime.

Yet it was not only Calderón's words that indicated how far relations had come: Mexico was now more important to the United States than ever before, with Calderón's election capturing more American newspaper headlines than perhaps any election in Mexico's history. The fact that

---

[42] Patty Reinart, "Calderón Assails Border Fence; President-elect of Mexico Says Economics Is Key to Solving Problem of Immigration," *Houston Chronicle*, November 9, 2006, sec. A, 9.

[43] Maura Reynolds and Sam Enriquez, "Calderón Pressures Bush on Immigration," *Los Angeles Times*, March 14, 2007, sec. A, 6.

[44] Maura Reynolds and Sam Enriquez, "Calderón Pressures Bush on Immigration," *Los Angeles Times*, March 14, 2007, sec. A, 6.

Mexico mattered to Washington was made even clearer by how often bilateral issues like trade and immigration came up during the 2004 and 2008 U.S. presidential campaigns.

While post–September 11 security issues would remain an undeniable component of America's policy toward Mexico, dialogue and cooperation had replaced the once skeptical and critical overtones of Cold War ties. Now, not only did Mexico matter, but it mattered permanently, as its importance to and throughout these three U.S. presidential administrations attest. Amigo diplomacy, for all the sidetracks and setbacks, was here to stay.

15

Conclusion

In September 2007, two members of the U.S. Congress, Senator Bernie Sanders (I-VT) and Congressman Mike Michaud (D-ME), led a delegation to Costa Rica that made the headlines. Their trip and the resulting responses illustrate the complex, interrelated issues that have come to characterize U.S. involvement in Latin America in the post–Cold War era.

The American congressmen traveled to the small Central American nation as Costa Ricans prepared to vote in a referendum on whether to ratify Costa Rica's participation in the Central American Free Trade Agreement (CAFTA). As long-standing opponents of free trade pacts such as NAFTA and CAFTA, Sanders and Michaud hoped that their visit would give a last-minute boost to the anti-CAFTA campaign in Costa Rica.

Leading up to the up-or-down vote, many Costa Ricans wanted to know whether the U.S. government would revoke Costa Rica's existing free trade privileges enjoyed through the Caribbean Basin Trade Partnership Act (CBTPA) if the country rejected CAFTA. CAFTA would make permanent many of the tariff privileges that Costa Rica enjoyed under CBTPA, but the agreement would also force Costa Rica to open up its markets to American goods. Even supporters of the anti-CAFTA campaign in Costa Rica still wanted to maintain the country's free trade access via CBTPA. Sanders and Michaud were in the country to reassure voters that Costa Rica would maintain its CBTPA privileges if the Costa Rican people rejected CAFTA.

The congressional visit provoked a strong response from the conservative, free market *Wall Street Journal* editorial page. Columnist Mary O'Grady started the fireworks when she wrote that the "visit from the gringos seems to have widely insulted the Costa Rican nation" because these two "protectionists" were promising to keep the U.S market open to Costa Rican goods even if CAFTA lost the vote.[1] O'Grady added that the two congressmen were being especially disingenuous because they were in no position to guarantee Costa Rica's continued duty-free access given that any change in Costa Rica's CBTPA status would have to come from the White House, not Congress. A follow-up *Journal* editorial argued that the two congressmen were attempting to influence the referendum shamelessly. "But why else go the tropics in the rainy season?" the writers asked rhetorically.[2]

Sanders swiftly responded to the *Journal*'s charges in a letter to the editor, in which he wrote that he was not meddling in the country's domestic affairs but rather supporting Costa Ricans' ability to exercise their "democratic rights" through the referendum and that if, "the people in a free, democratic and independent country like Costa Rica vote their conscience they should not be punished [through canceling Costa Rica's CBPTA privileges] by the world's superpower. That is not what democracy is about." Sanders added that his trip to Costa Rica "was not about telling the people there how to vote. That's their business, not mine."[3]

While this heated exchange might seem to read like one more spat between conservative proponents of free trade agreements and their protectionist opponents, more brewed beneath the surface. Not surprisingly, a significant part of Sanders and Michaud's opposition to CAFTA resulted from domestic political considerations. Both politicians firmly believed that these types of trade agreements were bad for the American worker, especially the American workers in the their congressional districts who stood to lose jobs. In this sense, Sanders and Michaud were advocating for the interests of the very citizens who had voted them into office, even if that meant traveling to Costa Rica to drum up support for the anti-CAFTA referendum.

Yet, in a fascinating twist, the anti-free-trade Sanders and Michaud were attempting to allay the fears of Costa Rican voters by assuring them that the country's duty-free access would *continue* through CBTPA. That is, they were at once advocating both for and against some sort of free trade between Costa Rica and the United States. On top of this, Sanders, when serving in the House of Representative in 2000, had voted against CBTPA renewal, the very program that he was now promoting.

On the other side of the political spectrum, the *Wall Street Journal*'s pro-free-trade editorial writers were finding themselves in an increasingly lonely

---

[1] Mary O'Grady, "Democrats vs. Central America" *Wall Street Journal*, October 3, 2007.

[2] "Weekend with Bernie," *Wall Street Journal*, October 4, 2007.

[3] Bernie Sanders. "Free Trade Agreement Means Impoverishment," letter to the editor. *Wall Street Journal*, October 4, 2007.

position among fellow Republicans. The same day as Sanders's letter to the editor, the same newspaper published a poll indicating that 60 percent of Republicans believed that free trade agreements have hurt the United States, a number only slightly lower than Democratic voters. An accompanying article cited the surprising financial support for Republican presidential candidate Ron Paul of Texas, who called free trade deals "a threat to our independence as a nation."[4] In their scathing critique of Sanders and Michaud, the *Journal* editorialists implied that opposition to CAFTA came only from left-wing Democrats (Sanders was an independent who caucused with the Democrats); in actuality, millions of Republicans shared these critical sentiments. When the Costa Ricans went to the polls on October 7, they approved CAFTA by a narrow majority of 51.6 percent, moving the treaty to the country's congress for implementing legislation.

The debate over CAFTA raises some interesting questions. Were Sanders and Michaud genuine in their support for CBPTA and opposition to CAFTA, or would they come to oppose the former once Costa Ricans rejected the latter? Was their visit an act of solidarity with Costa Rican voters and workers, as they contended? Or was the visit an unorthodox yet powerful reincarnation of the Big Stick, which saw American officials once again meddling in their "backyard?"

If there was any semblance of Big Stick in Sanders and Michaud's trip, it is a new version of the Big Stick, one that is more particular to the post–Cold War than prior eras. Without the overarching threat of communism, the United States will depend less on heavy-handed military interventions or covert operations and more on subtle, "postmodern" versions of "involvement" similar to the Costa Rica episode. At times, these efforts will produce positive results for the United States, and at other times they will backfire, as occurred in Bolivia in the first several years of this century. In addition, Washington will continue to disagree about the best course of action, and the motivation for U.S. actions in these cases will often be based in domestic political considerations.

So while in upcoming years the "gunboats" and CIA plots of earlier eras will remain largely dormant, in areas such as democracy, trade, narcotics, and terrorism, the United States will continue to play an integral and often controversial role in the events of the Western Hemisphere. As students of Latin American–U.S. policies in the post–Cold War era, it is less important whether we consider any particular episode or policy to be the Big Stick.

[4] John Harwood, "Republicans Grow Skeptical on Free Trade," *Wall Street Journal*, October 4, 2007.

Rather, the complexity and nuance in cases such as the Costa Rica–CAFTA referendum remind us that we must observe carefully and not let outdated assumptions and models automatically lead us to foregone conclusions.

It remains to be seen when the United States will enter the "next era" in its Latin American relations. Even after the transformative impact of the September 11, 2001, terrorist attacks, more recent U.S. policy in Latin America still follows the general trends set upon after the end of the Cold War. Thus, contrary to the contention that September 11 "changed everything," in Latin America policy, at least, U.S. policy is still "post–Cold War." But this could of course quickly change if, like the Cold War, a new "communism" emerged to capture the attention of U.S. policymakers.

For the time being, in a quest for the elusive "Goldilocks" formula, Washington will continue to seek the "just right" in its policies in Latin America. Critics will continue to contend that the United States is too involved or too uninvolved, too controlling or too apathetic. Given the United States' tremendous power and ability to influence outcomes, U.S. involvement in Latin America will continue to be surrounded by controversy and debate, no matter what policies Washington adopts.

Index